THE ART & THOUGHT OF THOMAS HARDY

On
A Darkling Plain

By

HARVEY CURTIS WEBSTER

THE UNIVERSITY OF CHICAGO PRESS

Cambridge: AT THE UNIVERSITY PRESS

THE UNIVERSITY OF CHICAGO PRESS, CHICAGO 37
Cambridge University Press, London, N.W. 1, England
W. J. Gage & Co., Limited, Toronto 2B, Canada

To

MY MOTHER

Preface

THERE have been a good many books that deal specifically with Hardy's philosophy—to cite only the best, the works of M. D'Exideuil, Mr. Brennecke, Miss Garwood, and Mme de Ridder-Barzin. Accurate brief accounts of the nature of his thought have been written, most notably, by Professor Lionel Stevenson, Professor Samuel C. Chew, and Mr. W. R. Rutland. But no book published since Mrs. Florence Hardy's biography of her husband has attempted to present the evolution of Hardy's thought and its effect upon his art. My study attempts to remedy this omission and to supply as comprehensive an account of the influences that affected Hardy's development as is at present possible.

It would be impossible to acknowledge here (though I try to do this in my notes) all that I owe to others who have written about Hardy and to those who have assisted me in both my research and the preparation of my manuscript. I do wish, however, to acknowledge my particular gratitude to Professor Carl J. Weber, who was kind enough to forward information about the Colby College collection of Hardyana; to Sir Sydney Cockerell, who allowed me to see his private collection of letters from Hardy and gave me permission to quote from one of them; to Mr. Willard Robertson, director of the American University Union in England, who extended to me innumerable courtesies; to Mr. Lovatt-Dickson, who helped me to come in contact with Hardy scholars in England; to Professors Earl L. Griggs, Paul Mueschke, Warner C. Rice, Clarence Thorpe, and Bennett Weaver, who gave valuable suggestions about the preparation of the doctoral dissertation which started me on this book; and, most of all, to Professor Howard Mumford Jones, whose mingled encouragement and criticism is largely responsible for whatever merit my study may have.

I also wish to thank Harper and Brothers for permission to quote from the novels of Thomas Hardy copyrighted in the United States; The Macmillan Company for permission to quote from *The Collected Poems of Thomas Hardy*, *Winter Words*, and *The Dynasts*, and to quote "Neutral Tones" and "Long Have I Framed Weak Fantasies of Thee," from *The Collected Poems of Thomas Hardy;* The Macmillan and Company, Limited, and the Estate of Thomas Hardy, for permission to quote from *The Early Life of Thomas Hardy*, *The Later Years of Thomas Hardy*, *The Dynasts*, and the poems and novels of Hardy, all copyrighted by them in the British Empire; and my wife, Lucille Jones Webster, for assistance that cannot adequately be acknowledged.

HARVEY CURTIS WEBSTER

CHICAGO, ILLINOIS
August 1, 1946

Table of Contents

I

THE STARTING-POINT

Page 1

II

FLUX AND REFLUX

Page 27

III

A YOUNG MAN'S VIEW OF EXISTENCE

Page 49

IV

MAN'S QUANDARY

Page 78

V

THE NATURE OF THE UNIVERSAL

Page 136

VI

TO THE BETTER

Page 161

VII
ANOTHER STARTING-POINT
Page 200

NOTES
Page 217

INDEX
Page 235

I

THE STARTING-POINT

"O Memory, where is now my faith,
One time a champion, now a wraith?"

—*Poems of the Past and the Present*

1

IT IS difficult to realize that Thomas Hardy, the discouraged and pessimistic old man, was ever young. To do so, we have to change back to a world that is pre-Darwinian, to an age confident of both itself and God; to a world which was moving, no doubt, toward the catastrophe of a world war that has led to another world war—but altogether unconsciously. We have to shift back to an age when futilitarianism was almost unheard of, when Hardy, the old man with pessimistic views, would have been a complete anomaly.

In his later years Hardy himself often found it difficult to recall what he had been in the 1840's and 1850's. Writing on his eighty-seventh birthday, in a poem significantly entitled "He Never Expected Much," he declares that the world has said to him, since childhood:

"I do not promise overmuch,
Child; overmuch;
Just neutral-tinted haps and such."

Two other poems, "Epitaph" (1917) and "For Life I Had Never Cared Greatly" (1922), express almost the same idea. Small wonder, then, that many critics agree with Arthur McDowall's belief that Hardy the young man and Hardy the mature artist were alike in "never expecting much."[1]

Great men are often unusual youths, but could Hardy have been as unusual as this? In McDowall's view, it is as if Hardy were himself the prototype for one of those boys who "seem to see all [life's] terrors before they are old enough . . . . to resist them . . . . [who represent] the beginning of the coming universal wish not to live." If one reads the remainder of the passage, this conception of Hardy's youth becomes even more unbelievable. For Hardy says that such boys as Father Time are of a "sort unknown in the last generation,"[2] and the "last generation," that of the 1840's, was the author's as well as Jude's.[3]

Indeed, if we look to his own characterizations of his youth elsewhere, we see that Hardy has done as much as anyone to perplex us. He speaks of his early years as a time before "I had learnt that the world was a welter of futile doing," as a period when he "was the midmost of [his] world."[4] Most of his children (and would he not think of his own childhood when writing about them?) look forward to the world as

> A pure delight, a beauty-spot
> Where all is gentle, true and just.[5]

With few exceptions his characters enter manhood full of faith in their capacity for realizing their illusions. All of them would subscribe to the view of nature Hardy attributes to his own youth— something "love alone had wrought . . . . for his pleasure."[6] Even when they are disillusioned later—and they all are—they would still say with their creator:

> "O Memory, where is now my youth,
> Who used to say that life was truth?
>
> . . . .
>
> "O Memory, where is now my joy,
> Who lived with me in sweet employ?"[7]

Both Chew[8] and Hedgcock[9] consequently believe that Hardy was an idealist who had become disillusioned. And G. R. Elliot even sees a "paradisaic tendency" in young Hardy. According to this interpretation, he yearned for "a comfortable harmony, social and spiritual, which wears the guise of human happiness but in which the essential conditions of human happiness are slurred or submerged."[10] Confusion seems to have become worse confounded.

2

However confusing the task of interpretation at first may seem, the facts upon which any interpretation must be based are simple enough.[11] Thomas Hardy was born in 1840, in Upper, or Higher, Bockhampton, a part of the Stinsford parish the reader of the novels will remember as Mellstock of *Under the Greenwood Tree*. Here he lived for the first sixteen years of his life, with his father, a fairly well-to-do stonemason and builder, and his mother, an ambitious, largely self-educated woman. Although he learned to read almost before he learned to walk, fragile health kept him from the village school until he was eight. Once he had started, he became a particular favorite of the lady who sponsored the school, and he soon showed himself a superior student in arithmetic and geography.

Encouraged by his mother, Hardy read a good deal when he was not in school. He discovered Dryden's *Virgil*, Johnson's *Rasselas*, and Bernardin de St. Pierre's *Paul and Virginia;* he dragged from a closet and read an account of the war with Napoleon—in a periodical, *A History of the Wars*, which was contemporaneous with the events recorded. Probably this is the first of a series of events that led to the writing of *The Dynasts* almost sixty years later.

At the age of nine he was considered strong enough to go to the larger and better Dorchester day school. Under an able teacher he advanced rapidly. At twelve he began to study Latin in the old Eton grammar, reading portions of Eutropius and Caesar. For his progress in mastering the language he won Beza's *Latin Testament*. As in the Stinsford school, he was good at figures, doing well in advanced arithmetic, geometry, algebra, and applied mathematics.

At home his more popular course in reading continued. He went through much of the work of G. P. R. James, W. H. Ainsworth,[12] Dumas *père*, James Grant, and Shakespeare—whose tragedies he liked because of their plots. Thanks to his practical mother, some of his out-of-school work was instructive. His sister's governess taught him French; out of Cassell's *The Popular Educator* he began to learn German, a task he was never to complete.

His everyday life was not exciting or exceptional. He attended the Stinsford "High Church" regularly, got the morning and evening services and a large portion of the "New Version of the Psalms" by heart. He taught a Sunday-school class; he played his violin at country dances; he went to a "Harvest Supper"; he spent a few days in London. His was the normal life of a country boy whose parents are moderately well off and fairly well educated.

At sixteen, although "he had just begun to be interested in French and the Latin classics,"[13] Hardy "cheerfully" agreed to his parents' wish that he become an apprentice to John Hicks, the Dorchester architect. As a consequence of this apprenticeship Hardy came into close contact with intelligent youths of his own age for the first time. Bastow, Hicks's other pupil, knew well both the ancient languages and Baptist theology. So did Bastow's friends, the sons of Perkins, the Dorchester Baptist minister. With these three, sometimes helped by Hicks and the poet William Barnes, Hardy studied the classics during his free time. Before his twentieth year he had studied several books of the *Aeneid*, some of Horace and Ovid, a few books of the *Iliad*, and the Greek Testament. Was there ever a great man with a youth less extraordinary?

3

At a first, deceptive glance Hardy's character seems quite as ordinary as his early biography. He was fond of play and studied the *Boy's Own Book*, a game manual, as conscientiously as he did his grammar. Like many another boy, he found learning the catechism a bore; his eyes often wandered away from the preacher's "on afternoons of drowsy calm." He liked playing the violin at dances; he liked to dance. He early fancied himself in love with the older, and very attractive, Lady of the Manor, who sponsored the village school; frequently he thought himself in love with girls more nearly his age.

His taste in literature, already mentioned in passing, does not show a precocious profundity. Indeed, *Hamlet* earned his critical disapproval because the ghost did not stay on the stage until the end! Although it would involve overlooking a good deal of evidence, a case could be made out for Hardy's being neither the boy who expected great things of life nor the boy who "never expected much."

Nevertheless, there were ways in which Hardy was more than ordinary. Most boys have at least one or two close friends, but Hardy generally avoided those his own age. He frequently played the fiddle at country fetes and was fond of dancing, but he danced rarely. With his Dorchester schoolmates he was friendly, never intimate. Popular with them, he still found their friendship "burdensome": "He loved being alone, but often, to his concealed discomfort, some of the other boys would volunteer to accompany him on his homeward journey to Bockhampton. How much this irked him he recalled long years after. He tried also to avoid being touched by his playmates. . . . . This peculiarity never left him."[14]

He taught Sunday school with the Stinsford vicar's two sons, but his contacts with them elsewhere were altogether casual. When he became an architect's pupil, he studied the Bible and discussed religion with Bastow and the Perkins boys, but he did not become intimate with any of them. It was not until his twentieth year, when he met Horace Moule, that he had a real friend outside the family circle. As Ellis reveals, traces of this reluctance to mix with people always remained with Hardy: "Rather than meet a stranger, in his last years, he would turn back at the approach of one and retrace his steps."[15]

So great a passion for solitude, undoubtedly peculiar in a boy and young man, would seem to indicate that Hardy did have something of the "melancholy temperament" many critics regard as the basis of his "pessimism." And, whatever our ultimate conclusion may be, it must be admitted that he had another characteristic we often associate with those who are melancholy. He was excessively sensitive.

As a child, Mrs. Florence Hardy tells us, "he was of ecstatic temperament, extraordinarily sensitive to music."[16] Three or four of the country dances his father played evenings made him cry. In later years he said that "like Calantha in Ford's *Broken Heart*, he danced on at these times to conceal his weeping."[17] A similar sensitiveness, this time more definitely motivated and more in keeping with his later writings, is revealed by two memories of his youth that "always haunted" Hardy.

One day a stone his father threw hit a half-frozen fieldfare and killed it. When Hardy picked it up, he discovered it to be "all skin and bone, practically starved."[18] He never forgot how the fieldfare's body felt in his hand. Nor did he ever forget the most striking example of human suffering he came upon.[19] He knew a sheep-shearing boy whose father made six shillings a week and cottage rent. The boy died of starvation, and an autopsy revealed nothing but raw turnips in his stomach. Such miseries of man and beast, the end products of a struggle for existence he only dimly understood, were always difficult for his sensitiveness to endure.

But his sensitiveness did not always lead to unhappiness. More prone than the average youth to feel the suffering of others, he was also more capable of joy. His delight in Nature is as evident in the poem "Domicilium," written sometime between his seventeenth and twentieth years, as it is in the frequent beautiful descriptions in his later work. There are no brighter stanzas in Hardy's *Collected Poems* than those that describe his early delight in Nature:

> When I early sought thee,
>   Omen-scouting,
>   All undoubting
> Love alone had wrought thee—
>
> Wrought thee for my pleasure,
> Planned thee as a measure
>   For expounding
>   And resounding
> Glad things that men treasure.[20]

Hardy's melancholy temperament, if such it was, evidently did not preclude intense enjoyment.

Nor did Hardy's temperament preclude a most flattering view of human nature. Exceptions to the flattering view there no doubt were. But he seems, like Othello and the sentimental novelists he read so much, to have divided human nature into two groups: those who deserve idealization and those who do not. He found more of those who approached the ideal than of those who decreased his faith in human nature.

He thought of his mother as "matchless in might . . . . with measureless scope endued."[21] In his copy of *Hamlet* his father's name and death date are written opposite the lines:

> Thou hast been
> As one, in suffering all, that suffers nothing,
> A man that fortune's buffets and rewards
> Hast ta'en with equal thanks.[22]

The Lady of the near-by Manor—who, as the patron of Hardy's earliest school, had taken a special interest in him—he worshiped this side of idolatry. Similarly, his early "love affairs" indicate a tendency to idealize. He fell in love with the daughter of a neighboring farmer. When he learned that she had gone to a boarding school in Weymouth, he went there Sunday after Sunday until he saw her. Although he was rewarded only by a shy smile, he remembered her even in his old age, writing the flattering poem "Louisa in the Lane" of her a few months before his death.

This inclination to think highly of human beings was always characteristic of Hardy—what characters did he treat unsympathetically? There were always men and women of whom he might speak as he did of his first wife:

> The city sleeps below. I sigh,
> For there dwells one, all testify,
> To match the maddest dream's desire.[23]

Certainly the writer of this poem, the idealizer of his parents, Louisa, and the manor lady, does not square too well with the usual notion of one who is melancholy to the point of pessimism.

For, most characteristically, the excessively melancholy person should be pensive and sad. He should, most of the time, be inclined to regard sunny days as but the putting-off of rain, birthdays as the preludes to funerals, good men as bad men in disguise, good fortune as a way of raising one's hopes too high. When Hardy grew older, some of these characteristics were his, but an adult's melancholy is a gradually acquired rather than an inherited trait. Indeed, if we are to believe modern psychology, melancholy is most generally a characteristic fathered by experience and environment upon a nature unusually sensitive.

If, instead of starting Hardy in the cradle with lackluster eyes, we see in him the potentiality for melancholy—even an unusual potentiality—I agree. The development of character is determined by the play of environment upon inherited tendencies. Obviously, something in Hardy's environment eventually did combine with his sensitiveness, his liking for solitude, and his lack of ambition to make him what he became. But did this happen early or late? Was he a confirmed melancholic when he went to Dorchester at sixteen? To London at twenty? Or did his melancholy develop still later? I think that we shall find that it did.

Certainly no one would have been more surprised than Hardy's parents to learn that either heredity or early environment made him into a confirmed melancholic. The one portrait of Thomas Hardy senior that has come down to us shows a stocky, keen-eyed, shaggy-haired man who seems plentifully supplied with energy even in his sixty-sixth year. Energy of a kind he certainly had always had. He was a great walker, fond of being in the open whenever possible. After a day's work he often fiddled at country dances and bridals with his brother or, later, with his son. Since his building and master-masoning business prospered moderately, and he had not absorbed the success philosophy of Samuel Smiles, he was always able to concentrate upon living as much as upon making a living.

His failure to get rich or to extend the family business—a failure that sometimes troubled his wife—is, one supposes, where the "spent social energy"[24] Hardy's second wife remarked upon comes in. He did not care about wealth. Having enough, he was content to live unambitiously, enjoying his music and the occasional collecting of old country jigs and hornpipes. Evidently he had time for an enjoyment of nature similar to his son's, for one of the few anecdotes that have been handed down tells of Thomas Hardy senior lying in hot weather "on a bank of thyme or camomile" and looking about while grasshoppers jumped over him.[25]

We do not know much about him as a father, save that his son idealized him. But he taught young Hardy to dance and to play the violin, communicated to his son some of his appreciation for nature, and helped him to a start as an architect. It is unlikely that such a father—as some critics imply[26]—dwelt mournfully upon the decline of the family since the days of Clement le Hardy, who founded the Dorchester grammar school in the fifteenth century, and Nelson's Captain Hardy.

Certainly Hardy's mother did not foster any sense that Hardy belonged to a race which had long since had its day. There was nothing remotely decadent about this yeoman's daughter, who was, according to the official biography, a woman of unusual ability, judgment, and energy, who read "every book she could lay hands on."[27] She was more ambitious than her husband. She frequently urged him to move away from remote Upper Bockhampton to a place where his building trade would become yet more prosperous. She was ambitious, too, for her son. She was responsible for the boy's removal to the well-taught Dorchester school and for his early taste for reading. Judging from her disapproval of her son's impracticality (of which no illustrations are given) and her dismay at his early lack of social ambition, one might even suppose that she tended to push her son too much.

But it should not be inferred that Mrs. Hardy was merely an ambitious mother. Her portrait, taken when she was in her sixties, although it fails to reveal the attractiveness of her youth, does give one the sense that she retained a capacity for enjoyment. From all accounts she could take a child's pleasure in amusing or exciting adventures. One anecdote, rather blurred in the telling, relates how she and young Thomas, full of laughter at the more conventional woman's surprise, burst in upon her sister disguised in cabbage nets. We learn, too, that when they took a trip to London together, Hardy and his mother were equally enthusiastic about tracing the course of Leonard Holt, the hero of *Old St. Pauls*, through the streets of London.[28]

Assuredly, Hardy, with the sophisticated perspective of maturity, did see his family and his class as declining. But it appears quite impossible, when we remember the normal youthful lack of historical perspective and what we know of Hardy's regard for his parents, that he became melancholy contemplating the declining fortunes of his family while he was still young.

Nor is it very likely that Hardy developed a melancholy view by perpetual contemplation of Egdon Heath, which almost reached the side of "the seven-roomed rambling house" where Hardy spent his first sixteen years, despite the fact that some critics have supposed this waste land a "dominant factor in Hardy's childhood."[29] For the Stinsford region, the Mellstock of *Under the Greenwood Tree*, is singularly beautiful. Near Hardy's home is the river Froom, whose "waters were clear as the pure River of Life . . . . , rapid as the shadow of a cloud."[30] Still nearer is the Yalbury Wood of the novels, where, in spring, "country people go to bed among nearly naked trees, are lulled to sleep by a fall of rain, and awake next morning among green ones . . . . , [where] the night-jar comes and strikes up for the summer his tune of one note."[31] Certainly it would be conclusive proof of Hardy's melancholy temperament if he altogether neglected the loveliness about him in his obsession with Egdon Heath. But the heath is only briefly described in his earliest poem and does not appear at all in a drawing he himself made of his birthplace.

If we rid ourselves of the preconceptions Hardy's magnificent description of Egdon naturally imposes, his home in Upper Bock-hampton helps, rather, to explain the delight Hardy expressed in "To Outer Nature." "High beeches" swept "against the roof," hanging a "veil of boughs." Wild honeysuckle climbed the walls. Everywhere around were "red roses, lilacs, variegated box."[32] And Dorsetshire as a whole has been described by an outsider as a "land literally flowing with milk and honey . . . . where rustic ways and speech and habits of thought live long, and the kindlier virtues are not forgotten."[33] If one recalls the descriptions of Dorsetshire-Wessex that occur in, say, *Under the Greenwood Tree*, remembers the poet William Barnes's invariably lovely Dorset, and recalls that Hardy was a normal child, not Father Time, the conjecture that Hardy grew melancholy staring at Egdon Heath must be dismissed.

6

Indeed, the further one examines Hardy's early environment, the more unaccountable become the various conjectures that Hardy was already developing a twilight view of life. Truly enough, the peasants were superstitious and unorthodox. Young Hardy may have known the postman of *Desperate Remedies* who hoped a time would come when "they'll do away wi' Goda-mighty altogether."[34] If he had had the intelligence of maturity in youth, he might have perceived that the superstitions of the peasants implied that "no supreme Will manifests itself [to them] as in control of the general scheme of things; there are only tremendous, inexplicable forces."[35]

But Hardy's parents were not peasants and were altogether orthodox Christians. They took care that their son attended two "High Church" services each Sunday. His contacts with the peasants were casual rather than intimate. What he saw of them was more likely to conform to the insight of William Barnes (whose poems, W. R. Rutland convincingly shows, he read in his early teens)[36] than to his own mature and somber insight. And the Reverend William Barnes, admirable poet that he was, was either unaware of peasant disbelief and pragmatism or unwilling to write about them. As a reading of his poems clearly shows, he found the Wessex peasant charming and delightful; an interesting subject for painstaking study of provincial peculiarities; good people; but never an incentive for mournful philosophizing or an inducement to other than a pleasant poetic melancholy.

Although it is true that Hardy later found the superstitions of the Wessex peasants artistically useful and felt that there was much truth in their "queer pragmatic view of Scriptural authority,"[37] in his youth he associated with the educated people about him—his parents, the schoolmaster and schoolmistress of his earliest schools, the vicar and his two sons, the Lady of the Manor—all of whom held views representative of the spirit of the time rather than of the beliefs peculiar to the Wessex peasant. The Wessex of William Barnes had not yet become the Wessex of Thomas Hardy.

7

If Hardy was influenced by the intellectual trends most current in his youth, an early pessimism would be altogether unaccountable. For it is not true, as Mme de Ridder-Barzin declares, that the English were more attached to the positive spirit of science than to religion during the thirties, that the Hegelianism of Strauss met ready welcome in England.[38] Nor is it legitimate to find, with Mlle Cazamian, that rationalism was dominant during the years between 1840 and 1860.[39] To do so is to confuse a growing, but still weak, progressive force with the characteristic religious thought of the time.

Far more characteristic of the religious thinking of the period than the isolated rationalism of a few positivists, a George Eliot or a Matthew Arnold, are the lectures sponsored by the three chief religious foundations of early and mid-nineteenth-century England: the Bampton, the Boyle, and the Hulsean. Although it is true that these lectures show a wide variety of opinions upon the primacy of reason, authority, or feeling in determining religious truth,[40] it is equally evident that all the lecturers agree on fundamental principles. As Clement Webb correctly concludes, all the lecturers made four outstanding assumptions: "(a) the transcendence of God; (b) the origin of the material world in an act of creation in time; (c) the claim of Scripture to be an authoritative revelation of truth otherwise unobtainable by man; (d) the happiness and salvation of individual souls as the supreme concern of religion."[41]

Indeed, these assumptions were still common to the majority of English churchmen in 1860. In this year, as a counterblast to the

〚 13 〛

Essays and Reviews (the manifesto of a few Broad Churchmen who held radical theological opinions), *Aids to Faith* and *Replies to "Essays and Reviews"* appeared. The first was edited by William Thomson, bishop of Gloucester and of Bristol, the second by Samuel Wilberforce, bishop of Oxford. Among the sixteen contributors to these volumes, there were four others who either were, or afterward became, bishops in the English Church. Each contributor emphatically believed in all the outstanding assumptions Webb has named. When one adds to this evidence the fact that eleven thousand clergy signed a declaration of belief in inspiration and eternal punishment in 1864,[42] he can hardly doubt that the essential orthodoxy of these essayists, and of the various lecturers, was representative of the norm in Anglican belief.

Moreover, the closer we come to Hardy's birth date, the more it becomes evident that the clergy paid heart rather than lip service to orthodox religious assumptions. The clergy that had, in the early decades of the century, been represented by such men as Henry Hawarth, who found it difficult to decide which was worse, enthusiasm or disbelief,[43] and Newman's bishop, who could not make up his mind whether he was a successor to the apostles or not,[44] became increasingly ardent in its conservative Christianity. Clergymen who were "on very easy terms with the world" were forced to become more devout and more intelligent theologically by the Oxford movement—which penetrated to Dorset in the very years in which Hardy was growing up.

Because the Oxford movement had succeeded so thoroughly, it would have been impossible for Newman to have decried the church (as he had in the thirties) during the period when Hardy was attending two High Church services. Mistiness was no longer regarded as the mother of wisdom.[45] Whether they agreed with the Puseyites or not, men now knew what they believed. An awakened church and an awakened clergy were everywhere conscious of the divine mission of the church and the supreme impor-

[[14]]

tance of man's communion with a God who transcends the natural order.

This awakening of the church is reflected in the poetry and fiction of the period. None of the novelists questioned scriptural truth, God's goodness, or the divine mission of the clergy. *Vanity Fair* (1847–48) shows the awful consequences of people living without God in the world.[46] Dickens continually tells us of the compensation heaven makes for this world's trials. "Think what earth is, compared with the world to which her young spirit has winged its early flight,"[47] one of his characters exclaims after the death of Little Nell. Similar passages might be taken from almost any novel of the period, and there are indications of a faith more devout in many of them. The poets who were best known—the two Brownings and Tennyson himself—never went beyond mild questioning, and they would have always agreed finally with Tennyson's wonder that he had listened to the doubting voice rather than with "him that said, 'Rejoice! rejoice!' "[48]

Although poets such as Matthew Arnold and Arthur Hugh Clough, although other men of considerable importance to the historian of the *progress* of the intellect, held unorthodox, occasionally antitheistic, views, and although the Noetics, the Broad Churchmen, the Coleridgeans, and the Radicals of the *Westminster Review* undermined the orthodoxy of the few and alarmed conservative theologians into long-titled replies, the general religious spirit from 1840 to 1860 was both orthodox and devout. Even the scientists bear testimony. Professor Agassiz was brought up under teachers who held that God had scattered fossils about the earth as a test of faith;[49] an Oxford teacher of high repute held, at about this time, that the typical vertebrate was multiplied all over the world as a proof of the Crucifixion;[50] in 1859, the year of the *Origin of Species*, Rawlinson, the Bampton lecturer, "gravely assumed the accuracy of the biblical chronology from Adam."[51] Skepticism and disbelief were alive, no doubt, but their vitality was not appreciated by the majority of Englishmen.

[15]

It is even proper to signalize the years from 1840 to 1860 as the last great heyday of fervent belief. The lukewarmness of the twenties and thirties overcome by the Oxford movement, there was everywhere a renewed interest in the significance of doctrine. What was before only said, now was felt. The supernatural world's contiguity to the world of man was appreciated as seldom before. God, all-good and all-powerful, was near to man, listening to his confession or prayer, granting absolution, planting the germ of spiritual growth in the child at baptism, renewing man's strength through the sacramental rite of the Holy Eucharist. If most of the English were unable to embrace the lyrical feeling that all's right with the world, they were devoutly certain that a living God, watching from above, was conscious of their sufferings and troubles and would, in this or the next world, right all.

8

Dorset, it is true, was a remote part of England. Even today it is difficult to get to Dorchester, its principal city. But Dorset was not the intellectually isolated district some of the writers on Hardy have supposed. The *Dorset County Chronicle* for the years between 1840 and 1860 is likely to startle anyone with preconceptions about the isolation of the region. Although one does not find evidence that either the most esoteric or the most radical thinking of the time was known in Dorset, it is clear to the point of obviousness that the readers of the county newspaper were familiar with the main tendencies in the religious thought of the period.

The weekly book column, until the very late fifties, does not pay much attention to secular literature (occasionally there are reviews of books as popular as *David Copperfield*), but there are detailed and discriminating reviews of the most important orthodox church periodicals and of many heavy tomes on theology. The *Churchman*, which was sympathetic to the Oxford movement, was reviewed regularly. The *Church of England Quarterly Review*—with which Samuel Wilberforce, a Tractarian sympathizer, was closely connected—was regularly given detailed summary. Although the frequently stupid perorations against popery contributed by both editors and readers reveal a provincialism and prejudice even Newman's most conservative followers would not have countenanced and although there is a tendency to gibe at the Puseyites at the same time that many of their ideas are accepted, there can be no doubt that the paper represented the general religious awakening and clarification for which the Oxford movement was responsible.

As phrases such as "our pure and apostolical branch of the Reformed Religion,"[52] reiterated again and again, reveal, Dorset was not afflicted with the muddy-mindedness of Newman's bishop who did not know whether he believed in the apostolic succession or not. As a characteristic comment upon *Eucharistica*—"we cannot too much admire the liturgical tone"[53]—demonstrates, Dorset had become sensitive to liturgical matters at the same time that the Church of England generally, following the Puseyites' lead, began to stress the importance of sacramental purity. As article after article and review after review reveal, Dorset shared the unimpeachable belief in the perfection of revealed religion that characterized Newman and his followers. "The history of the Church is the fulfillment of God's will for the salvation of man, the accomplishment of prophecies, the triumph of grace over the imperfections and sins of nature."[54] This might have been written by Newman; it was written by a contributor to the *Dorset County Chronicle*.

Accompanying this awakening of doctrinal awareness in Dorset was a resurgence of religious feeling. The laxity of Parson Raunham, who allowed his parishioners to do what they willed, was replaced by the more fervid Christianity of Parson Maybold. The single Sunday service that had been characteristic of Dorset generally before 1840 gave way to the observation of two services in four-fifths of the parishes of Dorset, Hardy's among them.[55] The poetry column of the *Dorset County Chronicle* began to be flooded with verses that revealed a staunchness of devotion that was equaled only by their bad metrics.

Whatever may be said of the mechanics of the lines, one cannot question the well-intentioned meaning of

> That call not education, which decries
> God and his truth, content the seed to strew
> Of moral maxims, and the mind imbue
> With elements which form the worldly wise.[56]

This was printed in 1840, but one might go on endlessly, quoting the stumbling lines and devout sentiments of the contributors to the *Chronicle* before 1860. But perhaps one more effusion, this time of 1855, will suffice:

> Oh! thou Omnipotent, Thy Voice we hear
> In the loud thunder rolling in the skies;
> We gaze upon Thy wondrous works with fear—
> Too grand, too glorious for our finite eyes.[57]

This feeling for an Omnipotence which surpasses and overshadows the finite characterized the educated Dorsetshire man. Hardy, his family, and the people with whom they most intimately associated were among these educated readers of the *Dorset County Chronicle*.

But we can come still closer in tracing the influence of a resurgent Anglicanism upon Hardy. About 1841 the amiable but not over-zealous Parson Murray (Raunham of *Under the Greenwood Tree*) was replaced by the vicar who appears as Maybold in Hardy's second novel.[58] His church in Stinsford, perhaps because he had come only recently from Oxford, was affected by the principles of the Tractarians. There was a morning and an evening service. Easygoing Christianity was replaced by ardent advocacy of High Church principles—although, it is clear, Hardy's vicar never went to the extreme of the radical Puseyites.[59]

In this church, where he regularly attended morning and evening service, taught Sunday school, and associated with the vicar's sons, Hardy became acquainted with a religion which, if it was conventional in its dogma, was not conventional in the ardor which accompanied the preaching of dogma. A little later, probably in Hardy's early teens, the influence of the Stinsford vicar was supplemented by frequent contact with Henry Moule, the vicar of near-by Fordington and a divine of some reputation throughout England.

It was entirely natural that Hardy should have become active in this church. His family had been prominent in the Stinsford parish for over a hundred years, and Hardy's father and mother both felt that their son should be reared according to "High Church principles." But the Hardy's were not religious fanatics. Hardy's mother was quite content that her son attend the nonconformist day school in Dorchester as long as he attended the Stinsford Anglican Church regularly. When "everybody" was suggesting Hardy would become a preacher, his mother had "many misgivings." Perhaps the absence of fanatical proselytizing made Hardy the more ready to accept Anglican teaching.

At any rate, there can be no doubt that Hardy grew into a convinced Anglican. While still quite young, he would wait for the moment when the evening sun intensified the Venetian red coloring of the staircase of his home to sing, "with great fervency," Dr. Watts's hymn "And Now Another Day Is Gone":

> I lay my body down to sleep:
>   Let angels guard my bed:
> And through the hours of darkness keep
>   Their watch around my head.

> With cheerful heart I close my eyes,
>   Since Thou wilt not remove;
> And in the morning let me rise
>   Rejoicing in Thy love.

When wet Sunday mornings kept him at home, he wrapped himself in a tablecloth and read the Morning Prayer standing on a chair, while his cousin played the part of the clerk and his grandmother served as congregation.

Moreover, Hardy taught Sunday school when he was fifteen and seriously considered entering the ministry as late as his twenty-fifth year.

Hardy's early devotion to religion is even more strongly evidenced by an episode of his first years as an architectural apprentice in Dorchester. One of his co-pupils, Bastow, who was an earnest Baptist, argued the necessity of adult baptism with Hardy. Bastow was so ardent a proselytizer that Hardy decided he must either give in or learn to meet his acquaintance's arguments effectively.

He sought out the vicar of his parish and asked for help. Referred to Hooker's *Ecclesiastical Polity*, Hardy read it—only to find it of no practical assistance. He consulted another vicar who lent him a handbook on the sacraments. Still unsatisfied, he examined as many books and notes on pedobaptism as he could find. When the two sons of Perkins, the Dorchester Baptist minister, joined Bastow in the effort to argue him down, Hardy gave up his reading of "heathen" authors—from whom he was just beginning to get pleasure—and worked steadily every night on the latest and most correct text of the Greek Testament he could buy. Certainly no young man who shared the "queer pragmatic faith" of the peasants and was indifferent to religion would have gone to such trouble to uphold a minor point in the Anglican credo.

The importance of religion to Hardy as a young man his poems confirm again and again. In "God's Funeral," after describing the procession of mourners for dead creeds, he declares:

> I could not buoy their faith: and yet
> Many I had known: with all I sympathized;
> And though struck speechless, I did not forget
> That what was mourned for, I, too, long had prized.[60]

In "The Impercipient at a Cathedral Service" Hardy speaks of the strange destiny that makes his comrades' faiths seem fantasies to him and protests against the charge that he is an unbeliever willingly:

> O, doth a bird *deprived* of wings
> Go earth-bound wilfully![61]

Again and again, throughout the collected poems, we hear this lament for a *loss* of faith. As late as the 1920's, Hardy's will to believe is manifested by his active interest in a movement to make "the Established Church comprehensive enough to include the majority of thinkers of the previous hundred years who *had lost* all belief in the supernatural."[62] Looking back upon the course of his development at a time when he was attacked unfairly and frequently as an enemy to religion, Hardy himself summarized the attitude toward Christianity the quotations above suggest:[63] "Although invidious critics had cast slurs upon him as Nonconformist, Agnostic, Atheist, Infidel, Immoralist, Heretic, Pessimist, or something else equally opprobrious in their eyes, they had never thought of calling him what they might have called him much more plausibly— churchy; *not in an intellectual sense, but in so far as instincts and emotions ruled.* As a child, to be a parson had been his dream; moreover he had had several clerical relatives who held livings; while his grandfather, father, uncle, brother, wife, cousin, and two sisters had been musicians in various churches over a period covering altogether more than a hundred years. He himself had frequently read the church lessons, and had at one time as a young man begun reading for Cambridge with a view to taking Orders."*

* My italics. Compare the above with: "after infinite trying to reconcile a scientific view of life with the emotional and spiritual so that they may not be interdestructive" (journal entry for May 9, 1881, *Early Life*, p. 192) and "a hymn rolls from a church-window, and the uncompromising No-Godist or Unconscious-Godist takes up the refrain" (journal entry for July 22, 1883, *ibid.*, p. 211).

Hardy's religious convictions, which he certainly must have felt intensely—how else account for the persistence of religious feeling?—can be defined with some clarity when we remember that he was a member of a church affected by the Oxford movement. He believed that the sacraments were more than mere forms, that they were important and direct means of communicating with God. Why, otherwise, was he so concerned with Bastow's arguments about baptism? He believed, with the Tractarians, that Scripture was a guide to truth otherwise unobtainable by man, that the Bible, including the story of man's origin related in Genesis, was literal truth. Otherwise, why the quotation of biblical texts in the argument over baptism? He believed in the apostolic descent of the clergy. Even "middle" churchmen so believed after the Oxford movement had run its course. He believed—all church members of his time did—in a transcendent God, omnipotent and beneficent, the guarantor of immortality, of the significance of each individual, and of the ultimate victory of justice.

Although such religious convictions are not necessarily accompanied by optimism—witness Jonathan Swift—there is evidence that Hardy tended to be optimistic. Certainly his attitude toward his family, toward the Lady of the Manor, and toward the early objects of his love indicates that he had a high regard for mankind in so far as he knew it. We can also see, from the poem "To Outer Nature," that he regarded Nature as an instrument for joy, as something which "love alone had wrought" for "his pleasure" and to "expound . . . . glad things that men treasure."

Furthermore, Hardy generally treats youth as a gay and hopeful period. In his poem "In Childbed," he has the mother, after warning the daughter of life's inevitable disillusionments, say,

> Yet, as you dream, so dreamt I
> When Life stretched forth its morning ray to me.[64]

In "The Unborn" he has the children look forward to the world as

>   A pure delight, a beauty-spot
>   Where all is gentle, true and just,
>   And darkness is unknown.[65]

With the exception of Father Time, all his young people—even
Jude—look forward hopefully to life. Like any other artist, Hardy
must be drawing upon his own experience in his interpretation.

Several autobiographical poems confirm this supposition. He refers to his childhood as a time before "I had learnt that the world
was a welter of futile doing."[66] He speaks of his youth as a period
when "I was the midmost of my world."[67] He asks:

>   "O Memory, where is now my hope
>   Who charged with deeds my skill and scope?"[68]

The preponderance of evidence and common sense alike lead us to
conclude that Hardy's youth was a period before the "necessity of
taking thought" had made the heavens gray,[69] when his insight into
the conditions of existence was so imperfect that he regarded life
hopefully.*

Indeed, there is evidence that Hardy had what Elliot calls a
"paradisaic tendency." Elliot believes that his tendency "derives
particularly from that kind of romanticism that found its extreme
expression in Shelley."[70] It is altogether possible that Hardy's view
of the world was influenced by Shelley, even in these early years.
That Hardy read some Shelley during this period we know.[71] We
also know, from numerous references to Shelley and from the frequent quotations from this poet in the novels, that Hardy was sym-

---

* Perhaps it is worth noting that Hardy's characters who do not occupy
themselves with thoughts on things in general are happy, while those who are
thinkers are unhappy ("The Dorsetshire Laborer," *Life and Art*, p. 21; *Tess*,
p. 11; *Hand of Ethelberta*, p. 391; *Woodlanders*, p. 8; *Laodicean*, p. 5; *Return of
the Native*, pp. 138, 139). This notion is probably the result of his own experience, for it was not until he began to think seriously that his own happiness
lessened. As he himself remarked, "[I] was a child till [I] was sixteen, a youth
till [I] was five and twenty, and a young man till [I] was nearly fifty" (*Early
Life*, p. 42). These periods roughly correspond to the time he spent exclusively
with his parents, the time which elapsed until he became an antitheist, and the
time it took him to give his philosophy final formulation.

pathetic with portions of the romantic poet's philosophy at a later period.[72] It is quite conceivable that his picture of what the world should be was colored by the paradisaic desires of Laon and Cythna.*

When we turn to those books Hardy read in these years that might have contradicted his paradisaic hopes, we find him, interestingly enough, neglecting them or overlooking their tragic implications. We know that he read Johnson's *Rasselas*, but one can find no reference to it in his journals and no allusion to it in his highly allusive novels. We know that he read the Bible, therefore presumably Ecclesiastes and Job, but there is no reason for supposing he was more fond of them than most youths—and I suspect that these are books which make their particular appeal to maturity. We know that he read, with great care, some of the *Iliad*. One might suspect, thinking of the later Hardy, that one of his favorite passages would be the pathetic scene between Priam and Achilles, where the very Hardyan passage, "This is the lot the Gods have spun for miserable men,"[73] occurs. Actually, however, the passages Hardy particularly admired at this time are almost purely rhetorical. His favorite passages were the speech of Phoenix (ix. 434–601), the fight of Hector and Ajax (xiv. 388–432), the descriptions of Achilles' appearance unarmed (xviii. 202–26), of the heavenly armor for Achilles (xviii. 468–617), and of the funeral games in honor of Patroclus (xxiii. 700 ff.).[74] Did he overlook the tragic implications of these works because they conflicted too much with the view of life he then held? Or did he simply fail to see anything but what he was conditioned to see?

At any rate, the novels of Ainsworth, James Grant, Bernardin de St. Pierre, G. P. R. James, and Dumas *père*, favorites of his youth,

* It is possible that the reading of Shelley, particularly the reading of *Queen Mab*, began the undermining of Hardy's religious convictions. I doubt this, however, because most mid-century readers of Shelley passed *Queen Mab* by as one of the poet's indiscretions; because Hardy never refers to the poem or Shelley's early rationalism; and because Hardy's continual reference to Shelley as a lyrical rather than as a philosophic poet leads me to believe that he undervalued the philosophic poetry.

all give the same specious and paradisaic view of life. There are two classes of people, the good and the bad. The good eventually prosper and marry the inconceivably lovely, faithful, and virtuous heroines; the bad always deserve their unhappy fate. The world is described as a place where poetic justice always prevails. Hardy's early view of life must have been affected by such reading.

Whatever the cause, there is no doubt that Hardy was always inclined to regard as universal the wish that earth be heaven. In *A Laodicean* he remarks that human nature is at bottom romantic.[75] If we interpret the word "romantic" to mean a desire for an impossibly perfect world, his novels bear out this statement. His lovers expect their sweethearts to be faultless. Angel Clare's love was "ethereal to a fault, imaginative to impracticability"; Egbert Mayne's love is worship of Geraldine, Smith idealizes Elfride, so does Knight; Dick Dewey idealizes Fancy. As Elfride remarks to Stephen Smith, it appears that men want to make a world to suit their happiness.[76] They are not content with things as they are (or even with any practical conception of what things may become) because they are looking for perfection.[77]

There are, of course, no contemporary autobiographical documents to prove definitely that Hardy had this "paradisaic tendency." But it is evident that he later expected much more of life than life readily grants. He thought of his wife as one to "match the maddest dream's desire." He wished that the delicious minute before meeting could be indefinitely prolonged. He believed that he should be unable to smile when his friend is in trouble. He thought that his loved one should be unhappy in his absence and think only of him.[78] One of the main criticisms he later made of the world is that there is a disproportion between what man expects and what man obtains.[79] It is hardly logical to suppose that this paradisaic attitude, a more usual accompaniment of youth than of maturity, suddenly burst into flower when Hardy became a man. This tendency must have been a part of him even when he was young. Far

[[25]]

from being one who "never expected much," he was a youth who expected too much.

Although there were undoubtedly discordant elements in his youthful philosophy—Hardy was aware of the presence of injustice; his long remembrance of the sheep-keeping boy's death of starvation and of the frozen fieldfare testify to that—he also believed that a personal and just God who was profoundly interested in the fate of human beings ruled the universe. He believed that the world and life were good; he was hopeful rather than gloomy.

But there were forces at work in Hardy and the world about him which were eventually to destroy his happy outlook. He was extremely sensitive to pain; he did not care much for companionship. For the time he was able to accept apparent injustice as either actual justice or injustice which God would eventually right. If, however, he were to lose his faith in God, such a reconciliation would become impossible. About him lived the peasants, who took their religion lightly, whose superstitious practices apparently concealed a belief in a malign force, whose fatalism suggested a ruling Power that cared little for man's fate. In the great world, far from Dorchester, with which he was soon to come in contact, Darwin was publishing the *Origin of Species*, and the "Seven against Christ" were publishing the radical *Essays and Reviews*.

If these forces in the outside world were to come in contact with Hardy's sensitiveness to pain and injustice, with his excessive belief in the goodness of the universe, he might come to believe that the peasant's view of life is closer to truth than his own. He would see that his romantic desires could not be gratified. He would become disillusioned, and the first step to the formation of a contradictory world view would be taken.

II

FLUX AND REFLUX

Next this strange message Darwin brings,
. . . .
We all are one with creeping things.

—*Winter Words*

1

IT WOULD, of course, be entirely wrong to assume that the London of the sixties was altogether different from the London of the preceding decades. Despite the fact that it was a period in which radical theologians did more to destroy the foundations of religious belief than they had ever done before, orthodoxy still seemed firmly intrenched. Although such Noetics and Latitudinarians as Milman,[1] Thirlwall,[2] and Martineau[3] had already disturbed the preponderantly orthodox theologians by their approximation of the methods of Feuerbach, Niebuhr, and Strauss;[4] although the most alertly "modern" were already aware of the extreme heterodoxy of Matthew Arnold,[5] George Henry Lewes,[6] and the *Westminister Review;*[7] and although the better-informed scientists and philosophers had known for some time of the metaphysical radicalism of Spencer[8] and the scientific radicalism of Chambers,[9] the majority of Englishmen remained undisturbed in their faith and naïve optimism even after Darwin and the authors of the *Essays and Reviews* became "notorious" figures.

Still, there can be no doubt that the publication of the *Origin of Species* and *Essays and Reviews* caused an intellectual upheaval that gave a distinctive mark to the years in which Hardy first came into contact with the trend of the times. . . . .

On November 24, 1859, Darwin's book was published unobtrusively. The danger of the book was not appreciated by the *Saturday Review*, which noticed it in a spirit of qualified approval exactly a month later. Truly enough, the critic remarks that some people will view the *Origin* with alarm, thinking that, like Chambers' *Vestiges of Creation*, it tends to "dispense with the agency of an intelligent Creator in the work of creation." But the *Saturday*'s reviewer will not be counted in this group. "No conceivable amount of evidence derived from the growth and structure of animals and plants would have the slightest bearing upon our conviction in regard to the origin of conscience, or man's belief in a Supreme Being and the immortality of his own soul."[10] Two days later Thomas Huxley cautiously reviewed the book in the London *Times:* Darwin "is as greedy of cases . . . . as any constitutional lawyer. . . . . The path he bids us follow professes to be . . . . a solid and broad bridge of facts. *If* it be so, it will carry us safely over many a chasm in our knowledge."[11] Meanwhile the public was quietly reading. On January 7, 1860, the first edition of twelve hundred and fifty copies being exhausted, a second edition of three thousand copies was issued. All was quiet until April, 1860.

The outcry began in the *British Quarterly*. The reader is asked to imagine a monkey at the zoo saying: "It is very true that we are clumsy, inelegant brutes. . . . . But . . . . just a word in your ear, gentlemen. Are you aware that you and we have come from the same stock—that we are all descended from one common ancestor—that we, vile, despicable brutes as you deem us, are in truth bone of your bone, and flesh of your flesh?"[12]

It is not likely that many of the public relished the suggestion. Nor was the *Edinburgh Review* article, reputedly by the geologist Owen, more calculated to gain satisfied adherents to the new theory, though its tone was more respectful.[13] By this time (April, 1860), as the radical *Westminster Review* remarks, "everybody has read Mr. Darwin's book, or, at least, has given an opinion upon its merits or demerits; pietists, whether lay or ecclesiastic, decry it with the mild railing which sounds so charitable; bigots denounce it with ignorant invective; old ladies, of both sexes, consider it a decidedly dangerous book, and even savans who have no better mud to throw, quote antiquated writers to show that its author is no better than an ape himself."[14] Or, as the more moderate *Saturday Review* remarks a month later: "The controversy excited by the appearance of Darwin's remarkable work on the *Origin of Species* has passed beyond the bounds of the study and lecture-room into the drawing-room and the public street."[15]

As the excitement manifested at the well-known debate between Huxley and Wilberforce, where the men cheered and the women waved handkerchiefs, shows, the *Saturday Review* did not exaggerate.[16] Nor was Bishop Wilberforce crushed by Huxley's famous retort. In the July number of the *Quarterly Review*, Wilberforce declared: "Mr. Darwin writes as a Christian, and we doubt not that he is one. We do not for a moment believe him to be one of those who retain in some corner of their hearts a secret unbelief which they dare not vent; and we therefore pray him to consider well the grounds on which we brand his speculations with the charge of such a tendency. First, then, he not obscurely declares that he applies his scheme of the principle of natural selection to Man himself. . . . . Man's derived supremacy over the earth . . . . man's free will and responsibility; the Incarnation of the Eternal Son; the indwelling of the Eternal Spirit, all are equally and utterly irreconcilable with the degrading notion of the brute origin of him who was created in the image of God."[17]

Some of the sound and fury abated after July, 1860. But it was at best a partial abatement. In February, 1861, *Blackwood's Magazine* reviewed Darwin in connection with a French book on spontaneous generation and in May published a half-humorous versification of the Darwinian hypothesis.[18] On June 22 the *Saturday Review*, writing on "Lyell and Tennyson," speaks of the poet's frequent use of the questionings about the universe which science has made such a prominent subject for discussion.[19] A third edition of the *Origin* was called for by the end of the year.[20] On October 18, 1862, the *Saturday Review*, noticing Darwin's work on the fertilization of orchids, speaks again of the furor raging about the *Origin of Species*.[21] In the same year, Spencer's *First Principles*, the complete embodiment of a naturalistic philosophy more radical than any that could be inferred from Darwin, was published.

Huxley's *Man's Place in Nature*, which states that "the attempt to draw a psychical distinction [between man and beast] is . . . . futile, and that even the highest faculties of feeling and of intellect begin to germinate in lower forms of life,"[22] Lyell's *Antiquity of Man*, guardedly favoring the transmutation theory,[23] and Dingle's *The Harmony of Revelation and Science* testify to the continued interest of real and pseudo-scientists in the entire question during 1863. The periodical press continued to make much of evolution, pro and con. The *Saturday Review* for 1864 contains three articles bearing directly upon the question, the last one of which, though admitting that perhaps Darwin is right, repeats the oft-recurring lament that the "ordinary mind feel[s] displeased at the ignominious suggestion that its personality is mysteriously related to that of the ape."[24] Between 1863 and 1872 three more editions of the *Origin* were called for.[25] The battle between such Darwinians as Huxley and Hooker and their more timid and conservative contemporaries continued far into the century.[26]

Early in 1861 Dean Church, writing to the American scientist, Asa Gray, remarked that the *Origin of Species* "would be the subject still of a great row, if there were not a much greater row going on about *Essays and Reviews*."[27] After having been temperately reviewed by the *Spectator* for April 7, 1860, the latter volume was the subject of a sensational article in the *Westminster Review* for October. The critic urged that the Essayists were hopelessly muddling conservative and progressive principles, that the tendency of their writings was definitely toward atheism, and that the authors were probably among the number of timid antitheists who abounded at Oxford and Cambridge. It concluded with the challenging statement: "Our account of this book would be incomplete unless we were to point to the reception it has received. It has passed through two editions, it has been read and discussed within and without the Church, with the hesitation of reflection or the pleasure of surprise. . . . . The authorities of the Universities are paralyzed, and incapable even of a protest. . . . . In the meantime, many of the younger members have received it with welcome and assent, many also with welcome but with slight assent. Indeed, no one that knows the religious state of the Universities could doubt that such a book would be eagerly welcomed, but welcomed only as a partial installment. Few, perhaps, are aware how far the decay of belief extends beneath those walls."[28]

Bishop Wilberforce, already a church hero in the Darwin controversy, stepped nobly forward to accept the challenge, agreed with the radical *Westminster*'s statement that the Essayists were tending toward atheism, and wrote in an article in the January (1861) *Quarterly Review:* "It is not true that the highest intellects revolt hopelessly against the old simple Christianity, and that it must either forfeit their adherence or submit to the reconstruction of the rationalist. The greatest, the most comprehensive, and the acutest intellects have received, and daily do receive, even as little children, without abatement, and without doubt, the whole Christian revelation."[29]

But the "highest intellects" were undoubtedly disturbed, as the continuous flow of articles testified. The *Edinburgh Review* came to the defense of the Essayists; the *Saturday Review* adopted a moderate attitude.[30] The *Essays and Reviews* reached an eighth edition by March, 1861, less than a year after its first publication.[31] Before 1861 had run its course, two bulky volumes—*Aids to Faith*, edited by the Lord Bishop of Gloucester and Bristol, and *Replies to "Essays and Reviews,"* prefaced by Bishop Wilberforce—and a host of small pamphlets with lengthy titles appeared. In short, as the *Saturday Review* declared,[32] "it is like the attempt to make oneself heard amidst the roaring of a tempest to uplift the feeble voice of reason amidst the storm that is raging about *Essays and Reviews*."* Or, as the writers of the *Life and Letters of Benjamin Jowett* affirm, "every diocese, archdeaconry, and rural deanery throughout the land became a busy hive for the manufacture of memorials against the notorious 'seven.' "[33]

It was a tempest which continued even after 1863. By provoking its share of replies, Bishop Colenso's *Examination of the Pentateuch* (1862–79), with its denial of the truth of Old Testament arithmetic, added more fuel to the flames. As late as December, 1863, the *Saturday Review*, commenting upon the decrease of young men as candidates for ordination, wrote: "Young men have read the *Essays and Reviews*, and more recently have perhaps puzzled their heads over Bishop Colenso's last edition of his *Arithmetic*, and the result is that they are (what is called) unsettled—i.e. look upon theology as a nebulous atmosphere, and on Holy Orders as a hazardous experiment, pecuniarily and intellectually."[34] The publication of John Stuart Mill's *Comte and Positivism* and the appearance of Lecky's *History of the Rise and Influence of the Spirit of Rationalism in Europe* and of Seeley's *Ecce homo*, all in 1865, surely did little to reassure the doubts of the wavering.

Unsettlement was not, of course, the effect of the *Origin* and the *Essays* upon all minds. The comment of *Fraser's Magazine* in 1860 doubtless represents the attitude of many: "No one need fear

---

* See also: "Every age must have its subject of religious controversy; and in ours the necessary fuel has been, to a partial extent, furnished by the discrepancy, real or supposed, which is alleged to exist between Revelation and the discoveries of science" (*Saturday Review*, XI [June 8, 1861], 589).

that the worship and faith to which that structure [the church] is dedicated, will be in any degree jeopardized by changes like those advocated in these *Essays and Reviews*.

> Our little systems have their day,
> They have their day and cease to be.
> They are but broken lights of Thee
> And Thou, O Lord, art more than they."[35]

There were undoubtedly many young men who agreed with Huxley's faith in natural selection: "Thoughtful men, once escaped from the blinding influence of traditional prejudice, will find in the lowly stock whence man has sprung, the best evidence of the splendour of his capacities; and will discern in his long progress through the Past a reasonable ground of faith in his attainment of a nobler Future."[36] But there was more than a little cause for Bishop Wilberforce's perturbation. He was probably right when he warned the young men of Oxford—as Newman had warned his contemporaries still earlier—that "the admission of doubts on subjects of pure criticism and history would lead to metaphysical doubts, and end in doubt of God."[37]

Wilberforce could have found justification in the lives of his younger contemporaries. During these years John Addington Symonds,[38] John Henry Green,[39] and Richard Jeffries[40] lost or nearly lost their faith. Lyell, Gray, and many other scientists, although they were convinced of the truth of evolution, "shuddered at the thought" of being cousin to an ape.[41] We have no way of telling how many more ordinary men were similarly troubled, but there can be no question that there were many such.

2

When we turn from the revolutionary developments of science and theology to the simple facts of Hardy's life from 1860 to 1865 —the years in which these revolutionary developments culminated

—it is at first difficult to see the ferment that must have been going on in his mind. In 1860, while still in Dorchester with another year or more of his apprenticeship ahead of him, Hardy began to think seriously about his professional future. Realizing the necessity of diligent application, he worked harder than usual and made many sketches for church restorations, perhaps believing that his future lay in this branch of architecture. Still, he could not abandon his other and, one infers, more pleasant activities. With his father and his uncle, he frequently played at country dances and observed—his future as a writer already a considered possibility?—peasant ways. Much of his free time, often made free at the expense of sleep, he spent with books. He read with interest Bagehot's *Estimates*, much poetry, parts of Homer and Virgil, some Aeschylus and Sophocles, the *Essays and Reviews*, and Darwin's *Origin of Species*.

The mention of Darwin, the Greek poets, and the Essayists suggests that the process which was to change Hardy from a devout young man to a believer in "crass Casualty" was already under way while he was in Dorchester, but there are no outer signs of perturbation. Once he had secured a position with the prominent London architect, Arthur Blomfield, he adopted a way of life that must have characterized many a young man about town. As the year of his settling in London coincided with the date of the Great Exhibition of 1862, he visited it frequently. He went to the National Gallery during many of his lunch hours. He attended the Italian operas at Her Majesty's and Covent Garden, where he heard the works of Rossini, Donizetti, Verdi, and Bellini; and the English opera, where he listened to the arias of Balfe, Wallace, and others. He sang in a church choir. He often saw Charles Kean and his wife in Shakespeare and went to all of Phelps's performances of the Elizabethan's plays. He danced at Almack's, the Cremorne, and the Argyll. He listened to Dickens read from his own works.

Nevertheless, in his growing preoccupation with the possibility of a career in letters, there are indications that he was no ordinary man about town. Even in Dorchester his reading evidenced this preoccupation; his continued effort to keep up with the literature of his age in spite of the distractions of London proves the seriousness of his intentions. He read a good deal of nineteenth-century prose: Ruskin's *Modern Painters*, Newman's *Apologia*, Thackeray's *Vanity Fair*, Trollope's *Barchester Towers*, Bulwer's *Pelham*, and the *Saturday Review*. He read much poetry: Shelley, as always; Byron's *Childe Harold*; Thomas Moore's *Lalla Rookh*; much Horace; other poets, ancient and modern, whose names are not supplied by the official biography. More than this, he continued his fugitive efforts as a writer, first begun when he wrote "Domicilium," sending some accounts of church restoration and a humorous skit to the *Dorset County Chronicle* before coming to London. He wrote verse frequently, undertaking, in addition to the writing of many short lyrics (a few of which are preserved), the rendering of Ecclesiastes into Spenserian stanzas. A prose sketch of his, "How I Built Myself a House," was accepted by *Chambers' Journal* and appeared in 1865.[42]

All this, however, gives us only a superficial picture of Hardy during this immensely important period of his life. There are more significant matters to consider. How did he come in contact with the spirit of the time that was to have so disenchanting an effect upon him? How did it happen that Hardy became one of the earliest readers of the *Origin of Species* and *Essays and Reviews*, neither of which is mentioned in the *Dorset Chronicle* until after Hardy had read them? How did it happen he broke company with those of whom Bishop Wilberforce could still speak in 1861 with much justification who "have received, and daily do receive, even as little children, without abatement and without doubt, the whole Christian revelation?"[43]

Unquestionably, Hardy's intimacy with Horace Mosley Moule, Cambridge fellow, writer for the *Saturday Review*, and son of the vicar of Fordington, was primarily responsible for his early contact with the thought of his time. For Moule was both Hardy's first intimate friend and a man of unusual intellectual achievements. Just before Hardy's intimacy with him, Moule had won the Hulsean prize at Cambridge for his book on *Christian Oratory;* his book had been favorably noticed by the press; and he had become a writer for the most prominent organ of the intelligentsia of the sixties.[44] It was not the least of his intellectual achievements that Moule was able to see something in Hardy—young, orthodox, and undeveloped—which deserved his time and his friendship from their first meeting in 1860 until, as it is said, discouraged by his inability to overcome dipsomania, he committed suicide in 1873.

The fact that Moule is said to have committed suicide brings one up with a start. Hardy's best friend a suicide? It looks as though one has come upon a very significant fact indeed. But it is difficult to do more than speculate about the effect of Moule's temperament upon Hardy. The correspondence of Hardy and his friend, extending over thirteen years, has been destroyed. To judge by the meager biographical evidence—most of it is hearsay—Moule was not a particularly melancholy person except when he became despondent about his excessive love for alcohol. Certainly his published writings—the Hulsean prize essay already mentioned, some verses published by the Fordington Times Society, a cram book on Roman history, and a heavily learned article on Achilles and Lancelot—do not reveal either unorthodoxy or pessimism. Perhaps their main importance is that they confirm what biographical evidence suggests, that Moule knew a great deal and was well informed about what was going on in intellectual circles in the 1860's. No doubt Moule's attacks of despondency and his suicidal tendency helped to confirm Hardy's twilight view of the universe. It seems, however, most probable that the information about the intellectual currents of the time Moule brought to Hardy and the older man's recommendation of specific books exerted an influence more important than any temperamental peculiarity.

Certainly Moule's influence upon the thinking of his friend must have been considerable. Not only was Moule thoroughly versed in the classical learning of his time; he was also a reader of those modern historians, who, after the method of Niebuhr, treated biblical history no more respectfully than they did the records of the ancient civilizations. In addition to his familiarity with older historians such as Gibbon and Niebuhr, he knew well Bunsen (later regarded by Englishmen as little better than a heretic), Milman, and Grote.[45] His own book, though nominally devout, shows that he was inclined to accept the newer school of historical criticism,[46] and his own verse, particularly in its juxtaposition to the redundant piety of the Fordington Times Society, suggests that he was more nominally than ardently religious.

Hardy, whose belief in such sacraments as baptism had perhaps been disturbed by his arguments with Bastow, must have talked frequently with Moule about the evidences for Christianity. He must have heard with interest of Bunsen's lenient treatment of heretics, Gibbon's ironic civility to Christianity, and Milman's naturalistic method of treating Gospel history. It is doubtful, however, whether Hardy was profoundly affected one way or the other by his early conversations with Moule. Since he was intent upon getting up his knowledge of both classical and biblical Greek and was extremely busy as an architect's pupil besides, he had little time for reading these writers. Unless his regard for truth was much less in this period than it later was, he would not have been satisfied by even a friend's unsubstantiated statements. Moule's most important influence upon Hardy lay in another direction.

Hardy had not been to London since his early childhood. Living in a provincial town, surrounded by provincial people, he had had little contact with the spirit of the time. Moule, spending most of his time in Cambridge and London, was thoroughly sensitive to contemporary trends of thought. A fellow at Cambridge and formerly a student at Oxford, Moule must have realized the important destructive action which Darwin's *Origin of Species* might have on religious belief; he probably had heard of the *Essays and Reviews* even before they were published and knew what a storm of protest they would arouse in orthodox circles. At any rate, we know that it was Moule who first introduced Hardy to the *Essays*, that it was probably Moule who first drew his attention to Darwin's work.[47] Still further one may conjecture that Moule, who was probably writing for the *Saturday Review* shortly after he first met Hardy, introduced him to this magazine, the most frequent recorder of the quarrel between faith and science in the sixties. It is even possible that Moule was influential in causing Hardy to come up to London in 1862, thus bringing him into even more direct contact with the most tempestuous assault the faith of man in God had ever endured in England. But it is unimportant for us to decide specifically what Moule introduced to Hardy. It is sufficient that we know he put Hardy *en rapport* with the radical religious and scientific thinking that had been going on while Hardy was still in Dorset and with the still more radical thinking of the 1860's.

3

It is difficult to say dogmatically with how much of the iconoclastic literature of the time Hardy was familiar. As Hardy read the *Saturday Review* regularly and was in constant contact with Moule, a contributor, it is probable that he had heard or read discussions of most of the religious and scientific literature I have mentioned. But there can be no question as to which of these books affected him most profoundly. For it is not only true that *Essays and Reviews* and the *Origin of Species* were the most notorious and influential books of the early sixties; it is also true that Hardy stated definitely that these books were of particular importance to him in his young manhood. When we examine these books carefully, it becomes evident that they could have destroyed his faith and forced him into the first formulation of his "pessimistic" philosophy, even if they had not been supplemented by other rationalistic literature.

One of the *Essays* Hardy read, Pattison's "Tendencies of Religious Thought in England, 1688–1750," as it is no more than an impartial historical survey, probably had little effect upon him. Jowett's essay, "On the Interpretation of Scripture," particularly in its remarks upon the *mis*interpretation of Scripture, contained sufficient iconoclasm to disturb Hardy more than a little. But the other, and more radical, essays must have caused more painful doubts to arise in his mind.

Frederick Temple declares that man has been developed by Rome, Asia, and Greece quite as much as by the Jewish people and their Bible. "Thus the Hebrews may be said to have disciplined the human conscience; Rome, the human will; Greece, the reason and taste; Asia, the spiritual imagination." Moreover, Temple finds the Bible "a history: even the doctrinal parts of it are cast in a historical form, and are best studied by considering them as records of the time at which they were written, and as conveying to us the highest and greatest religious life of that time. *Hence we use the Bible—some consciously, some unconsciously—not to override, but to evoke, the voice of conscience.*"[48]

Reading the second of the articles in the book, Hardy came upon the following: "The sacred writers acknowledge themselves men of like passions with ourselves, and we are promised illumination from the Spirit which dwelt in them. Hence, when we find our Prayer-book constructed on the idea of the Church being an inspired society instead of objecting that everyone of us is fallible, we should define inspiration consistently with the facts of Scripture and human nature." At the end of his essay, the author, Rowland Williams, approvingly quotes the words of Bunsen, " 'How long shall we bear this fiction of an *external* revelation?' "[49]

In the essay on the "National Church," Hardy discovered that 42 per cent of the people do not attend church, that the early Christian church included those who did not believe in immortality, that the skeptic should not be eternally damned, that there is doubt as to the authenticity of the Genesis account of creation, and that the national church should be liberalized until it includes both ideologists and literalists.[50] Nor were these the greatest "difficulties" the book presented to the young High Churchman. The Mosaic cosmogony, he read, conflicts sharply with the findings of science and is incorrect. Moses was really no more than an early, groping Newton who set down probability as certainty.[51] Hardy also read Baden Powell's declaration that miracles must be tested rationally in accordance with now-known laws and that the *Origin of Species* is an authority which supersedes the Mosaic record of creation.[52] Within the covers of this single volume of *Essays* Hardy met the full force of the period's rationalistic criticism of the conventional Christian faith.

As Hardy read the *Essays* before he examined Darwin's work, he was probably looking for evidence for or against the Mosaic records when he first read the *Origin*. As portions of the book that discredited the authenticity of revelation were frequently pointed out in the reviews, Hardy must have been led to certain significant passages: "I cannot doubt that the theory of descent with modification embraces all the members of the same great class or kingdom. I believe that animals are descended from at most only four or five progenitors, and plants from an equal or lesser number. Analogy would lead me one step farther, namely, to the belief that all animals and plants are descended from some prototype. But analogy may be a deceitful guide."[53]

But this was only one of Hardy's previous beliefs the *Origin* must have compelled him to renounce. Hardy had formerly interpreted nature as something "love alone had wrought." Darwin thought of nature as the scene of the struggle for existence: "Everyone had heard that when an American forest is cut down, a very different vegetation springs up; but it had been observed that ancient Indian ruins in the Southern United States, which must formerly have been cleared of trees, now display the same beautiful diversity and proportion of kinds as in the surrounding virgin forest. What a struggle must have gone on during long centuries between the several kinds of trees, each annually scattering its seeds by the thousand; what a war between insect and insect—between insects, snails, and other animals with birds and beasts of prey—all striving to increase, all feeding on each other, or on the trees, their seeds and seedlings, or on the other plants which first clothed the ground and thus checked the growth of the trees.

"We behold the face of nature bright with gladness, we often see superabundance of food; we do not see, or we forget, that the birds which are idly singing round us live mostly on insects or seeds, and are thus constantly destroying life; or we forget how largely these songsters, or their eggs, or their nestlings, are destroyed by birds and beasts of prey."[54] By an implication widely accepted, this struggle also applied to man. If Hardy accepted the Darwinian hypothesis, he would be compelled to change entirely his previous conception of the law which governed the universe.

Owing to his background and the distinct ideas of good and bad he had previously accepted, Hardy must have wondered how one could speak of the survivors as the fittest. As he would have interpreted this phrase himself, as any man who accepted the values that had been current in Hardy's world would have interpreted the phrase, it meant the survival of those who best deserved, in a human sense, to survive. But according to Darwin: "It may metaphorically be said that natural selection is daily and hourly scrutinizing, throughout the world, the slightest variation; rejecting those that are *bad*, preserving and adding up all that are *good;* silently and insensibly working, *whenever and wherever* opportunity offers, at the improvement of each organic being in relation to *its organic and inorganic conditions of life.*"[55]

Such a structural conception of "good" and "bad" was entirely at variance with the theistic and ethical interpretation Hardy had formerly given these words. Similarly, there was material in the *Origin* that must have caused him to doubt the actuality of the place he had previously allotted man, the end of all creation: "With respect to the belief that organic beings have been created beautiful for the delight of man. . . . . If beautiful objects had been created solely for man's gratification, it ought to be shown that before man appeared there was less beauty on the face of the earth than since he came on the stage. Were the beautiful volute and cone shells of the Eocene epoch, and the gracefully sculptured ammonites of the Secondary period, created that men might ages afterwards admire them in his cabinet?"[56]

Still, granting that all this must have been a severe shock to Hardy's traditional beliefs, it is legitimate to wonder why Hardy was unable to arrive at a faith similar to that of the clergyman Darwin quotes in the *Origin*. This man wrote that "he has gradually learnt to see that it is just as noble a conception of the Deity to believe that He created a few original forms capable of self-development into other and needful forms, as to believe that He required a fresh act of creation to supply the voids caused by the action of His law."[57] Why did not Hardy believe that the all-pervading destructiveness necessary to the survival of the fittest was compatible with the idea of a beneficent Deity, that the surviving types were actually the fittest? Why did he not accept the clergyman's belief and remain an unperturbed follower of a more "modern" Christianity?

There were elements in Hardy's background and character which distinguished him from the clergyman and most of his contemporaries in more ways than one. While he believed in Christianity, he repudiated the ideas behind the peasant mores as the philosophy of an inferior, less-educated group. If, however, he tended to accept the Darwinian account of the world's operation, his knowledge of the peasant's outlook would make the scientist's theory appear more credible at the same time that the scientist's hypothesis would make the peasant philosophy appear more probable. The peasants' superstitions which seem to posit a malicious rather than a beneficent force behind happenings, their bitter feeling that God sends bread to one house and children to another, their belief that nature scatters "heartless severities or overwhelming generosities in lawless caprice,"[58] would influence the effect the *Origin* would have upon Hardy.* Since the law of natural selection depends upon accidental variation to make the fittest survive, it would seem altogether likely that a kind of "lawless caprice" did govern human fortunes. Since the force which governs natural selection apparently cares for good and bad only in a structural sense, no reason appears why a malignant force, quite capable of sending bread to one home and children to another, might not have control of the universe.

Moreover, Hardy was inordinately sensitive to the pain and suffering of others. As an old man of eighty, he exclaimed against Mrs. Hardy's speaking of a "lovely, frosty morning"—"It is too inconsiderate of the birds' suffering."[59] Two of the most lasting impressions of his childhood, his painful remembrance of the frozen fieldfare and of the starved sheep-keeping boy, were connected with the cruelty of the struggle for existence. Such extreme sensitiveness would cause him to accept with greater reluctance than our clergyman, or even Thomas Huxley, the pain of the less organically fit.

* It should be noted, however, that the Wessex peasant in general is resigned or skeptical rather than bitter. As Lionel Johnson (*The Art of Thomas Hardy* [new ed.; London, 1923], p. 155) has expressed it: "The attitude of Mr. Hardy's country folk toward existing forms of worship, is that of customary adherence to the 'old ancient' ways, venerable by their establishment for three centuries; a religion of use and wont; not lightly to be renounced, not greatly to be revered, but to be accepted naturally, as a fact in the order of existing things."

Hardy had been reared on the edge of Edgon Heath; he had had, since childhood, a firsthand opportunity of observing all forms of nature, "striving to increase, feeding on each other." Excessively sensitive, the impressions the observed cruelty in nature made upon him were unusually deep and lasting. Reading in Darwin of the struggle going on in all nature integrated his hitherto dim and disconnected impressions of the cruel plan by which Nature works and made him even more sensitive than before to the pain involved in the continuation of life.

4

Hardy's reading of the Essayists, who undermined his faith, and of Darwin, who destroyed his faith, accounts for his coming to believe in the universal scope of "crass Casualty" as no other explanation can. Schopenhauer was not generally known in England during this period.[60] Hardy did not read German. He could not have accepted the peasant philosophy, unchecked and unconfirmed, as an accurate account of the working of the universe. The *Essays* and the *Origin* were based on sound evidence and sound arguments. The folk beliefs had less rational grounds of support than the Christian scheme in which Hardy had believed.

It is improbable, however, that these two books were the only ones to influence his change of outlook. We know that "as a young man [Hardy] had been among the earliest acclaimers of the *Origin of Species*," that he was much impressed by the *Essays and Reviews*;[61] we know that "Hardy, born in 1840, was nineteen when the *Origin of Species* was published, ... and his eager mind received, when at its most receptive stage, the shock of that school of thought which sought to supplant a beneficent God by a First Cause."[62] We know that the evolutionary hypothesis always remained fundamental in his philosophy. We do not know that Hardy was not affected by other books which moved in the same direction.

Hardy read John Stuart Mill's *On Liberty* before 1865.[63] The magnificent irony of Mill's treatment of Christian theory and Christian practice may have either prepared for or intensified the effect of his other reading—depending, of course, upon precisely when he read the essay. Certainly his reading of Mill's defense of liberty— parts of which he had by heart—must have encouraged him to believe in the importance of even unwelcome truth. For Mill's essay, which might almost as well have been entitled *On Truth* as *On Liberty*, abounds in the love of truth for truth's sake: "No one can be a great thinker who does not recognize, that as a thinker it is his first duty to follow his intellect to whatever conclusions it may lead."[64] It is difficult to resist the speculation that this was one of the passages Hardy memorized and that it was the unconscious basis for his later line, "if way to the Better there be, it exacts a full look at the Worst."

It must also have been in these years, as Rutland suggests, that Hardy first became acquainted with the work of Huxley and Spencer.[65] Aside from his interpretation of Darwin, which no doubt clarified much in Hardy's mind, it is likely that Huxley's most important effect was similar to that of Mill. He increased Hardy's bias for the truth at all costs. Indeed, it is quite likely that the admirable integrity of Huxley in his controversy with Wilberforce may have prejudiced Hardy against religion as well as in favor of truth.

If Hardy read *First Principles* or the earlier articles in which its main tenets were stated, Spencer may have given the *coup de grâce* to the young man's religious convictions, for he is certainly the most convincing and forceful expositor of naturalism to appear in the sixties. Indeed, Spencer's philosophy may have synthesized for Hardy the view of the universe Darwin and the Essayists were forcing upon him. But it is best not to be too dogmatic here. We cannot say for certain that Hardy assimilated Spencer until much later.[66] The creator of *The Dynasts* was quite capable of constructing a naturalistic system without Spencer's help.

Sometime during these years or those which immediately followed, Hardy learned enough about geology to be able to describe Knight's clinging precariously to a cliff where he faced the rock record of his neolithic predecessors. It is quite likely that Lyell's *Antiquity of Man* or his earlier *Principles of Geology* was the source of this knowledge. The former work was considered to be important enough for frequent discussion in the periodical press and was reviewed by the *Saturday Review*, which Hardy read regularly. By its tale of the vast periods of time necessary to the development of man, this science may have contributed to Hardy's feeling that man is insignificant. Perhaps, too, he studied astronomy between 1860 and 1865. It would be a natural adjunct to his other studies in natural science. Certainly he was familiar with astronomy when he embodied in *Two on a Tower* the "wish to set the emotional history of two infinitesmal lives against the stupendous background of the stellar universe."[67] His study of the astral universe may have convinced him that, not only man, but his world as well, is insignificant against the vastness of the solar immensities.

It is probable, too, that Hardy absorbed the destructive biblical criticism of Colenso as well as that of the Essayists. The father of his friend, Horace Moule, published in 1863 a reply to Colenso's *Examination of the Pentateuch*.[68] It is likely that Moule's best friend was familiar with the work the Fordington minister was criticizing. Perhaps he also became acquainted with the work of Ernest Renan. Numerous advertisements of the *Life of Jesus* appeared in the *Saturday Review*.[69] He may even have read a statement of Renan's which comes remarkably close to his own later view of the Immanent Will: "There is an obscure consciousness of the universe which tends to make itself, a secret spring which pushes possibilities into existence."[70] Conceivably, Hardy also read one of the earliest English reviews of the work of Arthur Schopenhauer.[71] But is is highly improbable that works his biographer fails to men-

tion[72] had an influence comparable to that of Darwin's hypothesis
and that of the *Essays and Reviews*.*

5

At the age of twenty Hardy was an orthodox believer, an optimist with a Shelleyan tendency to expect more of the world than he
reasonably could. He was studying his Greek Testament regularly;
he was keeping up his association with the High Church; he was
still in frequent contact with the sons of the Dorchester Baptist
minister. At twenty-five, after a long and gradual process of spiritual fermentation, Hardy renounced his long-cherished ambition to
enter the church, from "a conscientious feeling . . . . that he could
hardly take the step with honor while holding the views which on
examination he found himself to hold."[73] When he was twenty-six,
he wrote "Hap":

> Crass Casualty obstructs the sun and rain,
> And dicing Time for gladness casts a moan . . . .
> These purblind Doomsters had as readily strown
> Blisses about my pilgrimage as pain.[74]

In the intervening years Hardy read *Essays and Reviews*,[75] a sufficient cause for the abandonment of his orthodox convictions. His
reading of the *Origin of Species*[76] during the same period gave him
plentiful grounds for believing that the world, if it is the work of a
magnipotent Being, is not the work of a beneficent Creator who
cares for man and his values. Other books which he read and the
general temper of the period supplemented and confirmed the view

---

* It is, of course, also true that Hardy was very familiar with the Bible and
that his quotations from it and allusions to it show its thorough absorption. But
he used the Bible, as he also used Shakespeare and other poets, because he felt
reference to it would be stylistically useful. Later he did develop a particular
fondness for its most pessimistic books, as Rutland shows (*Thomas Hardy*,
pp. 4–6). But it would be difficult indeed, in view of average experience with
the Bible, to show that these pessimistic books prepared him for his heterodox
reading. More probably it was the other way around.

of the universe these works slowly impressed upon him. Hardy's extremely sensitive temperament, his unusual background, and the very ardency of his early faith were, of course, important conditioning factors in his change. But it was Darwin and the Essayists who started him toward *The Dynasts*, who changed him from one who expected a great deal of life to one who came to feel that life was cruel and not much worth the living.

At the end of this period, in the year in which he finally gave up his youthful "dream" of becoming a preacher, the following significant entries appear in Hardy's journal:

June 2, 1865. My twenty-fifth birthday. Not very cheerful. Feel as if I had lived a long time and done very little.

July 2, 1865. Worked at J. H. Newman's *Apologia*, which we have all been talking about lately. A great desire to be convinced by him, because Moule likes him so much. . . . . Only—and here comes the fatal catastrophe—there is no first link to his excellent chain of reasoning, and down you come headlong. . . . .[77]

One more note of the year I have placed out of its chronological order because it anticipates the poem which begins a new phase of Hardy's intellectual career:

May, 1865. The world does not despise us; it only neglects us.[78]

This is the idea he further developed in the poem "Hap."

III

A YOUNG MAN'S VIEW OF EXISTENCE

A senseless school, where we must give
Our lives that we may learn to live!
. . . .
A century which, if not sublime,
Will show, I doubt not, at its prime,
A scope above this blinkered time.

—Time's Laughingstocks

1

IT WOULD be interesting to know if, during the years between 1865 and 1870, Hardy read George Meredith's lines from *Modern Love:*

Ah, what a dusty answer gets the soul
When hot for certainties in this our life.

For, whether he read this uncharacteristic Meredithean passage or not, the lines characterize the latter half of Hardy's twenties with singular aptness. From his reading of Darwin and the Essayists he had already concluded that God probably does not exist and that, if he does exist, he does not care for the happiness of insignificant man. But Hardy was not content to rest in this position. He wished to think out all the metaphysical implications of his newly assimilated knowledge. He wished, if possible, to find some positive counterpart to these negative conclusions, a certainty, a positive faith which would enable him to believe in the eventual amelioration of things—a positive faith comparable to that of Huxley, Darwin, and most of the naturalistic thinkers of his age.

That such positive faiths were there for Hardy to find is incontrovertible. Neither the rationalistic Essayists nor their German predecessors were as much disturbed by their conclusions as Hardy was. They were at one with Frederick Temple and Connop Thirlwall in a belief that the world was being progressively educated by God and that his later lessons might "well transcend His earlier." Likewise, the scientists who destroyed Hardy's faith in man's significance and the benevolence of the universe were without exception men of robust faith. To all of them the progress of science was a source of immense gratification. Like William Whewell, they looked back proudly on "the line of vast progress,"[1] or, like the co-discoverer of evolution, Alfred Russell Wallace, they looked upon the nineteenth as "the Wonderful Century."[2] When they "dipt into the future," they saw the "wonder that would be," a "Parliament of Man," a "Federation of the World."

The philosophers, too, viewed the nineteenth century and the future with confidence. Materialist and idealist were united in a common faith in progress, if in nothing else. William Godwin, the inheritor of the eighteenth-century faith in man's educability, the faith that had produced Lessing's *The Education of the Human Race* and the works of Herder and Condorcet, believed in man's essentially rational nature so thoroughly that he advanced the dogma of perfectibility—a doctrine with which Hardy was perhaps familiar because of its diffusion through the poetry of his favorite, Shelley. Although he was as much opposed to eighteenth-century rationalism as Godwin was in favor of it and less inclined to expansive optimism, Samuel Taylor Coleridge believed equally in ultimate progress—the result of the action of a "living Power" that "meets man face to face in nature, and communes with the spiritual principle in him."[3] Through the poetry of Wordsworth,[4] if not through reading of Coleridge's philosophy, Hardy was familiar with this optimistic and idealistic faith. Similarly, since he evidences his admiration for Carlyle by listing one of his essays as a "cure for despair,"[5] Hardy must have known of Carlyle's faith in the universe as a miraculous revelation of God, of his belief that society would pass from a living past to a living future through the mediation of great men. And there were other thinkers, equally optimistic, with whom Hardy must have had at least secondhand acquaintance.

Even if he was not familiar with the widely diffused thought of Bentham, Hardy knew Mill's confidence in the ultimate regeneration of society through the free play of individualism. Indeed, as he quotes in *Jude* the passage I quote below, as the section "Of Individuality" is listed as another "cure for despair," there can be little doubt that he felt at least temporarily invigorated by Mill's characteristic injunction: "He who lets the world, or his own portion of it, choose his plan of life for him, has no need of any other faculty than the ape-like one of imitation. He who chooses his plan for himself, employs all his faculties."[6] Moreover, as Comte is an author Mill frequently quotes, and as his thought was readily accessible at second hand in the frequent propagandizing of his followers in England, Hardy must have had some acquaintance with the essential doctrines of Comte's philosophy. And if he did know him, why, one wonders, could he not have been braced by his contact with positivism, as Frederick Harrison was, and come to feel that a "*relative* synthesis admits that *absolutely*, *in rerum naturâ*, the Earth is an infinitesmal bubble, and Man, a very feeble casual, and faulty organism. . . . . But *relatively* . . . . this Earth is to us mites the true centre of the World, and Humanity is far the noblest, strongest, most permanent organism that we can prove to inhabit it"?[7]

Why did Hardy turn against the current of his age, rejecting the confident optimism of the philosophers, scientists, and theologians, the positive faith of Tennyson and Browning in

> one far-off divine event
> To which the whole creation moves,

to concur with the relatively isolated group of thinkers—Byron, Benjamin Constant, Lamartine, Arnold, Clough, Senancour, Leopardi—who felt either continually or at times that the "world is an opus posthumum" created to "make eternity less burthensome to His immense existence"?[8] This last question calls all the more for an answer when we realize that Hardy nowhere mentions familiarity with any of these pessimistic thinkers during the time in which his own pessimistic synthesis was taking shape.

Although this question cannot be answered quickly and easily by falling back upon a hypothetical melancholy temperament, we already know part of the answer. Hardy's peculiar background, the unusual ardency of his early faith, and his extreme sensitiveness help to account for his developing a world view altogether different from those common to his time. But this explanation does seem partial rather than whole. It accounts for Hardy's adoption of the philosophy one finds in "Hap," not for the persistence of the philosophy. It is evident that there must have been other conditioning factors that account for the tenacity with which he held to his somber view of existence.

2

During 1866 and the first part of 1867, Hardy continued both his work with Blomfield and his effort to become a man of letters. As numerous notes of these years indicate, he came to feel more and more that his interests and his talents were primarily literary. Because he had the protean curiosity of an artist, he found it difficult to concentrate upon one subject alone. But "in architecture men who are clever in details are bunglers in generalities," and "more conducive to success in life than the desire for much knowledge is the being satisfied with ignorance on irrelevant subjects."[9] Since he was more interested in irrelevant subjects than in architecture, from six to twelve o'clock every evening he tried to prepare himself for a career in literature. Believing that poetry epitomized the knowledge of generalities he coveted, he read nothing else.

But his efforts to make himself a man of letters were at first discouraging. His poems were uniformly rejected. Although he thought for a time of writing blank-verse plays for both profit and pleasure and actually secured an introduction to the manager of the Haymarket Theater, practical consideration of his lack of training for such a career caused him to abandon the project. Despairing of popular success in poetry, he continued to write verse only because the inward compulsion was still strong. Unable to decide upon which occupation he should concentrate, he continued to work hard at both architecture and literature until his health suffered. Blomfield, an employer unusually sensitive to the welfare of his employees, suggested that he find less arduous work in his native county so that he could recuperate. When, in July, 1867, an offer arrived from his old employer, Hicks, Hardy returned to Dorset.

Away from the hurly-burly of the city, his health and spirits improved. He still hoped for a literary career. He thought over, more carefully this time, his chances for success as a writer. West Country life he felt he knew better than most writers. He also knew, from personal experience, the plight of an isolated student in London, trying to become famous. Feeling that these contrasting materials might be worked into a successful novel—and novels were paying much more than poetry—he began *The Poor Man and the Lady*. But this decision did not mean that he at once became satisfied with either himself or his prospects. He still had to work at architecture. His mind was not altogether made up. His love for poetry, always greater than his affection for prose, continued. He wrote more lyrics. He began a long narrative poem on the Battle of the Nile. He was still sufficiently moody to set down in his journal three cures for despair: Wordsworth's "Resolution and Independence," Mill's "Of Individuality," and Carlyle's "Jean Paul Richter." In the main, however, he was in good enough spirits to read and write a great deal. As he was himself becoming a writer of prose, he read prose as well as poetry. He studied Walpole, Thackeray, and Macaulay at the same time that he read Shakespeare, Whitman, and Virgil. Before the end of 1868 he finished his first novel and sent it to Alexander Macmillan.

To a less sensitive person Macmillan's generally complimentary letter[10] would have been distinct encouragement, but Hardy noticed the publisher's qualified disapproval more than his praise. He then took the manuscript to Chapman and Hall and had what he feared was an unsatisfactory interview. Leaving the novel with the publishers, he returned to Dorset—still undecided whether he should concentrate upon prose, poetry, or architecture.

But even in Dorset, generally so soothing to his nerves, he could not settle down. In 1869 he returned to London to inquire about his manuscript. After seeing Chapman and Hall and coming to an agreement with them about the publication of the book, he returned to Dorset, in high spirits over a seemingly settled career in letters. But a letter from his publishers called him to the city in the winter. They asked him to talk over his book with their reader, George Meredith, and he, perhaps remembering the recent reception of his own *Modern Love* (1862), advised Hardy against printing his promising, but too radical, novel. Meredith suggested that the young man either "tone down" his book or abandon it for the present and start another tale with a more sensational plot. Hardy was where he had been before—undecided as to what he should do.

While he was in London, word came that Hicks was dead. Crickmay, a Weymouth architect who bought Hicks's practice, asked Hardy to help him. He accepted. In Weymouth, which now became the center of his activities, Hardy's spirits revived still another time. He went frequently to the dancing pavilion with the friend who is later presented as Springrove in *Desperate Remedies*. For hours at a time he would swim and lie on the beach, letting the sun bake the discouragement out of him. Finally, he decided to take

Meredith's advice and, abandoning his more serious novel as too advanced for its time, began work on the novel with a more complicated plot. At times his heart was actually light.

Feeling that he would get ahead on his book more rapidly at home, he returned to Stinsford early in 1870. Almost immediately after arriving there he was asked to undertake a church restoration in Cornwall for Crickmay. Because his novel was still unfinished, he refused for the moment. When, however, he had completed *Desperate Remedies* (March, 1870) and packed it off to Macmillan for a reading, he decided to accept Crickmay's offer. He was still uncertain what his true profession was to be.

In addition to his uncomfortable perplexity about what he could do and his recurring distrust of his own capacities, Hardy must have been troubled, consciously or unconsciously, by his anomalous social position during these years. Although it is not necessary to agree with Rebecca West's too cutting remark—"He came half from the yeoman class and half from the laboring class; and was very eager to be above criticism and range himself firmly with the yeoman class"[11]—it is undoubtedly true that his class position was an uncomfortable one. Intellectually he belonged with the highest class in English society; there was no possibility whatever of his even mixing with this group at this time. Although he at times felt a definite sympathy with the aspirations of the more advanced of the working class—as we shall see when we examine *The Poor Man and the Lady*—he was not of them, and it was precisely those parts of his first novel which showed greatest sympathy for the workers that brought most condemnation from the publishers upon whom he would have to depend for a literary career. For the middle class he never had much sympathy; their commercialism and their petty play for petty social advantages were altogether antithetical to his own indifference to worldly success.

So, while Matthew Arnold and Meredith could feel themselves allied with the more intelligent of the patricians; while Dickens,

Mrs. Gaskell, George Eliot, and Thomas Huxley could feel their literary or scientific efforts a part of the progressive efforts of the most humane members of the middle class; and while even such a poet as Ernest Jones, himself a worker, could find consolation in being one of a class in whose ultimate liberation he had confidence, Hardy found himself a member of a declining group in society, the yeoman class, and most sympathetic with the most static groups in the English society of his day, the peasants and small farmers. Add to this the fact that he was now old enough to realize that his particular family, the Hardys, had been in decline since the days of the Hardy who had founded the Dorchester grammar school, and one can readily see the basis for Granville Hicks's suggestion that Hardy's position in the society of his day was an important contributing factor to the persistence of his disenchantment.[12]

His dissatisfaction with architecture, his distrust of his own powers, his social isolation, and his inability to decide upon a proper course in life must have intensified the disillusionment effected by his loss of faith in God and in man's exalted place in nature. Disillusionment, Stuart Pratt Sherman once said, has "three distinct phases: a disillusionment about love and human relationships; a disillusionment about [one's] powers and [one's] career; and a disillusionment about God and the universe." With Hardy these phases came in a different order. He lost his faith in God and the universe before the other disillusionments were well begun. Hardy lost faith in his ability and his career between his twenty-fifth and his thirtieth years. Although here one is on more hazardous ground, it appears probable that Hardy's disillusionment with love and human relationships came at about the same time.

Of course, it is more than likely that Hardy was started toward this last disenchantment much earlier. The character of his early love affairs and his idealization of the people he knew intimately show that his disillusionment did not go far in the first twenty years of his life, but the lack of any considerable body of contemporary evidence makes it impossible to be dogmatic. However, it is certain that Hardy's attitude toward love and human relationships did change in the years we are now considering.

On March 11, 1865, he wrote: "The woman at a first interview will know as much of the man as he will know of her on the wedding morning; whilst she will know as little of him then as he knew of her when they first shook hands. Her knowledge will have come upon her like a flood, and have as gradually soaked away." A little later, in April, he wrote: "There is not that regular gradation among womankind that there is among men. You may meet 999 exactly alike and then the thousandth—not a little better, but far above them." Such partial disenchantment did not cause any unnatural aversion, however. On June 2, 1865, he declared: "Walked about by moonlight in the evening. Wondered what woman, if any, I should be thinking about in five years' time."[13]

Nevertheless, Hardy's disillusionment about love and human relationships generally was a serious one. Partly, I feel, this process was the result of personal experience. Because the emotion communicated is so intense, it is difficult to regard "Neutral Tones" as other than autobiographical:

> We stood by a pond that winter day,
> And the sun was white, as though chidden of God,
> And a few leaves lay on the starving sod;
> —They had fallen from an ash and were gray.
>
> Your eyes to me were as eyes that rove
> Over tedious riddles of years ago;
> And some words played between us to and fro
> On which lost the more by our love.
>
> The smile on your mouth was the deadest thing
> Alive enough to have strength to die;
> And a grin of bitterness swept thereby
> Like an ominous bird a-wing. . . . .
>
> Since then, keen lessons that love deceives,
> And wrings with wrong, have shaped to me
> Your face, and the God-curst sun, and a tree
> And a pond edged with grayish leaves.[14]

But, whether part of his disenchantment was personal or not, Hardy was certainly acquiring a vicarious knowledge of the unhappiness love may cause. One of his later poems, based on an incident of 185–, centers about Sergeant M——'s remorse for a wartime rape. Another poem, referring to a happening of 186–, tells of a student of architecture, presumably Hardy, coming upon a lady weeping before a memorial brass where her name is engraved beside that of her husband. Under her name is the inscription "faithful till my last breath." Far from weeping because she must still live on alone, the lady cries because she fears her new husband may see the memorial and doubt her faithfulness to him.[15] Several other poems, actually written between 1865 and 1870, show a similar disillusionment. "Amabel" (1865) bewails the "ruined hues" and "custom-straitened views" of a woman once idealized. "Postponement" (1866) points to the transitoriness of love. "She to Him" (1866) emphasizes man's cruel treatment of a woman who has lost her beauty. "Her Dilemma" (1866) shows the unwilling but inevitable cruelty of a woman to a man she does not find physically attractive. "Revulsion" (1866) is an abjuration of love forever, since, to win, one risks the chance of losing, and to lose is unbearable pain.[16]

Perhaps it was through what he heard or observed of lovers that Hardy suffered his first disillusionment with human relationships. Certainly, the incident of 185– Hardy later made into "The Chapel-Organist" might have had such an effect. Compelled by poverty to live by petty, degrading amours, a chapel organist gets her one consolation from her playing. The bigoted church members, whose niggardliness has driven her to her affairs with men, take away her position when talk about her begins to circulate widely. She commits suicide.[17] Another poem, based upon an incident of the sixties, tells of a girl about to have an illegitimate child. Despite her mother's efforts, the man who is responsible refuses to marry her. Because of fear of a society that is both hypocritical and self-righteous, the girl takes an herb supposed to effect abortion and dies.[18] Certainly Hardy's knowledge of these tragedies did not make his view of either love or human relationships unduly glamorous.

Nor was Hardy's disenchantment limited to the relations of lovers with each other and with society. Not only did he lose faith in Christianity; he also began to lose faith in the integrity of Christians. In his notebook for 1868 he records: "The village sermon. If it was very bad the parish concluded that he (the vicar) wrote it himself; if very good, that his wife wrote it; if middling, that he bought it, so that they could have a nap without offending him."[19] The half-humorous tone of this remark was not found in the "sweeping satire" of modern Christianity included in *The Poor Man and the Lady* (1868). In this same novel Hardy also sweepingly satirized domestic and political morals and the vulgarity of the middle class and portrayed, in darkest colors, the heedlessness of the upper classes to lower-class misery and the "frivolity, heartlessness and selfishness" of Londoners.[20]

3

Hardy's disillusioning experiences with a wide variety of men and women and his own unsuccessful search for a satisfactory position in life were probably the most important new influences to impel him toward pessimism. His reading and the intellectual climate had a much less significant effect than they had in the period described in the previous chapter. Perhaps this was because the period itself was quieter. Although Huxley published his *Lay Sermons* (1870), Spencer his *Principles of Biology* (1867), and Arnold his *Culture and Anarchy* (1867–69), the general tone of the period is better represented by the unimpeachable but not very disturbing novels of Trollope, Tennyson's "The Holy Grail" (1869), and Browning's *The Ring and the Book* (1868).

If Hardy read any or all of these books (and there is no record of his reading any of them), there is no indication that they affected him in the least. The more conventional and orthodox publications certainly did not change the direction of his thought. What effect the other works may have had could not have been much more than the general one of adding to the impetus of the rationalistic literature of the preceding period.

But there is one writer of this period who did importantly affect Hardy. Long afterward Hardy recalled his first reading of *Poems and Ballads* (1866):

> O that far morning of a summer day
> When, down a terraced street whose pavements lay
> Glassing the sunshine into my bent eyes,
> I walked and read with a quick glad surprise
>   New words, in classic guise,—
>
> The passionate pages of his earlier years,
> Fraught with hot sighs, sad laughters, kisses, tears;
> Fresh-fluted notes, yet from a minstrel who
> Blew them not naïvely, but as one who knew
>   Full well why thus he blew.[21]

It at once occurs to the reader that Swinburne's militant antitheism and his flouting of conventions may have had a definite effect upon Hardy. Reading *Poems and Ballads*, Hardy came upon many vigorous denunciations of the Providence against which he himself rebelled. Indeed, we know that he was much impressed by "Anactoria,"[22] later one of his favorite poems, and we may suppose that he was particularly moved by such lines as the following:

> Were I made as he
> Who hath made all things to break them one by one,
> If my feet trod upon the stars and sun
> And souls of men as his have alway trod,
> God knows I might be crueller than God.
> . . . .

> Is not his incense bitterness, his meat
> Murder? his hidden face and iron feet
> Hath not man known, and felt them on their way
> Threaten and trample all things and every day?[23]

Quite possibly, too, his reading of *Poems and Ballads* sent Hardy back to *Atalanta in Calydon*, where he came across a rebellious chorus that might do as much to cure, for the time, his moody despair as anything Wordsworth, Carlyle, or Mill ever wrote—because Swinburne had evidently passed through a similar despair and come from it with renewed courage:

> Because thou art cruel and men are piteous,
> And our hands labour, and thine hand scattereth;
> Lo, with hearts rent and knees made tremulous,
> Lo, with ephemeral lips and casual breath,
>   At least we witness of thee ere we die
> That these things are not otherwise, but thus:
> That each man in his heart sigheth, and saith
>   That all men even as I,
> All we are against thee, against thee, O God
>   most high.[24]

At any rate, in the first of these passages, Hardy read what he himself had felt but had never so well expressed.

On the emotional side, Swinburne's poetry certainly strengthened Hardy's antitheistic convictions and, perhaps, as we shall see, influenced him to rebel against the whole social order in *The Poor Man and the Lady*. But on the intellectual side Swinburne's influence was negligible. Despite the fact that he wished that he might, Hardy was never able to believe in a "vengeful God" who wished man's unhappiness and could be defied. Hardy's "purblind Doomsters" have little in common with Swinburne's God, and Hardy's early philosophy only superficially resembles Swinburne's combination of republicanism and paganism.

As a consequence of his experiences, vicarious and otherwise, and the reinterpretation of life forced upon him by his reading of

Swinburne and others, Hardy became increasingly melancholy. On July 13, 1866, he commented: "A man's grief has a touch of the ludicrous unless it is so great as to be awful."[25] In this same year he wrote two of the most poignant expressions of the bitter disillusionment he was to feel for many years—"Hap" and "A Young Man's Epigram on Existence." As the latter poem shows, life was becoming for him

> A senseless school where we must give
> Our lives that we may learn to live.[26]

On February 18, 1867, Hardy felt it necessary that he "remember that Evil dies as well as Good."[27] In the same year he wrote "Heiress and Architect," a poem that shows the futility of bright expectations about the future, and "A Young Man's Exhortation." The latter poem, after speaking of the cloying of joys, the sureness of death, and the swift passage of love in a fashion reminiscent of Swinburne, concludes that a "determined deftness" is necessary to eke out any joy from existence.[28] In the autumn of 1868 he made an entry in his journal which suggests his dominant mood: "How people will laugh in the midst of a misery! Some would soon get to whistle in Hell."[29] It was during these years—years in which it was all but impossible for him to see the ludicrous in any man's grief or understand any man's ability to whistle in the midst of misery—that Hardy first recorded his "reading of life."

4

Although numerous critics have endeavored to make them so, Hardy's "readings" have little resemblance to a system of philosophy. In his 1895 Preface to *Jude* he declares that this novel, like his others, is "simply an endeavor to give shape and coherence to a series of seemings, or personal impressions, the question of their consistency or their discordance, of their permanence or their transitoriness, being regarded as not of the first moment."[30] The same idea he expresses a little differently in the Preface to *Poems of the Past and Present* (1901): "Unadjusted impressions have their value, and the road to a true philosophy of life seems to lie in humbly recording diverse readings of its phenomena as they are forced upon us by chance and change."[31] This caution, which Hardy never tired of iterating, has been unduly neglected by orderly minded critics intent upon fitting Hardy's thought to the systematic thinking of Schopenhauer or some other philosopher.[32]

Hardy's thought, in this as in later periods, was amazingly inconsistent if one judges it by strict logical canons. Although there can be no doubt about the generally pessimistic outlook embodied in the poems of these years, his first novel reveals an almost revolutionary ardor for social change. He is not consistent in his use of a term for his First Principle. Sometimes he refers to this power simply as Nature; sometimes as Chance; in one poem, he refers to "purblind Doomsters" as the controlling forces. A similar lack of co-ordination is to be found in the subordinate parts of his "philosophy." From some of his poems it appears that women are a near-embodiment of the *idea;* from others it appears that they are a near-embodiment of the principle of evil. Love itself sometimes seems mere desire, sometimes an ideal passion.

It is true that none of these apparent inconsistencies is sufficiently great to trouble any but the lovers of irreproachable system. While a formal philosopher cannot be both a pessimist and a meliorist, the artist is likely to be both at different times. The philosopher, properly so called, must be careful to use his terms consistently. Such fidelity is not required of the more metaphorically minded artist. The philosopher considers the unity which underlies things; he regards love as a whole and is more concerned with woman than with women. The artist is interested in individual differences, particular instances of love, and of women. Still, whether he admits it or not, there is generally an underlying consistency in the outlook of the artist—as there is to an unusual degree in even Hardy's thinking. Generally he is pessimistic; most frequently he regards women as other than ideal. Whether he refers to his First Principle as Nature, Chance, or "crass Casualty," it always has essentially the same characteristics.

In the strictest sense, Hardy's Chance is not a First Principle at all. A First Principle controls, while the word "chance" implies the absence of a controlling force. Hardy's term is really a personification of the way the world and its activities appear to nescient man. The poet has not yet arrived at any conclusions as to the ultimate nature of the power which controls the world's destiny, but, since he does know how this power operates, he uses a word that stands for the way in which the primal force appears to work in place of a name which would describe the thing-in-itself. He has not yet attained the vision which later enables him to call his First Principle the "Immanent Will." He does not use the language of the Spirit of the Years but merely declares that all works in accordance with "luckless, tragic Chance—in [our] more human tongue."[33]

When we remember the world view implied in the *Origin of Species* (which did, we recall, resemble the Wessex peasant outlook), it becomes easier to understand Hardy's adoption of such a "First Principle." According to Darwin, living species survive or fail to survive in accordance with the principle of natural selection. Accidental variations enable some species to succeed in their environment. If a species does not happen to develop variations which enable it to survive, it perishes. Chance, then (so it would appear to a species endowed with the ability to think out a set of values), seems to be the deciding factor in survival. If, however, it could be shown that accident favored those species which, in accordance with man-made values, most deserved to survive, there would be no particular reason for a human being to feel disturbed. Accidental variations which worked justly would indicate a just First Principle —would indicate, in fact, that variations are not accidental in any ultimate sense but part of an ethical plan, similar to the Genesis view of creation wherein outer nature and other species are sub-ordinated to their ethical superior, Man. Darwin, however, does not show this to be true. The survivors are the fittest only in the sense that they are best adapted to their environment. Insects may survive long after man has gone under in the struggle for existence, and the species which survive may be precisely those that a human being would say were unfit for survival. Human ethics are not recognized by the law of Nature.

There is, of course, the possibility that might equals right, that survival values equal human values. Nietzsche sometimes believed this to be true. Darwin did not deny it. But here is where Hardy's own experience and character enter the equation. Hardy did not feel that the survivors were always the fittest. He believed that the law which determines survival operates without regard for human criteria of fitness. Accidental variations, which do not show the action of a just controlling Force in their operation, are responsible for all that man and the world are.

"Hap" (1866) most clearly expresses Hardy's early "meta-physic." If misery occurs, it is not the work of a vengeful God who enjoys human suffering. There is no power which controls or cares for human happiness or unhappiness. Accident, "crass Casualty," and "dicing Time" are responsible for fortune and misfortune. Nat-ural law is not directed by conscious intelligence that contemplates the emergence of man. It is mere Chance that man as he is and the world as it is exist rather than an altogether different world other-wise inhabited; it is Chance that accounts for man's consciousness, man's values, and man's suffering. It might equally well have hap-pened that man would have been unconscious, or possessed of other sets of values, or incapable of suffering—as far as natural law's un-conscious and purely hypothetical wishes are concerned.

Such a "metaphysic" is common to all of Hardy's writings of this period. In "At a Bridal" (1866) he comments that Nature does not care if man "all . . . . sovereign types unknows." In "She to

Him" (1866) he speaks of "Sportsman Time," who does not care at all for man's desire to preserve youth, beauty, and intelligence, but only "rears his brood to kill." "The Two Men" (1866) illustrates Hardy's conviction that it is a matter of indifference to the universe whether the virtuous or the vicious prosper. Indeed, so much does this conviction pervade Hardy's poetry that it appears even in an essentially happy poem such as "Ditty" (1870). The lover who happily finds the ideal woman might just as easily have missed meeting his love, for, happy or unhappy, we are all "bond-servants of Chance."[34]

It is true that indifferent Nature does not plot unhappiness; but man, as he is portrayed in Hardy's early poems, is generally unhappy. For the accidental variations which have brought man to his present structural state have also brought a consciousness which causes him to desire and to suffer. We have no record in this period of an indictment of consciousness as clear as the following: "Law has produced in man a child who cannot but constantly reproach its parent for doing much and yet not all, and constantly say to such parent that it would have been better never to have begun doing than to have *over*done so indecisively; that is, than to have created so far beyond all apparent first intention (on the emotional side), without mending matters by a second intent and execution, to eliminate the evils of the blunder of overdoing. The emotions have no place in a world of defect, and it is a cruel injustice that they should have developed in it."[35]

But it is clear that Hardy felt in this period what he did not explicitly state until later. Hardy wishes to have a complete *Einfühlung* with the troubles of his friend. He finds it impossible. A girl in the country wishes to be in the city. She cannot be there. The City Shopwoman desires a lover and a cottage in the country. Both are unattainable. The Heiress wishes to preserve her beauty and her love. It is impossible. A young man wishes that he could have realized when he first saw the name of a now beloved actress that she was worthy of his affection![36] All these situations are presented as items in an indictment of the universe rather than as indictments of man's unreasonable desires.

Of course, it is obvious to us that many of these wishes are more than a sensible man would ask of life. Few people expect or desire complete *Einfühlung* with another, the eternal preservation of love and beauty, or the immediate perception of the lovely essence for which a name may stand. Instead of arraigning the universe, one might well attribute these failures to obtain satisfaction to an unrealistic view of life. Perhaps because Hardy still retained much of his earlier desire for a world altogether fairer than the one in which he found himself, he is always in sympathy with the desirer. Or one might attack the social conditions which prevent the city and the country woman from doing as they would. As the passage above indicates, Hardy did not realize even later that the fault was perhaps that of either society or the individual himself. He believed that desires should be satisfiable if they are present in one's consciousness. Despite the fact that he does not state this idea as explicitly as he later did, it is obvious that Hardy felt "the intolerable antilogy of making figments feel." For, at the end of the "Dream of the City Shopwoman," he has her say what he was later to reiterate:

> O God, that creatures framed to feel
> A yearning nature's strong appeal
> Should writhe on this eternal wheel
>   In rayless grime;
>
> And vainly note, with wan regret,
> Each star of early promise set;
> Till Death relieves, and they forget
>   Their one Life's time![37]

In this Chance-governed universe, where men are constantly tormented by unrealizable desires, Nature is not careful of the single life. All that Nature values is the continuation of existence. So, Hardy tells us in "Amabel" (1865) that "though Love cease [in a particular case], Love's race shows no decrease."[38] Nature is not concerned about the cessation or continuance of love in individual instances. She demands only that love and propagation continue. Again, it is a matter of indifference to Nature whether two people who would breed "high-purposed" children should marry or not. She does not object if these two people wed the unfit or if the "race all such sovereign types [in the human scale of values] unknows."[39] So, too, with the success of men in more ordinary matters. "The Two Men" are altogether different. One rates

> the Market's sordid war
> As something scarce worth living for,

and strives

> to mend the mortal lot
> And sweeten sorrow. . . . .

The other

> liked the winnings of the mart
> But wearied of the working part.[40]

Both died in a "pauper sty." Nature's complete indifference allows the good and the bad to perish alike. Individual worth means nothing in a scheme which cares only for the perpetuation of the race.

As most of Hardy's early poems deal with love, the cruel working of Chance is most notably illustrated in his treatment of this passion. Love, as Hardy sees it, clearly depends on physical attraction. There is no rational cause for man's attraction to woman or for woman's attraction to man. Sexual selection appears to operate much the same with human beings as with the species Darwin analyzed. "Generally, the most vigorous males . . . . leave the most progeny."[41] There is no humanly intelligible standard that accounts for this process of selection. Probably it is Hardy's reading of the section on "Sexual Selection" in the *Origin of Species* and his vicarious experience with love that account for his naturalistic interpretation.

He is very consistent. In "Amabel" (1865) the lover idealizes his beloved only until "warmth . . . . wane[s]." "Her Dilemma" (1866), specifically attributed to Nature, is a woman's inability to feel attracted to one who loves her. "She to Him" (1866) is a woman's complaint that love passes with the passage of beauty, that the more commendable traits, in an ethical sense, are not sufficient to hold love when "Sportsman Time" brings on old age. "The Dawn after the Dance" (1869) takes as its theme the decrease of love after sexual intercourse. Passion spent and Nature's purpose served, love ends.[42]

Unfortunately, too, physical attraction is accompanied by a peculiarly human characteristic. As a result of the same Chance-directed process of natural selection which accounts for the development of the peculiar qualities of men and animals, human beings idealize those they love. So, until "warmth wanes," the lover thinks highly of Amabel. So the "immortal" lines once felt to apply to the woman of "Her Initials" (1869) soon seem inappropriate. In similar fashion, "At Waking" tells of a woman once regarded as a "prize" who now seems but one of "earth's poor average kind," and "The Dawn after the Dance" describes the change from love that seemed "sweet sempiternal spinning" to no love at all after the love is physically consummated.[43] As it is possible that physical attraction may occasionally lead to one who deserves idealization, disillusionment is not the inevitable accompaniment of love. But Chance, as it is interpreted by Hardy in his earlier poems, rarely leads to a compatible union between man and woman.

Still another reason for the unhappiness that almost inevitably accompanies love is the inconstancy of both men and women. Although, as in "Neutral Tones" (1867), men and women occasionally cease to love at the same time, Nature does not generally provide for such coincident cessation. "She to Him" tells of the pain suffered by a woman whose love continues after the man's has passed.[44] An inherent tendency to faithlessness is implied in all but two of Hardy's early love poems.

The two exceptions to the rule, "Postponement" (1866) and "A Poor Man and a Lady" (1868),[45] do indicate, however, the danger of too consistently grounding Hardy's pessimism about love in the inherent nature of things. In both these poems Hardy clearly shows that disparity in position and wealth are responsible for the failure of the lovers to come together happily. These poems recall the necessity of taking seriously Hardy's admission that he is no systematic philosopher and point to another aspect of his thinking. Nevertheless, it is true that Hardy's pessimism about love is usually based upon cosmic rather than social causes.

Almost invariably, Chance accounts for the pain so constantly associated with love. Man, exercising his reason, would prefer that compatibility should be the basis for love; Nature cares for neither man's wishes nor man's ethic and dictates that physical attraction should be the basis for mating. Despite man's wish that there should be a sound basis for his inherent tendency to idealize the one loved, Nature, wishing only that "Love's race show no decrease," does not care whether idealization is a false trick of the imagination or not. Constancy, likewise, is a human value rather than something firmly based upon the nature of things. Nature cares only that man serve her purpose. Whether lovers gratify each other by faithfulness or pain each other by unfaithfulness, she does not care.

This pessimism about love which emphasizes the almost certain brevity of passion, which leads to the almost certain realization that the lover must say

> That the prize I drew
> Is a blank to me![46]

D'Exideuil attributes to the influence of Schopenhauer's *Metaphysic of Love* and Darwin's *Descent of Man*.[47] Since Hardy was not acquainted with Schopenhauer during this period and since Darwin's *Descent of Man* was not published until 1871, it is obvious that Hardy's pessimism about love had other sources. His experiences, vicarious and otherwise, and the implications which he himself found in Darwin's treatment of sexual selection in the *Origin of Species*, were responsible for the early development of this form of pessimism. Similar factors, too intangible for their effect to be defined with precision, and the world view implied in Darwin's treatment of natural selection, account for the other pessimistic elements in Hardy's early philosophy.

<h2 style="text-align:center">5</h2>

It is, however, a mistake to regard Hardy's early outlook as an entirely pessimistic one. Even if one demands a logical coherence which Hardy himself disclaimed, it is well to remember it does not inevitably follow that a Chance-directed universe should be the worst of all possible worlds. In Hardy's universe the bad most frequently fail, although the good rarely succeed. The lazy, selfish character in "The Two Men" also ends up in a "pauper sty." In "The Fire at Tranter Sweatley's" (1866), Accident intervenes to make a happy marriage out of an unhappy one. Although Hardy realizes that he is a bond servant of Chance and might just as easily have missed meeting his wife-to-be, he does meet her.[48] Chance can be responsible for happiness as well as for unhappiness.

Even in this early period, when Hardy must have been particularly oppressed by his disenchantment, he does not feel that the world is in a hopeless state. Perhaps inspired by the vigorous optimism of most of his contemporaries, he believed in progress. Truly enough, progress seemed to him to go at a much slower pace than his contemporaries would have admitted. "Had the teachings of experience," he wrote on April 29, 1867, "grown cumulatively with the age of the world we should have been ere now as great as Gods."[49] A progress so slow comes too late to make his own life much sweeter. Nevertheless, he thought in 1867 of

> A century which, if not sublime,
> Will show, I doubt not, at its prime,
> A scope above this blinkered time.[50]

Nor did Hardy feel that human beings are generally unworthy. Even those who serve Nature's ostensibly cruel purpose, such as the woman who cannot reciprocate the love of a dying man, shame "to prize a world conditioned thus." Man is too good for the world into which he is born. Indeed, there are many men and women who deserve even romantic idealization. Such, surely, was the actress, the *idea* incarnate of Rosalind, to whom he addressed two poems in 1867. From the poems later addressed to his future wife, we can be reasonably certain that he regarded her as another such.[51] Indeed, with the few exceptions already noted, the men and women portrayed in his early writings are generally regarded as admirable. Although his optimism about the laws which govern the world and man has, for the most part, failed him, his optimistic view of most men and women continued.

Perhaps because he felt that human nature has much that is good in it and that there is therefore hope for amelioration in a world where the "purblind Doomsters" are indifferent rather than malign, Hardy's writings manifest a desire to better the world. Although he does not feel that any remedy can be devised for man's possession of unrealizable desires, for the injustice of the wholly unethical struggle for existence, or for the cruelty Nature's indifference has allowed to become a frequent accompaniment of love, he does believe that there is a possibility of bettering social conditions. Indeed, if one regards a wish thoroughly to change society as an indication of optimism, one might make out a very good case for Hardy's having been, when he wrote *The Poor Man and the Lady*, considerably more sanguine than most of his contemporaries.

Despite the fact that the portion of *The Poor Man and the Lady* which was separately published as *An Indiscretion in the Life of an Heiress* justifies Hardy's wisdom in not reprinting this piece, students of Hardy's thought owe a considerable debt to the ingenuity of Carl Weber and of W. R. Rutland[52] in reconstructing the content of Hardy's first novel. For one evidently finds in this novel, side by side, both the pessimism and the meliorism that were always to characterize Hardy's work. But even the pessimistic portion of the book, a tale of a poor man who does not live happily ever after with the woman he loves, is in some respects importantly uncharacteristic of the writer of the early poems. For the villain of the piece is not so much Chance as social circumstance.

Will Strong loves Miss Allamont, the daughter of the squire who employs Strong's parents on his Dorset estate, and she returns his love. Because they are intensely class conscious, the squire and his wife will not consider the possibility of a marriage between their daughter and the son of a "peasant." The two lovers are forbidden to meet. Thinking he may be able to win the parents' favor by success in the world outside, Strong goes to London, where he becomes both a successful architect and an exponent of working-class politics. Miss Allamont, coming to London with her family, happens to pass where Will is addressing a meeting in Trafalgar Square and is temporarily repelled by her lover's radical views. A chance meeting, however, throws them together again. They reconcile their differences and repledge their love. But the opposition of the parents and the feeble health of Miss Allamont (accentuated by the excitement of her conflict with her parents) prevent the happy consummation of their love. Miss Allamont dies, and Strong is left inconsolable.

The pessimistic conclusion of the tale, the death of the young lady, and the rather frequent accidents upon which the action hinges are typical of the later Hardy. But it was not typical of Hardy in his later novels to place so much importance upon class differences as a cause of unhappiness. If it had not been for the social prejudices of the parents, Strong and Miss Allamont might very well have lived happily ever after. Other portions of the novel are even less typical of the mature novelist.

Indeed, what we know of that part of the book which is not taken up with Will and Miss Allamont's love would lead us to suppose that Hardy did find, for a time, a positive faith capable of compensating for his other disillusionments. For, in addition to what has been outlined above, the novel contained satire on domestic and political morals, satire on the frivolity of the upper class and its heedlessness of lower-class suffering. It decried the heartlessness and selfishness of Londoners and displayed, as a whole, a "socialistic, not to say revolutionary," tendency.[53]

Remembering G. M. Young's conjecture that socialism in the Victorian age could be made to mean "everything which a respectable man saw reason to disapprove of or to fear"[54] and the amazingly temperate conduct of radical Felix Holt, who took the stump to persuade the workers *not* to agitate for suffrage, it seems unlikely that the novel contained anything remotely comparable to the radicalism of modern proletarian fiction. But it is evident, even from our necessarily limited knowledge of the radical portions of the novel (which were completely destroyed),[55] that Hardy, whose sympathies are with Will Strong throughout the action, for a time thought seriously of radical politics and aligned himself with some shade of working-class opinion.

This temporary sympathy with a positive philosophy, with, moreover, a positive philosophy more comprehensive than any he later felt drawn to, is not difficult to understand when we remember that Hardy was not, after all, a contented adherent of a negative philosophy. He was constantly searching, both in these years and later, for a positive philosophy which was not based on illusions. During the years that immediately preceded the writing of *The Poor Man and the Lady*, which Hardy began in 1867, it did seem as though there was more hope for an equitable society based upon the interests of all social classes than there had been since the hopeful years immediately preceding the passage of the first Reform Bill.

This movement for social reform—a movement that remained unparalleled until the eighties—owed no small part of its success to the working-class movement which Will Strong espoused. After a period of relative absence of class strife following the death of chartism and the increased prosperity that followed the repeal of the Corn Laws, the working-class movement became important once again in the sixties. The First International was founded in London in 1864. By 1865 it was sufficiently strong for the Cobdenites to approach it with an appeal for co-operation. In 1866 the London Trades Council and the London Working Men's Association were formed. Early in 1867, while Hardy was still in the capital, working-class demonstrations occurred in scores of industrial towns, and there were meetings in Trafalgar Square (where Hardy's own hero spoke to a crowd of workingmen) and a serious riot in Hyde Park.[56] Indeed, the Tories were afraid that there might be a revolution if nothing was done, and this fear in part accounted for the passage of the Reform Bill of 1867.

These semirevolutionary outbreaks and the unusual importance of the working-class movement in the three years preceding the composition of *The Poor Man and the Lady* were undoubtedly important in determining the socialistic tone of the book. It is, however, probable that Hardy was also moved by certain literary influences. We do not know that he read any of the novels of Kingsley or Mrs. Gaskell, or that he was familiar with Dickens' *Hard Times* or George Eliot's *Felix Holt*, although he may have known all these books. But we may suppose that he had, by this time, become familiar with the socialistic poems of Shelley, and we know that he was reading with sympathy and pleasure the poetry of Swinburne in the year that preceded the start of his first novel. It is highly probable that such poems as Swinburne's "To Victor Hugo" and "A Song in Time of Revolution" intensified and influenced the direction of his social sympathies. The reading of such lines as,

> The poor and the halt and the blind are keen
> and mighty and fleet:
> Like the noise of the blowing of wind is the
> sound of the noise of their feet.
>
> The wind has the sound of a laugh in the clamour
> of days and of deeds:
> The priests are scattered like chaff, and the
> rulers broken like reeds,[57]

may even have been responsible for the beginning of Hardy's interest in the contemporary working-class movement.

At any rate, Hardy's faith in radicalism was evidently short-lived. The dying-down of revolutionary ardor after the passage of the second Reform Bill was undoubtedly partly responsible for the brevity of his faith in the proletariat. To an even greater extent, probably, he was influenced by the reception his "radical" novel met from the publishers and publishers' readers.[58] It became obvious to him that the time was not yet ripe for even literary radicalism. One presumes, for there is no tinge of "socialism" in anything Hardy later wrote, that he finally decided his hope for fundamental social change was as much an illusion as his belief in the beneficence of God had been previously. In any case, he abandoned the idea of publishing *The Poor Man and the Lady* as a whole and never printed more than an emasculated version of it. For the time, at least, he turned to the more profitable, if less congenial, task of writing a novel with a complicated plot.

6

A few of the poems and his brief excursion into radicalism set aside, the general tone of Hardy's reading of life was, throughout this period, exceedingly somber. Even in the years in which he wrote *The Poor Man and the Lady*, which was itself sufficiently somber in its conclusion, he continued to present a twilight view of life in his poetry. "Neutral Tones," "Heiress and Architect," "Her Reproach," "A Young Man's Exhortation," and "Retty's Phases," all of them representative of the melancholy outlook that was becoming more and more a part of him, were written in the same years in which Hardy wrote his first novel.

For an artist with no pretension to philosophic schematism, Hardy presented a singularly consistent Weltanschauung between 1865 and 1870. Chance allows happiness and unhappiness to be distributed almost at random. Man has desires which the nature of things prevents him from fulfilling. The struggle for existence, directed by an indifferent Nature, does not ordinarily result in success for the most deserving. Love causes pain far more often than it does joy. Perhaps, in the distant future, something can be done to ameliorate conditions. Perhaps the next century, at its prime, will be better than the present one. But, in general, the world in which "crass Casualty obscures the sun and rain" is a "senseless school" in which only dolts learn lessons that "leave no time for prizes." Such is the unmistakable dominant impression.

IV

MAN'S QUANDARY

That old-fashioned reveling in the general situation grows less and less possible as we uncover the defects of natural laws. . . . .

—The Return of the Native

1

ON MARCH 7, 1870, Hardy arrived at St. Juliot Rectory, Cornwall, to deliver and explain Crickmay's plans for the reconstruction of the church. Too firmly convinced that the world is a senseless school to feel absolute delight as he approached the rectory, still he could not feel that an altogether dreary experience awaited him. He was in the poetic country of "Lyonnesse," "preeminently . . . . the region of dream and mystery" where the "ghostly birds, the pall-like sea, the frothy wind, the eternal soliloquy of the waters, the bloom of purple cast that seems to exhale from the shoreward precipices, in themselves lend to the scene an atmosphere like the twilight of a night vision."[1]

When he reached the rectory, he was met by a "young lady in brown" who immediately impressed him with her capacity for enjoyment and her faith in life. Since the young lady, Emma Lavinia Gifford, had been away from people of her own class for some time, she had been looking forward to the architect's visit as a relief from dull routine. Prepared to like him from the start, she was impressed by his "familiar appearance," "his soft voice." When she discovered that there was a poem written on the commonplace blueprint in his pocket, she began to feel that he must be an unusual, as well as an attractive, young man.

During the evenings of his stay Emma Gifford sang duets with her sister, the rector's wife. As Hardy had always been fond of music and as the songs were romantically suited to the spot, the songs added to the charms of the singers. During the daytime he and Emma Gifford explored as much of the surrounding country as they could. One time, attracted by the legends of Arthur and his court, they visited Tintagel. Another day they went to Beeny Cliff, Emma Gifford riding on her brown horse so gracefully that it seemed a part of her. On the way home from this ride—it was to be his last day at the rectory—Hardy quoted to himself Tennyson's lines

> The tender grace of a day that is past
> Can never come back to me.

Although he was thoroughly convinced that he was in love, his old melancholy would not let him believe that he would carry back from Cornwall anything but the memory of a short and unusual happiness.

But, when the morning of his departure came,[2]

> She looked like a bird from a cloud
>   On the clammy lawn,
> Moving alone, bare-browed
>   In the dim of dawn.
>
> The candles alight in the room
>   For my parting meal
> Made all things without doors loom
>   Strange, ghostly, unreal.
>
> The hour itself was a ghost,
>   And it seemed to me then
> As of chances the chance furthermost
>   I should see her again.

.   .   .   .

"I am leaving you . . . . Farewell!" I said,
    As I followed her on
By an alley bare boughs overspread;
    "I soon must be gone!"

Even then the scale might have been turned
    Against love by a feather,
—But crimson one cheek of her burned
    When we came in together.[3]

And so:

When I came back from Lyonnesse
    With magic in my eyes,
    All marked with mute surmise
My radiance rare and fathomless,
When I came back from Lyonnesse
    With magic in my eyes![4]

Their love progressed with a smoothness that would have an-
gered Hardy's later Spirit Sinister. Hardy was strongly attracted
to the girl whose "so living" appearance contrasted strikingly with
the moody melancholy of his own face. In many ways she seemed to
be almost his counterpart. Like him, she was moved by romantic
Cornwall; she, too, could write of this "beautiful seacoast," describing "the wild Atlantic Ocean rolling in with its magnificent
waves and spray, its white gulls, and black choughs and grey puf-
fins, its cliffs and rocks, and gorgeous sunsettings, sparkling red-
ness in a track widening from the horizon to the shore."[5] Like him,
she was an amateur musician and an avid reader. Because of her interest in literature and her love for Hardy, she encouraged him to
follow his bent for writing. When, discouraged by the failure of
his earliest novels, Hardy declared that they could only be married
if he devoted himself exclusively to architecture, Emma Gifford
persuaded him to continue with his fiction.

During the four years of their engagement Hardy spent most of
his time in Dorchester, while Emma Gifford remained in Cornwall. But they were together as much as time and money permitted.

As they were both amateur artists, they would often walk to Boscastle Harbor when Hardy visited at the rectory and go down "the beautiful Valency valley" to sketch. Similarly attracted by the Arthurian legend, they returned to King Arthur's Castle, Tintagel, when they had time for a longer excursion than that of Hardy's first visit. Whatever they did with their days, evenings there were always music and the reading-aloud of romantic poetry. Each time that he saw her, each excursion that he took with her, Hardy became more convinced that there was a sound basis of compatibility for their love.

Perhaps it was his fiancée's differences from himself that completed her attractiveness. She took a refreshing pleasure in tiny achievements. When she heard that she had been skilful in her plastering of the foundation stone to the church Hardy was restoring, she was immensely pleased—so pleased that she remembered this trifle even when she became an old woman. She liked the attention her ability as a horsewoman attracted: "Fanny [her horse] and I were one creature, and very happy. She was a lovely brown color too, stopping where she liked, to drink or munch, I often getting off sketching and gathering flowers. The villagers stopped to gaze when I rushed down the hills, and a butterman laid down his basket once to exclaim loudly. No one except myself dared to ride in such a fashion."[6] Even more than by such naïve vanity, Hardy must have been drawn to her by her faith in God and life— a faith that he would have liked to have kept but had lost. Emma Gifford felt that an "Unseen Power of great benevolence" directed her ways, that a "strange unearthly brilliance shines around our path, penetrating and dispersing difficulties with its warmth and glow."[7] Perhaps Hardy thought he would learn the secret of her faith.

In 1874 they were married. Then began that period which was to culminate, after a first exciting trip to the Continent (all the more enjoyable because of his wife's naïveté and slighter knowledge), in

the "Sturminster Newton Idyll" (1874–78), "our happiest time."[8]
It is difficult to suspend disbelief when we read the lines Hardy
wrote about his wife:

> For there dwells one, all testify,
> To match the maddest dream's desire:
> What swain with her would not aspire
> To walk the world, yea, sit but nigh
>   On Beechen Cliff![9]

Has the young man who had seemed so near complete disillusionment, who had written, in 1866,

> So may I live no junctive law fulfilling,
> And my heart's table bear no woman's name,[10]

been able to realize one of his paradisaic wishes?

One begins to wonder about the usual interpretation of that
period of Hardy's development which culminated with the publication of *The Return of the Native* in 1878. If these were the years of a
love that contrasts altogether with that of Clym and Eustacia, how
can one account for the invariable interpretation of his novels as
pessimistic? How did his life in general go? Did his philosophy remain essentially the same despite this experience? Do his novels
really illustrate the same somber outlook that we found in his
poems? For, whether his world view has changed or not, it is obvious that there is a change for the better in his own life.

2

Hardy was becoming more reconciled to his everyday life as
well. In his own struggle for existence he was successful. After
1873 he was able to abandon architecture because of his success as
a novelist. Though the writing of fiction was less satisfying than
the writing of poetry, it was infinitely better than daily boredom
with tedious architectural details.

He was not, as both he himself and his critics have occasionally implied, indifferent to worldly recognition. He cared little for the accumulation of money, but he was as sensitive to public blame or praise as he was to suffering. When, in 1871, *Desperate Remedies* was sharply reviewed, he had wished that he were dead. But now the tide was turning. Taking an excursion to Oxford with his fiancée in 1873, he was surprised to see, in a newspaper shop, a flattering review of *A Pair of Blue Eyes* in the same magazine that had "snuffed out" his first published novel. The thrill this review gave Emma Gifford, Hardy fully shared.

This was only the start to his literary success. Leslie Stephen asked him to write a serial for the *Cornhill Magazine*. When the novel *Far from the Madding Crowd* anonymously appeared in 1874, it was thought to be by the most eminent of living novelists, George Eliot. Almost without exception the English reviews were favorable.[11] In the winter of 1875 the *Revue des deux mondes* published an enthusiastic account of Hardy's first four novels. Even before the *Revue* article, Hardy had been considered important enough for a translation of his second novel, *Under the Greenwood Tree*, to be published in Paris.

His more distinguished contemporaries began to accept him as a writer of the first rank. Coventry Patmore wrote that he "regretted at almost every page [of *A Pair of Blue Eyes*] that such unequaled beauty and power should not have assured themselves the immortality which would have been impressed upon them by the form of verse." Hardy became friendly enough with many noted men and women to be often in their company. He became acquainted with Stephen's wife—the daughter of Thackeray—Frederick Greenwood, Henry Irving, Alexander Macmillan, and Huxley. He became an intimate friend of the wife of Barry Cornwall, Mrs. Proctor, who "used to tell him that sometimes after avowing to Americans her acquaintance with a long list of famous bygone people, she had been compelled to deny knowledge of certain others she had equally well known, to re-establish her listeners' wavering faith in her veracity."[12]

A new and happier mood manifested itself in many ways. Sometimes his journals enable us to catch him as he mixed amusedly with the peasants, chuckling over anecdotes remarkably similar to those we find in his books: "Met J. D., one of the old Mellstock fiddlers—who kept me talking interminably: a man who speaks neither truth nor lies, but a sort of Not Proven compound which is very relishable. Told me of Jack ———, who spent all the money he had—sixpence—at the Oak Inn, took his sixpence out of the till when the landlady's back was turned, and spent it over again; then stole it again, and again spent it, till he had had a real skinful. 'Was too honest to take any money but his own,' said J.D."[13] Again we see him watching alertly the changing colors of Egdon Heath, listening attentively to the calls of birds or the sounds the wind makes: "The thin grasses, more or less coating the hill, were touched by the wind in breezes of differing powers, and almost of differing natures—one rubbing the blades heavily, another raking them piercingly, another brushing them like a soft broom. The instinctive act of human kind was to stand and listen, and learn how the trees on the right and the trees on the left wailed or chaunted to each other in the regular antiphonies of a cathedral choir; how hedges and other shapes to leeward then caught the note, lowering it to the tenderest sob; and how the hurrying gust then plunged into the south, to be heard no more."[14]

There were even times when he showed a verve that would have done credit to his wife. Sitting in his writing-room one day, he heard a street barrel organ playing a quadrille which had once been a favorite. A pleasantly rakish friend of Hardy's at Dorchester had made it attractive by telling how he had danced to its music at the Cremorne and the Argyll, two of the popular London dance halls. But Hardy did not know its name. When he heard it outside in the street, he threw down his pen, and his wife, a moment later, saw him running hatless down Brodrick Road, disappearing into a by-street. Hardy ran at the organ-grinder with such eagerness that the latter, looking frightened, began to shuffle off. "Hardy called out, 'What's the name of that tune?' The grinder—a young foreigner—exclaimed trembling . . . . 'Quad-ree-ya! quad-ree-ya!' and pointed to the index in front of the instrument."[15] A few minutes later, Hardy, no wiser but much amused, was relating the incident to his wife. It seems as though Hardy had borrowed his wife's pleasure in minutiae, as though he had acquired much of her zest for "mere living." Yet the novel he left off writing to "fly" after the organ-grinder was probably *The Return of the Native*, where he writes: "The truth seems to be that a long line of disillusive centuries has permanently displaced the Hellenic idea of life, or whatever it may be called. What the Greeks only suspected we know well; what their Aeschylus imagined our nursery children feel. That old-fashioned reveling in the general situation grows less and less possible as we uncover the defects of natural laws, and see the quandary that man is in by their operation."[16]

Hardy was unable to escape from himself and his knowledge of the world. He had been singularly fortunate in his marriage; material success and congenial associates had made his individual life easier to live; he was able to enjoy the passing hour, the passing nature of beauty, the passing smile over the word antics of his peasant Dogberrys and Verges. But the iron was in his blood. He could not repress his knowledge of the world and its cruel laws. The undertone of sadness persists in spite of everything:

To sorrow
I bade good morrow,
And thought to leave her far away behind;
But cheerly, cheerly,
She loves me dearly;
She is so constant to me, and so kind.
I would deceive her,
And so leave her,
But ah! she is so constant and so kind.[17]

Still, because we know of the many reasons why Hardy might have been, and frequently was, happy, it is difficult to understand the persistence of his twilight view of life. It is true that he was painfully disillusioned—but have not others become serene in spite of such an experience? It is true that he was disappointed in his early attempts to make a career—but did he not become successful? It seems that there should be some mental or physical sickness, some hopeless struggle against poverty, to account for Hardy's constancy to sorrow. It is a surprise to learn that he was not a victim of alcoholism and melancholia like James Thomson. A life of successive material disappointments, like Swift's, seems necessary to explain his view of life. Baffled to find Hardy generally healthy and never in material need, one is likely to suppose, with Hedgcock, that Hardy was a lonely recluse who avoided society with Schopenhauerian misanthropy; that his steadfast pessimism can be explained by his not mixing with people as his optimistic contemporary, George Meredith, did.[18]

There is some truth in this last surmise—Hardy was appalled by the constant going-out into society demanded of the novelist—but he was not a lonely recluse. As he himself pointed out in the margin of Hedgcock's study, for three decades he spent three or four months of the year in London.[19] As he was by choice a member of the Savile Club and enjoyed being with his great contemporaries, we can be sure that society did not repel him.

Hedgcock approaches the truth more nearly when he remarks that Hardy, an artist, had both a more extensive and a more intensive sympathy with other people's sufferings than the ordinary man.[20] The preternatural sensitiveness that later caused him to say that speaking of a lovely frosty morning was too inconsiderate of the birds showed itself frequently in these, his happiest, years. On May 1, 1877, Hardy wrote in his journal: "A man comes every evening to the cliff in front of our house to see the sun set, timing himself to arrive a few minutes before the descent. Last night he came, but there was a cloud. His disappointment."[21] No doubt Hardy had noticed and vicariously shared the man's enjoyment of previous sunsets, but, significantly, it was only the man's disappointment that Hardy felt strongly enough to record.

Writing in 1876, in the midst of what he called his happiest time, Hardy himself expressed a further reason for his perpetually recurring melancholy: " 'All is vanity,' saith the Preacher. But if all were only vanity, who would mind? Alas, it is too often worse than vanity; agony, darkness, death also.

"A man would never laugh were he not to forget his situation, or were he not one who never has learnt it. After risibility from comedy, how often does the thoughtful mind reproach itself for forgetting the truth? Laughter always means blindness—either from defect, choice, or accident."[22]

Not only was Hardy extremely sensitive; he was as determined as the contemporary scientists he admired to face facts, even when he could not find facts that led to an optimism such as Huxley's or Spencer's. He was resolved, in the words of his later poem, that "if way to the Better there be, it exacts a full look at the Worst."[23] Looking the Worst in the face, he saw all about him the suffering produced by the endless process of evolution which had produced man and encumbered him with ideals he could not realize. Sensitive, intelligent, and honest, Hardy could not easily forget Nature's apparent cruelty. So, in the very year in which he gaily pursued the organ-grinder, he wrote in his journal: "Woke before it was light. Felt I had not enough staying power to hold my own in the world."[24]

So also, in the year of his election to the Savile Club, in the year which added a gay champagne party in Irving's dressing-room to an already large number of happy experiences, Hardy wrote of the quandary man is in by the operation of natural laws and felt that the time is near "if it has not actually arrived, when the chastened sublimity of a moor, a sea, or a mountain will be all of nature that is absolutely in keeping with the moods of the more thinking among mankind."[25] What he would like to believe—and sometimes did—was constantly at war with what his intellect told him to be the truth. He could not escape the painful consciousness of the "cursed condition of humanity." Born under one law, he felt himself bound by another.

4

What many of the best intellects were discovering or reiterating as truth between 1870 and 1878 was not likely to make Hardy optimistic, whatever its effect upon his less sensitive contemporaries. The iconoclastic forces that had been resting, perhaps *pour mieux sauter*, during the preceding five years, assumed an importance comparable to that they had had in the years immediately following the publication of Darwin's *Origin of Species*.

In 1873, articles by Francis Newman and Leslie Stephen, which decried the failure to accept unorthodox conclusions because they are negative rather than positive, were printed in the *Fortnightly Review*. At about the same time Romanes' *Candid Examination of Theism*, which concluded that science made belief in a God both beneficent and omnipotent impossible, was written. Before 1878, when James Knowles started to edit the *Nineteenth Century* as an organ of unorthodoxy, articles and books by John Morley, John Stuart Mill, and others gave agnosticism a reputability it had never enjoyed before.

These books and articles were far more widely read than their analogues in preceding years. It is significant that W. R. Greg's *Creed of Christendom* (1851) reached its third edition in 1873 and its eighth in 1883. The vogue of heterodox books by Winwood Reade, Cassell, and Arnold—all of which were frequently reissued during this period—show the spirit of the time, as does the publication of

Browning's *La Saisiaz* (1878), the second series of *Poems and Ballads* (1878), and *The City of Dreadful Night* (1874). There was even a lending-library novel, Mrs. Lynn Linton's *Under Which Lord*, that dealt with the problem of whether a woman should remain true to an agnostic husband.

As would be expected in a period when radical theology was continually gaining strength, the Darwinian hypothesis and its implications about man's origin became still more widely known. Darwin's own *Descent of Man* (1871) was the most complete statement of man's place in nature to appear during the decade, but it was supported and sometimes carried to more extreme conclusions by the speeches and publications of Huxley, Clifford, and Tyndall. Clifford, in his *Body and Mind* (1874), even went so far as to maintain that the proof of animal automatism will eventually become so complete that the existence of God will be susceptible to disproof.

Although most historians of philosophy regard the Hegelians and the Neo-Kantians as the most notable philosophers of the seventies, it suggests the importance of the materialists and naturalists that they were always regarded as the chief enemy. And if Spencer was not the most popular philosopher of the period, he was certainly the most notorious. His continued influence was perhaps still most forcibly felt in the wide diffusion of the ideas of *First Principles*, but his *Principles of Sociology*, still dear to the heart of many a rugged individualist, could not have been without considerable effect in a period pronouncedly capitalistic.

Probably as a result of the philosophy of Spencer, which was never very welcome to the thin-skinned, and of the iconoclasm of both liberal theologians and scientists, pessimism became more prevalent than it had ever been before. The first evidence of its increasing importance is found in an article on "Schopenhauer and Darwinism" in the *Journal of Anthropology* for January, 1871. In August of the same year an article on "Optimism and Pessimism" appeared in the *Contemporary Review*. Before 1878, four other essays dealing with either Schopenhauer, Von Hartmann, or the general subject of pessimism were published in journals with fairly wide circulation.[26] In 1877 three significant books were importantly concerned with pessimism: Helen Zimmern's *Arthur Schopenhauer* (a biography), Bowen's *Modern History from Descartes to Schopenhauer*, and Sully's *Pessimism*. It is true that most of these studies were either expository or opposed to Schopenhauer and his followers (Sully, for example, concludes that a George Eliot–like meliorism is more legitimate than pessimism). But it is also true—particularly when we take these articles and books in connection with the scientific, theological, and philosophical unorthodoxy of the time—that the very appearance of studies of pessimism is an important revelation of the intellectual temper between 1870 and 1878.

5

How much of the thought of the period importantly affected Hardy the incomplete records of his reading make it difficult to say. The official biography mentions his reading only one of the authors discussed above during the years before *The Return of the Native*—Leslie Stephen. Hardy's own statement positively denies a knowledge of Schopenhauer during these years,[27] and every element of his philosophy can be accounted for without assuming an influence by the German philosopher. It is difficult to believe, however, when we remember how much of the time Hardy was in London, that he was completely unaffected by the spirit of the time. Although we can trace no specific parallels between the thought of most of his contemporaries and the thought of Hardy, it seems unlikely that he would have continued to be as pessimistic as he was if his reading of rationalistic literature had stopped in 1865. It is improbable that Hardy should have gained sufficient intellectual impetus from the *Origin of Species* and the *Essays and Reviews* to carry him through the various developments perceptible in his philosophy during the seventies. It is likely that the persistence of the iconoclastic forces he first met when he was in his early twenties affected his intellectual development. Indeed, it is possible that some of these thinkers had a more specific effect than Hardy's biographer realized.

Rutland makes out a good case for the influence of both Spencer and J. S. Mill upon the ultimate shape of Hardy's philosophy, but it does not seem probable that their influence was upon Hardy's concept of the Immanent Will. As Rutland points out, there is a passage about an "inscrutable Power, manifested to us through all phenomena" in the fifth chapter of *First Principles* that sounds much like Hardy's later conception of the Will. But Hardy himself does not reach any definite conclusion about the precise nature of the ultimate reality beyond phenomena during the seventies. If Spencer did have such an influence, the effect did not manifest itself until later. Similarly with the passage in Mill's "Theism," where Mill states that mind can be produced unconsciously.[28] Hardy himself nowhere shows until much later that he was aware that mind could be produced unconsciously.

Since Mrs. Hardy speaks of Leslie Stephen as the "man whose philosophy . . . . [influenced Hardy's] for many years, indeed, more than that of any other contemporary,"[29] and since Hardy was frequently in contact with Stephen in the seventies, it is necessary to examine this possibility with some care. First of all, it must be admitted that Hardy had ample opportunity to become acquainted with Stephen's ideas. Stephen admired Hardy's earlier work sufficiently to ask him to contribute *Far from the Madding Crowd* to the *Cornhill Magazine*. In 1875 this business association developed into a friendship. Hardy and Stephen were frequently together; they discussed matters metaphysical and moral.

But a careful comparison of the works of the two men fails to show that Stephen influenced the shape of any of Hardy's fundamental ideas. True enough, there are passages in "Are We Christians?" (1873) remarkably similar to the parts of Mill's ironic discussion of Christianity in *On Liberty* Hardy had earlier approved. It is also unquestionable that Hardy agreed with the main argument of *An*

Agnostic's Apology. God rewards the "good and the bad, and gives equal reward to the free agent and the slave of fate." "To escape from Agnosticism we become Pantheists; then the divine reality must be the counterpart of phenomenal nature, and all the difficulties [about the presence of evil] recur." Hardy also agreed with the essential ideas of Stephen's *The Science of Ethics*. Stephen transfers the struggle for existence to social and political phenomena. He maintains that feeling is the ultimate basis for conduct—not reason; he believes that a slow progress is perceptible in human development.[30]

Although Hardy had not expressed these ideas in as precise and philosophic a form as Stephen had, and although Hardy may not have been aware that he was an agnostic when he neither affirmed nor denied the existence of God in his earlier work, it is nevertheless true that he believed in all of Stephen's fundamental premises before Stephen published any of the works I have mentioned or made the novelist's acquaintance. "The Two Men" (1867) and other poems show the equivalent rewards received by good and bad. In his earliest work Hardy shows implicitly that an identification of his First Principle (in so far as he admits one) with Nature intensifies the problem of evil rather than solves it. As a result of his own thinking about the consequences of Darwinism, Hardy early realized that the struggle for existence applies to society. Similarly, it can be shown from Hardy's early poems that he believed feeling to be basic in conduct and expected mankind to progress, though such progress, he believed, would be slow.

With Stephen's cause-and-effect determinism,[31] Hardy does not definitely agree or disagree between 1870 and 1878. He does not state his belief in a deterministic philosophy unmistakably until after the publication of *The Return of the Native*. It is quite likely that Stephen's determinism, along with the deterministic implications of Darwinism, was an important factor in helping Hardy to later formulate his own view. However, during the years we are now considering, Stephen's influence can have been only that of defining and confirming Hardy's previous convictions. He lent support to conclusions Hardy had previously drawn and made it less possible for him to change to a more conventional and optimistic interpretation of existence.

The common source of Stephen's and Hardy's ideas, scientific theory, continued to be important to Hardy's thought. There is no indication that science presented new difficulties, but there is ample evidence that the evolutionary hypothesis was still active in determining the nature of his outlook. In addition to frequent references to general science,[32] Hardy often speaks of the important effect scientific discovery has had upon man's conception of the universe. One of the most magnificent literary descriptions of the evolutionary process—unequaled, I believe, until Thomas Mann wrote *The Magic Mountain*—occurs in *A Pair of Blue Eyes* (1873). It is followed, significantly, by the already quoted passage about Nature's indifference. Nature is read "as a person with a curious temper; as one who does not scatter kindnesses and cruelties alternately, impartially, and in order, but heartless severities or overwhelming generosities in lawless caprice. Man's case is always that of the prodigal's favorite or the miser's pensioner."[33] Likewise, in *The Return of the Native* (1878), Hardy comments: "That old-fashioned reveling in the general situation grows less and less possible as we uncover the defects of natural law, and see the quandary that man is in by their operation."[34] It is these defects of natural law and the quandary in which they place man which form the intellectual basis for Hardy's pessimism in this as in the previous period. How thoroughly true this is becomes increasingly evident as we examine the novels.

6

From what we know of *The Poor Man and the Lady*, it must have been a fair presentation of the philosophy Hardy held to between 1865 and 1870. Because his first novel was criticized severely for its dead earnestness and because Hardy took the advice of George

Meredith that he moderate his criticism until he had gained a public, *Desperate Remedies* (1871) represents his outlook less adequately. As J. W. Beach and others have pointed out, Hardy probably took Meredith's suggestion that he write a novel of exciting interest seriously enough to model his own book after the popular novels of Wilkie Collins.[35] Certainly there were no better models for a young man about to write an exciting and popular novel than *The Woman in White* (1860) and *The Moonstone* (1868), which were among the most commonly read books of the decade that preceded the publication of *Desperate Remedies*.

At any rate, Hardy's first novel employs all the devices Collins used so well. From the time the reader's curiosity is first aroused by the story of the strange love of Cytherea's father until the moment when the villain Manston is captured, suspense and mystification are constantly used. To the suspense Hardy added a goodly measure of exciting incident. Indeed, one sometimes feels that Hardy also took Ouida for his master, so many are the melodramatic incidents in the book. A few pages after the book's beginning, Graye senior falls to his death from the top of a church tower. Before the plot finally unwinds, there have been a murder, a suicide, the appearance of a ghost, an attempt at rape, and a rousing good fight between successful lover Springrove and the villain, Manston. Perhaps for fear the reader's interest might lag, the author interspersed between these happenings Cytherea Aldclyffe's attempt to force her namesake to marry her bastard son, death rattles in the night, a marriage on Friday the thirteenth, a strange disease, and a breathless pursuit of Manston and Cytherea Graye to save the latter's honor. Even the use of coincidence and accident may have arisen partly out of respect for the practice of the sensational novelists Hardy was imitating. The frequent accidental meetings of *The Woman in White* and the almost uninterrupted chain of accidental happenings which make up *Armadale* (1866) would seem, at first glance, a sufficient reason for Hardy's use of these devices.

But because Hardy's early novel owes so much to the sensational novelists it need not be assumed that it lacks altogether the considered philosophy of the writer of "Hap." It is Chance—now become more the power behind accidental happenings than the symbol for Nature's indifference that it was earlier—that brings Cytherea Graye her position with her father's sweetheart, Cytherea Aldclyffe; Chance that accounts for the meeting of Manston and Cytherea and of Edward Springrove and Cytherea. If Manston had not misread his timetable, if the fire had not occurred on the night his wife came to him, Manston would not have been a murderer or his crime would not have been detected. If Springrove had arrived a few hours sooner, Cytherea would have probably refused to marry Manston in the first place. If the porter had revealed his secret somewhat earlier, Owen and Springrove would not have had to pursue Manston and Cytherea on their wedding journey. All these accidental occurrences might, it is true, be paralleled in other novels of the period. But there was no other novelist of the time who insisted so much upon the significance of the insignificant and the seemingly invisible means at work to bring about coincidence.[36] This insistence is characteristic of Hardy and of no one else.

Similarly, although some of the characters are conventional enough types, to be paralleled in many of the novels of the period, the peasants, Edward Springrove, Cytherea Aldclyffe, and Manston, plainly reveal that Hardy was responsible for their creation. The peasants of *Desperate Remedies* show this most clearly, perhaps. Although it is no doubt true that Hardy's peasants deserve, for the most part, the great praise they have received from the critics, and it is equally true that they talk and act like the real peasants they are drawn from, it seems, in this novel, that Hardy's portrayal reveals his own philosophy as often as it does the peasants'. Probably the peasants were frequently fatalistic and antitheistic, but it is unlikely that they were as much concerned with expressing those beliefs as Hardy makes them out to be. The peasant postman thinks that God will soon be abolished. Crickett maintains stoutly that God sends bread to one home and children, without the bread, to another. Whenever four or five peasants are gathered together, their conversation seems to turn upon fate. Farmer Baker and Farmer Springrove (Edward's father) watch a man come down the street with Manston's coffin. Baker says: "Why should we not stand still, says I to myself, and fling a quiet eye upon the Why and Wherefores, before the end o' it all, and we go down into the mouldering-place and are forgotten?" Springrove rejoins: " 'Tis a feeling that will come. But 'twont bear looking into. Ther's a back'ard current in the world, and we must do our utmost to advance in order just to bide where we be."[37]

The artistic effect of such a colloquoy is admirable. It serves as a comment on passing events and, like a Greek chorus, gives a significance to a particular event that it would not have had otherwise. But these dialogues leave one wondering whether he is listening to characteristic peasant talk or to Hardy, denied the opportunity of expressing his thought in his own right, using the peasants as his medium.

There may be some question as to whether Hardy is expressing a portion of his reading of life through the peasants. There can be no doubt that he is exemplifying portions of his philosophy through the speech and action of Springrove. Like his creator, Springrove is an architect and an idealist. He is constantly in search of the "something wanting," of his "alter ego." As his father once says, he is looking for perfection in things when there is none. Because of his idealistic propensities, he does not get ahead very fast in architecture. Because, like most Hardyan young men, he idealizes upon first falling in love, he later becomes disillusioned.[38] Although Hardy, wishing to please a conventional public, gave Springrove his loved one before the end of the book and promised that they should live happily ever after, Springrove is, in at least the first half of the book, an admirable example of a typical Hardy character—one who finds that ideal desires are unrealizable and comes to realize "the intolerable antilogy of making figments feel."

In another sense, Manston and Cytherea Aldclyffe typify Hardy's point of view. Apparently because the novelist believed that "crass Casualty" or an indifferent Nature was responsible for the vagaries of human beings, he treats these "evil" characters with unusual sympathy. They are not a conventional villain and villainess. A comparison with Collins' Count Fosco immediately shows the reader their individuality. Despite the fact that Cytherea Aldclyffe is often cruel in her treatment of her namesake and is the mother of a bastard, Hardy contrives to gain her the reader's sympathy. During the first half of the book the same is true of Manston. He is drawn to Cytherea Graye by an irresistible attraction rather than by inherent villainy. He tries to restrain his desire. He has attractive qualities, mental and moral, and is occasionally kind in a truly disinterested fashion.[39] His degeneration into an ordinary thriller villain in the latter portion of the book, no doubt necessitated by the type of tale Hardy was telling, is not adequately prepared for and leaves the reader unconvinced.

In addition to managing to infuse some of his reading of life into the handling of his characters, Hardy also succeeds in making them follow the pattern of his "sexual pessimism" to a degree surprising in so conventional a novel. The fact that Springrove and Cytherea fall in love at first sight is not unusual, but Hardy's emphasis upon the physical basis of their mutual attraction is not frequently paralleled in nineteenth-century fiction. It is the same with Manston and Cytherea Graye. Although Cytherea does not really admire Manston, he exerts a "fascination" over her. She feels "in his power" because of some almost irresistible attraction he can make her feel. Indeed, Hardy tells us in so many words that it is the law of "natural selection" which accounts for Manston's attractiveness to women. Likewise, the Darwinian reason for many of Cytherea's actions is fairly clear. With an instinct natural to her sex, she cultivates the pose that most becomes her. She is attracted by the "strength" and physical attractiveness of Springrove.[40] Many of her actions are consciously coquettish. Feeble though she is as a realistic character, she is dominated by the same fundamental impulses Hardy gives to his later, more believable, women. Her actions do not cause any heartbreaks in *Desperate Remedies*, but actions similar to hers wreak havoc in the novelist's later, less conventional, books.

Desperate Remedies is, then, a mixture of conventional thriller writing and typically Hardyan treatment. The devices by which the reader's attention is kept are probably the fruit of a study of the sensational novels of the period. But the actual subject matter, barring the more stunningly sensational incidents, is characteristic of Hardy. Nowhere else in contemporary fiction would one have found a disillusioned idealist like Springrove, such antitheistic peasants, such readily excusable villains, such pointed use of accident and coincidence, so frank a treatment of the process of sexual selection. Although one must agree with Hardy's own estimate that "the principles observed in its composition are, no doubt, too exclusively those in which mystery, entanglement, surprise, and moral obliquity are depended on for exciting interest," he must also grant that Hardy managed to introduce into the book enough of his reading of life to make it "not unworthy of a little longer preservation."[41]

7

In some ways *Under the Greenwood Tree* (1872) is Hardy's least characteristic novel. There are no sensational incidents.[42] A rather mild curiosity as to who will win Fancy is the closest approach to the continual use of suspense in the preceding novel. If the author was conscious of any literary indebtedness, he probably felt obligation to Miss Mitford's *Our Village* and Mrs. Gaskell's *Cranford*, for, whether this is an effect consciously intended or not, the novel suggests a skilful blending of Miss Mitford's use of scene and Mrs. Gaskell's use of simple characterization. In my opinion, it surpasses both these books in its faithful presentation of country life.

But the novel is even less illustrative of the author's philosophy than *Desperate Remedies*. One finds no character whose aspirations are high and unrealizable, no abnormally fatalistic or anti-Christian peasants, no references to Chance, and but one coincidence. Hardy's characteristic reading of life appears only in the disentanglement of the love plot that centers about the schoolmistress, Fancy Day.

Parson Maybold, Tranter-To-Be Dick Dewy, and wealthy Farmer Shinar all love Fancy Day before they have had any opportunity to discover whether she deserves their love. Despite the fact that the reader soon realizes clearly that idealization of Fancy is a mistake, Maybold and Dick infer the highest possible merit from Fancy's beauty. It takes each of them some time to recognize her coquetry and her continuous desire to have all men at her feet. For her part, she obviously enjoys having Maybold, Dick, and Shinar in love with her at the same time, even going considerably out of her way to make Farmer Shinar, the suitor she is drawn to least, propose. Her love for Dick, who finally wins her, is never sufficiently overwhelming to keep her from trying to attract as many suitors as possible. Although the author remarks in the conventional manner that Dick and Fancy are likely to be happy, the reader expects the hero to suffer many uneasy hours. There can be no doubt that Parson Maybold (possibly Shinar as well) suffers both disillusionment and disappointment because of Fancy's choice.[43]

The extremely problematical happiness love brings, Hardy often points out indirectly. When Fancy refuses to go nutting with Dick because she wishes to make a beautiful dress for the Longpuddle men (in whom she professes no interest) to admire, Hardy comments: "It is just possible that a few more blue dresses on the Longpuddle young men's account would have clarified Dick's brain entirely, and made him once more a free man." Hardy's entire account of Fancy's character and actions assures us that he agreed with Reuben Dewy's comment upon the love of women: "She'll swear she's dying for thee, and she is dying for thee, and she will die for thee; but she'll fling a look over t'other shoulder at another young feller, though never leaving off dying for thee just the same."[44]

But the questionable advantages of love are most clearly pointed out in the portrayal of two married couples, the families of the hero and the heroine. The Days hardly speak to each other. The Dewys continually indulge in a passionless process of mutual reproach. As his treatment of the marriages in the novel shows, Hardy was fully aware of the irony present in the thoughts of Dick Dewy about his family: "Dick wondered how it was that when people were married they could be so blind to romance; and was quite certain that if he ever took to wife that dear impossible Fancy, he and she would never be so dreadfully practical and undemonstrative of the Passion as his father and mother were. The most extraordinary thing was that all the fathers and mothers he knew were just as undemonstrative as his own."[45]

Either because Hardy was himself unusually happy in his love for Emma Gifford or because he continued to feel the necessity of moderation until he had found an audience, or for both of these reasons, he never allows the more somber aspects of his world view to be emphasized. It is quite possible that the casual reader, or the reader unacquainted with Hardy's early outlook, would be altogether unaware of the author's pessimistic view of love. As Hardy himself has said, the novel was written "lightly, even . . . . farcically and flippantly at times." He made no attempt at a "deeper, more essential, more transcendent handling."[46] Nevertheless, as a delicate and amusing picture of country life, it has few, if any, equals in English fiction.

8

A Pair of Blue Eyes (1873) lacks the exciting action which carries the reader through *Desperate Remedies* and the perfection of treatment one finds in *Under the Greenwood Tree*, but it foreshadows the mature Hardy much more clearly than either of these works. The novelist is still seeking a method, but his technical dependence on other models is much less than it was in his first novel, and his aim is more serious than it was in either of his first books.

As they were in *Desperate Remedies*, the peasant characters are a chorus which comments upon passing events, but they are no longer obvious expositors of the author's point of view. As in *Under the Greenwood Tree*, their fatalistic and antitheistic remarks come only when they naturally would come.[47] Moreover, the peasant scenes have become an integral part of the story rather than an obtrusive appendage. They help prepare the reader for Elfride's marriage with Luxellian. They add to the realistic atmosphere of the novel. They afford relief from the more tragic scenes in the book.

Most of the technical devices Hardy took over from the popular novelists of the period are used less frequently than in *Desperate Remedies*. Mrs. Jethway's curse upon Elfride and the heroine's nearly fatal fall from a tower remind one of the sensationalism of many of Hardy's contemporaries. But such incidents occur less often than they did in *Desperate Remedies*. At least once, in the justly praised scene where Knight nearly falls from a cliff, a potentially sensational event is handled with admirable restraint. Nor does Hardy rely as much upon mysterious happenings for suspense as he did in his first published novel. With the exception of the mystery surrounding Smith's origin in the early pages of the book and Swancourt's mystifying encounters with his wife-to-be, suspense depends solely upon the reader's curiosity about the fate of naturally conceived characters in a realistic situation. One technical device which Hardy found in the novels of the day and retained for reasons

[101]

self, we find again—the use of accident and coin-
~~gh~~ it is true that he overworks this device, piling co-
~~coincidence~~ until it is impossible for the best-dis-
~~suspend~~ disbelief entirely, it is also true that his use
~~coincidence~~ is integrated with his reading of life to
~~than~~ it was in *Desperate Remedies*.

In spite of the fact that this novel contains stylistic incongruities which one does not find in *Under the Greenwood Tree* and a more floundering construction than *Desperate Remedies*, its more serious "criticism of life" earns it more extensive treatment than either of its predecessors. Although, as in the earlier books, Hardy is primarily concerned with his pessimism about love, there are two important differences between this novel and the two that antedate it. The pessimism is carried to its logical conclusion in spite of the conventions of the contemporary novel. The exposition of Hardy's entire viewpoint is clearer, more detailed, and more convincing than it had been before.

All the important characters feel or might feel the disproportion between desire and the possibility of desire's realization. Elfride sighs for the unattainable and is inevitably disappointed. Smith longs for an ideal love with Elfride, but her finite fickleness and her innate desire to find a man unquestionably her superior cause Smith to be disappointed. But it is Knight, the superior man, who most realizes and suffers most from the antilogy involved in man's finite capacities and infinite longings. It is he who says that a high soul brings a man to the workhouse, and, if his own "high soul" does not quite bring him to such a pass, his success is scarcely more satisfactory than that of the worthy character in "The Two Men." Afflicted with the characteristic malaise of Hardy's characters, he wishes to make the world suit his happiness. He wants to be the first and only man in a woman's heart and to have the complete confidence of whomever he may love. Carried away, like most of Hardy's lovers, by physical attractiveness, he believes he has found the *idea* incarnate in Elfride, only to discover her an ordinary woman. This is the most important disenchantment he suffers, but it is not the only one. Where he would have wished an intellectual equal for a friend, Circumstance gives him the boyishly charming but not very intelligent Smith. He would like to take all knowledge as his province, but he is forced to conclude that man must content himself with the little he can acquire in a hurrying world. He is constantly and consciously a sufferer because he realizes that "such an appreciative breadth as a sentient being possesses should [not] be committed to the frail casket of a body."[48]

Knight's case anticipates what may be said of the sexual pessimism of the book. The focal point for the lovers of the novel is Elfride Swancourt. She is attractive, coquettish, and thoughtless. Because she is thoughtless, Elfride allows young Jethway to love her. Because she cannot return his love, he becomes so unhappy that he refuses to struggle against an illness that overtakes him and so dies. Then, for a while, Elfride is attracted by Smith's "prettiness" and believes that she loves him. But when Knight comes to see her and her father in Smith's absence, she is irresistibly attracted by his greater masculinity. Although she tries to retain her love for Smith, her lack of farsightedness (common among women, Hardy tells us)[49] allows her to continue to see Knight until her liking for Smith and her conscientious wish to be faithful disappear together. When Knight deserts her as she has deserted her two former lovers, she becomes truly unhappy, but she marries Lord Luxellian and is partially consoled by the luxury she enjoys with him.

If Elfride, because of her continual desire to subdue men and her preference for masterfulness, typifies Hardy's view of women in love, so are the male characters typical of Hardy's men when they love. From beauty they infer the possession of all other desirable qualities. They imagine Elfride the *idea* of woman made real. Whereas a writer who had himself less paradisaic tendencies than Hardy might deplore this impossible search for the infinite in a

[[103]]

finite world, Hardy does not. Such a sequence seems to him the inevitable result of natural law. Woman aspires to conquer man; woman is thoughtless; woman generally changes from love of a handsome face to love of a masterful personality—"the most vigorous males usually leave the most numerous progeny," said Darwin. Man mistakes physical beauty for a divine omen of perfection; he idealizes; he becomes disillusioned. The result of the cycle is pain for everyone involved. Thus Jethway, Smith, Elfride, and Knight suffer. So the battle of the sexes and Nature's process of natural selection operate, it seems to Hardy.

For the unhappiness which is found in *A Pair of Blue Eyes* natural law is primarily responsible. But there is a force not under the control of any apparent set of laws that contributes to the unhappiness of the characters. If Stephen Smith had not made a mistake in getting his marriage license, Elfride would have married him. If Mrs. Jethway had not seen Elfride and Smith get off a train together, Elfride might not have been exposed to Knight. The enumeration of such "ifs" could be indefinitely extended. Thirty-seven similar accidents, all of them more or less importantly related to the fate of the characters, occur in the novel. It almost seems as if a malign external force, quite different from the "crass Casualty" that might bring either gladness or moans, is co-operating with natural law to make unhappiness general.

Nor are these the only forces which contribute to man's inability to find satisfaction. Circumstance, a "Doomster" that had not appeared before and that roughly corresponds to the influence of environment, is also responsible for much of man's misery. Circumstance dictated that Knight should find no friend better than Stephen Smith. Circumstance is held responsible for Knight's having become a reviewer. Circumstance overpowered Elfride's purposes and caused her to marry Lord Luxellian.[50]

Working in conjunction, Circumstance, Chance, and natural law govern the universe inimically to man's purposes. Although Hardy does not believe that these powers are actively antagonistic to man, their effect is the same as that of malicious forces. Their strength and their character are symbolized by the forces of Nature which Knight sees opposed to him as he clings precariously to the cliff's edge. They are indifferent to man's fate and to man's happiness. The world was planned for purposes that man cannot possibly believe are sympathetic with his own desires.

Still, even in such a universe, Hardy does not see all as vanity. At the same time that he shows how sorry the condition of man is, he also makes us realize that there are some remediable ills and that there is at least a limited opportunity for happiness. An effort to remedy one of these remediable ills, in fact, forms a minor theme of the book. Stephen Smith's parents—like Hardy's—are of yeoman stock, socially beneath the pretentiously aristocratic Swancourts. The Reverend Mr. Swancourt feels himself far superior to Stephen; even Elfride, while she is still in love with Smith, is affected by the virus of class snobbery. Hardy ridicules this claim to superiority by his satiric portraits of the upper class[51] and by his presentation of Swancourt's absurd preoccupation with his own genealogical excellence. He leaves us in no doubt as to Smith's actual equality with the Swancourts, father and daughter.

More important than such incidental social criticism is Hardy's indirect plea for more imaginative sympathy in personal relationships. Although he recognizes the deficiencies of Elfride and shows her thoughtless cruelty to Smith and Jethway, he nevertheless sympathizes with her sincere love for Knight. He deplores Knight's preoccupation with abstractions—a preoccupation which makes it impossible for him to see that Elfride, although imperfect, is truly devoted to him. Apropos of Knight's desertion of Elfride, Hardy indignantly declares that men accept evidence not worthy to convict a dog when they are suspicious in love. At the end of the book, Knight, both older and wiser, points out the lesson which his relations with Elfride have taught him: "Since we don't know half the

meliorism by means of satire.

reasons that made her do as she did, ... how can we say, even now, that she was not pure and true in heart?"[52] This rather too obvious pointing of the story indicates that Hardy wished the reader to realize the importance and simple justice of imaginative sympathy.

A Pair of Blue Eyes is neither the best nor the most complete exposition of Hardy's essential philosophy to come between 1870 and 1878, but the book gains in both breadth and depth from the seriousness of its interpretation of life. Nor is one too generally aware that the book is an illustration of a philosophy. Whether one approves of Knight's search for the ideal in an imperfect world or not, it is a credible human experience, and Knight is sufficiently individualized to save him from being a mere illustration of the antilogy of making figments feel. Despite her domination by natural law and her propensity for creating unhappiness, Elfride is not only real—she is pathetic and attractive as well. With the exception of Swancourt, even the minor characters appear to be actual human beings. Nor does there seem to be anything forced about the course love takes. The evils which result are nonetheless credible because they sometimes do not occur and because they also exemplify a part of Hardy's philosophy. Even the operation of accident is not altogether unbelievable. In a novel with a happy conclusion, the ordinary reader would accept most of the accidental happenings.

Further, it seems rather futile to raise, with some critics, the conventional objection that the characters rarely come in direct conflict with one another. It is true enough that Smith and Knight, though they love Elfride, never contend against each other; it is true that all the direct conflicts are minor ones, such as the conflict between Elfride and her father over her engagement to Smith and of the Widow Jethway and Elfride over the concealment of the latter's secret. What conflict occurs is between the characters and the forces which direct the universe: Accident, Circumstance, and natural law. But it is perfectly credible that such should be the case.

A similar conflict appears in Greek drama and in the lives of many people. Since the characters tend to submit without a struggle to the forces which oppose them, it must be called a pathetic tale rather than a tragedy (where there is more contention between characters and fate)—but this does not mean that Hardy's novel therefore becomes inferior. It merely means that the author is not writing tragedy.

What actually makes the novel only partially successful is the immaturity of its workmanship. Hardy desires to dispose of Stephen Smith for a while so that Knight can win away Elfride's affection. Therefore, Smith secures a totally unexpected position in India and is thus put out of the way, but the reader remains incredulous. Hardy wishes to get both Stephen and Knight to the tomb of Elfride. Therefore, he has Knight and Smith accidentally meet in London, accidentally talk of Elfride, accidentally ride the same train, and—accidentally—board the train on which Elfride's coffin is taken to her home. It is not the fact that these are coincidences that is bad. It is that these are unnecessary and gratuitous coincidences, introduced not because they illustrate the author's philosophy but because the author was unable to get the two men to meet over Elfride's grave in a more natural and credible fashion. Such incredible incidents, of which there are too many, mar the book and force the reader to agree that there is an "immaturity in [the novel's] workmanship."[53] As an early illustration of Hardy's views the book is of interest and importance, but as a work of art it deserves one of the lower places in the canon of Hardy's works.

9

Evidently the mistakes of *A Pair of Blue Eyes* were both necessary and profitable steps in Hardy's development as an artist, for in *Far from the Madding Crowd* (1874) one finds him finally in command of his method. Sensational incidents, such as the fire which

Gabriel Oak puts out almost single-handed, the seduction of Fanny, and the madness of Boldwood, still appear, but they are not emphasized for their own sake and are handled with restrained artistry. As in *A Pair of Blue Eyes*, the peasants are an integral part of the novel's scheme. Sometimes their conversations help to give the pastoral atmosphere the story requires. Occasionally they help to clarify a situation or enlarge our conception of a character. Frequently they serve as comic relief. Although accidental occurrences play an important part in the development of the plot, they are not piled up as in *A Pair of Blue Eyes*. When they come, they have an inevitability which makes the reader accept them willingly. The reader's interest is stimulated, primarily, by the realistic portrayal of country scenes and folk and by the naturalness with which realistic characters play their part in a believable situation.

Moreover, the novel expresses the most balanced view of life Hardy presented between 1870 and 1878. His desire to establish a reputation did not force him to smooth over unhappy events as in his first two publications. Perhaps because he had himself achieved a temporary philosophic equilibrium, he does not overemphasize the tragedy of life as he does in *A Pair of Blue Eyes*. Although the misery of a Chance-governed universe is amply apparent, it is also obvious that happiness is a possibility, too. The reader who generally feels that Hardy stacks the cards against his characters should except this novel.

In general outline it resembles *A Pair of Blue Eyes*. Just as Elfride was loved successively by Jethway, Smith, and Knight, so Bathsheba Everdene is loved successively by Oak, Boldwood, and Troy. In *Far from the Madding Crowd*, however, Bathsheba finally marries the man who seems best suited to her, and there is an additional, though related, love story—that of Troy and Fanny Robin. The actions and motives of the characters are similar to those found in the preceding novel. In every case, physical attraction is responsible for the beginning of love. Although she is generally more admirable and intelligent than Elfride, Bathsheba is nevertheless coquettish, vain, and thoughtless. She wishes to subject men to her. She is attracted by superior mental or physical force.[54]

Near the beginning of the novel, Oak sees Bathsheba and falls in love with her. Bathsheba does not love him at first, but she goes out of her way to make him woo her. When he proposes, she rejects him; indeed, she is tacitly occupied with attracting and rejecting him until the last pages of the book. After Oak has proposed and has been rejected a second time, Bathsheba is attracted by Boldwood's supposed lack of interest in women and thoughtlessly sends him a valentine that declares her love—just to see what will happen. When her valentine causes Boldwood to fall in love with her and to propose, she repents her thoughtless action and tries to decide to marry him. But Sergeant Troy then appears. Although he is the moral and intellectual inferior of all the other men she knows, she cannot resist his fascination and marries him. Boldwood is driven into a literally mad agony. Because Troy is naturally fickle and because he repents having deserted Fanny Robin, he, too, is unhappy in the marriage. When Bathsheba sees the mistake her marriage to Troy is, she also becomes inconsolable.

The story finally ends happily, but the potential evils of love are emphasized more than they have been in the preceding novels: "It appears that ordinary men take wives because possession is not possible without marriage, and that ordinary women accept husbands because marriage is not possible without possession."[55]

In this pessimistic statement one detects a departure from good Darwinism that is characteristic of both Hardy and his period, for Hardy's women, although they are drawn to the men irresistibly, retain a Victorian nicety about the consummation of love. Nevertheless, the biological basis of Hardy's sexual pessimism stands clearly revealed. Indeed, one of the characters, Sergeant Troy, makes a speech that epitomizes the evils which result from "love" in both this and other novels of the Wessex series: "Probably some one man on an average falls in love with each ordinary woman. She can marry him; he is content and leads a useful life. Such women as you a hundred men always covet—your eyes bewitch scores on scores into an unavailing fancy for you—you can only marry one of that many. Out of these say twenty will endeavor to drown the bitterness of despised love in drink; twenty more will mope away their lives without a wish or attempt to make a mark in the world, because they have no ambition apart from their attachment to you; twenty more—the susceptible person myself among them,—will be always draggling after you, getting where they may just see you, doing desperate things. . . . . The rest may try to get over their passion with more or less success. But all of these men will be saddened. And not only these ninety-nine men, but the ninety-nine women they might have married are saddened with them. . . . . That's why I say that a woman so charming as yourself, Miss Everdene, is hardly a blessing to her race."[56] Although the eloquent Troy exaggerates more than a little, and Hardy himself would be inclined to equate more nearly the ordinary and the extraordinary woman, the fates of Fanny, Boldwood, Oak, and Troy himself are illustrations of the underlying thought of the passage. It could even be said that all the men and women in the Wessex novels either would, or should, recognize the essential truth of the Sergeant's words.

However, as in *A Pair of Blue Eyes*, natural law cannot be blamed for all the misfortunes of the characters. Chance happenings—the accidents and coincidences that neither the characters nor the author are able to account for by their understanding of natural law—help to make the characters unhappy. If Fanny Robin and Troy had understood each other as to the church in which they were to marry, if the result of the Bible-tossing that determined the sending of the valentine to Boldwood had been other than it was, if Bathsheba had not been deceived by the various coincidences which seemed to prove Troy's death—the lives of all involved would have been more contented. Their unhappiness is caused by both natural law and by what seems to be Chance.

One of the characters, Fanny Robin, owes her tragic fate not only to Chance, which prevented Troy and herself from finding the same church and marrying, and to natural law which attracted her to Troy and Troy to her, but also to Circumstance—this time made manifest in the pharisaic attitude of society generally to a "fallen woman." In the novels we have already treated there have been slight protests against the power of Circumstance, which Hardy evidently considered alterable when it takes the form of social conventions such as exaggerated class snobbery; but we have had nothing remotely comparable to Hardy's indignant protest against the cruelty of society to Fanny. On a smaller scale Fanny's story is the analogue of *Tess*, the tale of a pure woman who suffers unjustly. Fanny loves Troy, is intimate with him, becomes pregnant, and is deserted. In Hardy's vivid picture of her outcast state—where no one save a dog will help her—we have his first forceful protest against "man's inhumanity to man" and a definite indication of his wish to obviate remediable ills.

Moreover, although it is true that Boldwood's madness and deportation for the murder of Troy, the murder itself, the disappointment in the love of Oak for Bathsheba, and much of Fanny's suffering are caused by the magnipotent forces that govern or fail to govern Hardy's universe, the book as a whole cannot be called unrelievedly pessimistic even if one excepts the author's protest against Fanny's treatment by society. At the end of the book the two most admirable characters finally marry. As the author himself points out, they should be happy, for "theirs was that substantial affection which arises (if any arises at all) when the two who are thrown together begin first by knowing the rougher sides of each other's character, and not the best till further on, the romance growing up in the interstices of a mass of hard prosaic reality. This good-fellowship—*camaraderie*—usually occurring through similarity of pursuits, is unfortunately seldom superadded to love between the sexes, because men and women associate, not in their labours, but in their pleasures merely. Where, however, happy circumstance permits its development, the compounded feeling proves itself to be the only love which is strong as death."[57]

In yet another sense the tone of this novel is more hopeful. Always before, what conflicts have occurred have been markedly unequal. In *Desperate Remedies* neither Cytherea, Owen, nor Springrove makes any notable effort to resist bad fortune. When good fortune comes, it is thrown in their laps. One might say the same of *Under the Greenwood Tree*, while in *A Pair of Blue Eyes* there is not a single character who boldly resists the fate that tries to overcome him. In *Far from the Madding Crowd*, it is true, Bathsheba, Boldwood, Fanny, and Troy submit rather passively to Circumstance, but Oak does not. He is the first of Hardy's characters to succeed by dogged resistance to fate. When we first see him, he is fairly well to do, the owner of a large flock of sheep. An accident causes him to lose his flock, but, since he refuses to accept this passively, he eventually prospers again. So, also, in love. Although he is at first unable to win Bathsheba, his persistence eventually succeeds. He is not, of course, in any sense a subject for either Horatio Alger or Samuel Smiles—one of the reasons he does so well is that he does not have unattainable ambitions and can accept the inevitable—but he is a strong character. Even when his fortunes are at the worst, we feel that he is one whom "misfortune has inured rather than subdued."[58] His struggle with fortune approaches the condition of an equal battle.

Among the early novels, *Far from the Madding Crowd* is both the best-balanced exposition of Hardy's philosophy since *The Poor Man and the Lady*, and the most successful work of art. Faced by the indifferent, seemingly inimical, forces of Chance, Circumstance, and natural law, the characters experience more unhappiness than happiness. But one does not feel that the forces opposed to man are either unnatural in their operation or, inevitably, preventers of content. Through the knowledge that success is possible to one like Oak, who accepts the universe but refuses to be easily subdued, and through the knowledge that much of Fanny Robin's misfortune is due to the heartlessness of society rather than to Nature's inevitable cruelty, one sees that it is not an altogether hopeless world in which men live. As this realistic interpretation of life is joined by a command of technique such as the novelist had not shown previously, it is not surprising that this novel has been almost universally judged one of the best Hardy has written.

10

The Hand of Ethelberta is, I believe, Hardy's poorest novel. The false aesthetic theory which guided Hardy in writing the book, that improbable events are acceptable to the lighthearted reader when the characters appear real, in part accounts for the failure of the novel.[59] For, however real a character may be in conception, he becomes unreal when his actions are incredible.

The plot consists of a chain of unbelievable incidents. Although Ethelberta's father is a butler, she marries into the nobility. After her husband's death and the withdrawal of his mother's protection, she launches single-handed a campaign for social recognition. She becomes a successful public teller of her own tales; members of the nobility sue for her hand; she succeeds in marrying a fabulously wealthy lord. As if to pile improbability upon improbability, Hardy joins to this unlikely situation an unsurpassable succession of highly improbable coincidences and accidents. The characters almost invariably meet by chance; whenever Ethelberta especially wishes a character not to meet another character, he does, or almost does. The coincidence which caps the climax finds all the lovers together in one house, listening to Ethelberta's conversation with the lord she finally accepts. It is possible—though unlikely—

〚 113 〛

that such a chain of coincidences could have been made plausible; it is certain that Hardy did not make them so.

But the improbable events do not account by themselves alone for the novel's failure. Hardy is not only dealing with an incredible plot; he is also working in a milieu with which he is not familiar and in a spirit altogether unconsonant with his somber reading of life. A comparison of the scenes intended for high comedy with the successful comedy of *The Egoist*, or even of *The New Republic*, immediately shows how ill at ease Hardy was when he attempted to be urbane or witty. The characters are not only mere types;* they are also uninteresting types that have been overworked in both drama and novel. The witticisms are forced and wooden. The effort spent upon the composition of the epigrams is so readily perceptible that the reader almost takes to chewing his pencil out of sympathy. Moreover, Hardy attempts to give to the atmosphere a light gaiety of which he had become temperamentally incapable. He never successfully represses the eternal note of sadness, and, even when it is partially repressed, the reader is too conscious of the effort this suppression required. The only effective portion of the novel is the last hundred pages, in which Ethelberta's brothers, Christopher Julian, and the younger Mountclere pursue the heroine and her noble husband. There is some excitement, at least, in these pages. As much cannot be said of the rest of the book.

Nonetheless, the characteristic Hardy philosophy is expressed. Life is a battle in which the deserving rarely prosper. The sly and sensual Mountclere succeeds where Julian fails. Ethelberta's chance for happiness, even though her ambition is realized, is highly problematical. Even the most cheerful characters point out the unlikeli-

* An exception must be made of the Chickerells, who, although they apparently owe something to Hardy's reading of Dickens, are without exact parallels in nineteenth-century fiction. This does not make them less dull. Neigh is the usual worldly-wise man, Ladywell a somewhat more serious version of Dickens' Winkle. If it were not true that the sly sensualists of Restoration comedy were often amusing, one would suggest them as the ancestors of Lord Mountclere.

hood of realizing happiness. Ethelberta says that only the blind are cheerful. Julian remarks about the impishness of the gods who allow those who care little about their fate to succeed and force those who try for success to fail. At the most propitious moment, the same character says elsewhere, sorrow is so near that the wise man should not allow his spirits to rise above mere cheerfulness.[60] That the world is depicted as such a world despite Hardy's intention to write comedy is another reason for the failure of the book.

Most of the muted unhappiness in the book is the result of love. Ethelberta, like Elfride and Bathsheba, is the cause, but she is far more consciously responsible for her actions than are the other two women. She definitely intends to catch men in her "cherry net." She emphasizes her charm consciously, for she knows that the heart hot with passions is the same in Pall Mall as in Wessex. She knows the value of feigned indifference, but she also sees that she must go out of her way to bring men to her upon occasion. Further, her motives are more practical and reasoned than those that inspire the usual Hardyan woman. She wants to marry for money so that she will be able to make life easy for herself and for her family. Although an almost Atalantean force draws her to Julian,[61] the most deserving and the poorest of her lovers, her practical sense is sufficiently strong to suppress natural desire. She does not, however, have a sufficient sense of kindliness to keep her from coquetting with Julian. Knowing that she will not marry him, she nevertheless goes out of her way to attract him.

With other men she is far more ruthless. She skilfully contrives to get the love of three marriageable bachelors, Ladywell, Neigh, and Mountclere. But when she makes up her mind that Mountclere, a lord and fabulously wealthy, will give her what she wants, she casts off the other two with no thought for their feelings. Although the attempt to play lightly upon human emotions keeps Hardy from emphasizing the pain the lovers feel, it is evident that Neigh, Ladywell, and Julian are made unhappy. Ethelberta is no more fortunate, for Mountclere and his social position fail to bring the anticipated satisfaction.

Chance dominates the scene less than in most of Hardy's novels. There are numerous accidental occurrences, but they do not notably affect the course of the story. Ethelberta's conflict is with society rather than with Chance. She is, to a degree unusual in the Wessex novels, the master of her fate. Although, with characteristic irony, the author makes us see that she does not much value what she gets when she gets it, he does allow her to make her life as she wills it—despite the forces Hardy's more considered judgment believed opposed to her. The only important action of Chance in the book is a kind one—the bringing-together of Picotee and Julian.

Hardy's social criticism is not so effectively presented as it was in *Far from the Madding Crowd*, but it ranges over a wider field than it has in any of his earlier publications. Single lines often hit at some modern and remediable fallacy. We wrongly regard increase of size as symbolic of progress. We are worshipers of Mammon. The lower class should receive artistic education *à la* Ruskin. The excessive specialization of the modern tradesman is deplored. The condition of the poor, particularly of those in London, is lamented. A mean of common justice in one's relations with others is much better than the alternation of foolishly kind and unjustly harsh conduct that characterizes the action of such aristocrats as Lady Petherwin.[62]

Hardy gives more extensive treatment to two protestant themes he had treated before. Like Knight in *A Pair of Blue Eyes*, Ethelberta remarks that half-knowledge of a life misjudges. Ethelberta's own life is an intended example. But this appeal for greater imaginative sympathy is not so noteworthy as the attack upon class snobbishness. Although Ethelberta is a servant's daughter, she is at least the equal of Lord Mountclere. Snobbery is altogether unjustified on the part of a declining, corrupt, and useless aristocracy. The lower-class characters are uniformly portrayed as more admirable than the ineffective members of the rich, landed portion of society. Some indication of the importance of these criticisms in Hardy's intention may be gathered from his later opinion that his primary aim was an attack upon class consciousness and from his ironical request that his readers pardon "a writer for presenting the sons and daughters of Mr. and Mrs. Chickerell [the butler and his wife] as beings who come within the scope of a congenial regard."[63]

Indeed, for all its technical ineffectiveness, the book is important because it demonstrates the continuation of the early radical strain in Hardy. Although it would certainly be a mistake to consider socialistic a novel in which the Alger-like rise of a member of the working class is the most notable feature, one does see that Hardy's social sympathies continue to be with the classes of society that are at the bottom rather than at the top of the heap. One might even hazard the speculation, although it involves a too considerable number of "ifs," that, if Hardy had known the working class as a whole better and the aristocracy better, if he had felt an encouragement in the spirit of the time and the purse of the publishers, he might have anticipated the modern school of proletarian fiction by a good many years. But such speculations would lead us almost endlessly astray from Hardy as he was and the times as they were, for the logical consequence of such speculations would be the further supposition that Hardy would have directed more of his time to arraigning society, less to the criticism of the universe, that he would have become more like William Morris and less like Thomas Hardy.

In a final critical analysis little can be said for *The Hand of Ethelberta*. With such a philosophy as Hardy held, he was incapable of achieving high comedy. Because he wished to achieve it, he could not do justice to his own point of view. Because he followed a faulty aesthetic, he was unable to treat the material at hand with a convincing technique. It is a novel of wooden characters and unnatural incident. Had it not been written by Hardy, it would long ago have ceased to be of interest even to scholars. Had it not contained some illustrations of Hardy's philosophy and further proof that Hardy wished to direct a good deal of his criticism at society—thus recalling the author of *The Poor Man and the Lady* and foreshadowing the author of *Tess* and *Jude*—it would not deserve such remembrance.

11

As innumerable critics have pointed out, *The Return of the Native* (1878) is the best of the early Wessex novels. None of the technical defects we have found in the earlier books appears. The memorable characters it contains, the effective dramatic structure of the whole, the singleness of effect the novel achieves—all these qualities justify the judgment of the critics. Since the admirable critiques of other writers make critical comment a hauling of coals to Newcastle, I shall concern myself altogether with another aspect of the novel. For *The Return of the Native*, while it is not so fair an interpretation of Hardy's reading of life as *Far from the Madding Crowd*, is yet the most effective and complete illustration of the pessimism most people and most critics have considered to be typical of Hardy.

But, before going into the book as a whole, it seems worth while to ask why *The Return of the Native* is not only pessimistic—that we already understand—but the most pessimistic of the early novels. In his first novel, *The Poor Man and the Lady*, there was evidently an approximate equilibrium between Hardy's presentation of cosmic and social evils. Although in the two novels that followed, Hardy tried only to establish his reputation, and, though *A Pair of Blue Eyes* is recognizably in the spirit of *The Return of the Native*, in *Far from the Madding Crowd* we approach again an equilibrium between an arraignment of the universe and an arraignment of society. In *The Hand of Ethelberta* it might even be said that Hardy's criticism of society is more important than his quarrel with the universe. It would seem, then, that there was a definite tendency, during these his happiest years, toward the re-establishment of the equilibrium that characterized his earliest work. Why do we find the almost unrelieved somberness of *The Return of the Native* while we are still in the years Hardy considered his happiest? Why is there this sudden break from the effort to balance social and cosmic evils?

I believe that this was largely the result of the reception *The Hand of Ethelberta* received. Hardy again sent up a trial balloon, similar to his first novel in the force of its social criticism. He wished to see if he was now sufficiently established as an author to do what he could not do in 1868. He wished to see how the public would receive a protest against the prevailing social norm. But the public received *The Hand of Ethelberta* coldly. Leslie Stephen's enthusiasm for Hardy as a contributor to the *Cornhill Magazine* diminished. Evidently society was not ready, as yet, for an attack upon its ways, or so it seemed to Hardy. Not realizing that the indifference both of the public and of the critics to *The Hand of Ethelberta* was in large part due to nothing more revolutionary than its artistic deficiencies,[64] Hardy began to feel with Clym, in *The Return of the Native*, that efforts at social amelioration offered little present hope for success. As a consequence of this dampening of hope for social reform, he was thrown back upon a deeper pessimism. For, when one lives in a world where one is a lonely and unheard voice crying out against social injustice, when one lives in a world where even moderate criticism is unacceptable, what alternative is there to arraigning the nature of the universe itself?

This hypothesis is, I recognize, difficult to support. There is no statement in the official biography that Hardy felt a loss of social hope after publishing *The Hand of Ethelberta*. But it was in the year of *The Return of the Native* that he abandoned definitely all hope of having his early "revolutionary" novel published as a whole and had the most innocuous parts of it printed in the *New Quarterly Magazine*. Does not the conjunction of his loss of hope that his early novel could be published in its entirety and the deeper somberness of *The Return of the Native* point to a decrease in Hardy's hope for social amelioration? Would not an intensification of pessimism be the logical consequence of a dwindling faith in social progress? I can think of no other adequate explanation.

At any rate, it is unquestionable that *The Return of the Native* is the most pessimistic of the early novels. From the first description of Egdon Heath until the close of the story, this dreary and unfertile waste seems to symbolize the indifference with which Nature views the pathetic fate of human beings. Occasionally the reader is likely to look upon the long-enduring barrenness and apparent purposelessness of the heath as a sign of its kinship to man, to feel that it is like man, slighted and enduring. More frequently, its somber beauty, which, Hardy tells us, is the only kind of beauty that thinking mankind can any longer appreciate, reminds us that man is of no more significance than an insect against its far-extending barrenness.[65] It is the unsympathetic background for the human scene. What happens to man is not its concern. Like the forces of Nature, it has participated passively in man's slow and unhappy progress through disillusive centuries, unconcerned with the joys or sorrows of petty humankind.

What the dreary atmosphere of Egdon Heath makes us feel, the author's interpolations emphasize. The modern facial expression portrays a "view of life as a thing to be put up with." A long train of disillusive centuries have shown the defects of natural law and the quandary in which their operation has placed man. Life causes one to set aside the vision of what ought to be and induces a listless making the best of the world as it is.[66]

More than in any other Hardy novel, we feel the power of the forces that control man's destiny. Heartless Circumstance, this time *not* viewed as an environment that can be contended against, has placed Eustacia Vye in a situation in which her gifts are a plague rather than a blessing.[67] Natural law leads man from one mistake to another. Chance, in the shape of accident and coincidence, joins itself with these other unsympathetic powers to assure man's un-

[[120]]

happiness. Diggory Venn accidentally misunderstands the terms of Mrs. Yeobright's bequest to Clym and Thomasin. As a consequence, Eustacia and Mrs. Yeobright misunderstand each other, and Clym and his mother quarrel openly. Mrs. Yeobright comes to see Clym to attempt a reconciliation. When she knocks at his door, Eustacia hears Clym say "mother" and does not know that he is talking in his sleep. Mrs. Yeobright believes her son refuses her entrance and starts her weary journey home. She tells of her son's treatment to the passing Johnny Nonsuch, who later tells Clym of her bitter reproaches—which no one would have known otherwise, for she lies down to rest, is bitten by an adder, and dies before reaching her home. Clym's feeling that he and Eustacia are guilty of what a chain of coincidences actually caused is responsible for the estrangement of the two. And when a letter that might have ended their misunderstanding comes to Eustacia, she does not find it but goes to her unhappy and accidental death. Undoubtedly Hardy believes that there is nothing actively malign in Egdon Heath, in natural law, or in the play of Circumstance or accident; but the very indifference of these forces to the fate of human beings results in such unhappiness that we are likely to assume that sinister gods control the action.

Against the somber atmosphere of an indifferent and Chance-guided universe, the characters move in accordance with natural law. Eustacia's physical attractiveness compels the love of Charley, Clym, and Wildeve. By a similar force Eustacia is drawn to Wildeve and Clym. None of them is fitted for each other, but their imaginations cause them to believe that their ideas of each other are real.[68] Disillusionment and pain result.

Because a desire for an all-consuming passion dominates Eustacia, she forgets the realities of Wildeve's character. When she realizes how badly her judgment has erred, her disillusionment causes her to suffer. But, as there is still no better man near her and she wishes to feel the power of her attractiveness, she calls Wildeve to her again on the evening of his marriage to Thomasin. The result does not bring her happiness; it brings discontent to Wildeve and to Thomasin. When Clym Yeobright returns from Paris, her imagination and her desire for an all-consuming love and a life of splendor color her conception of him. Eustacia's beauty causes Clym to misjudge her similarly. Their marriage is, of course, unsatisfactory.

It is not only to themselves that the actions of the lovers bring pain. Wildeve cannot forget Eustacia. Although he is married to Thomasin, he cannot be satisfied with her. So Thomasin is unhappily married, too. Because Eustacia's beauty exerts a power, even when she does not will it consciously, she attracts the boy, Charley, and makes him unhappy by her complete disregard of the feelings she arouses in him. Clym's love for Eustacia conflicts with his love for his mother. His decision to follow Eustacia leaves his mother almost literally heartbroken. Fate, in the shape of coincidence, completes the process Clym's love for Eustacia started.

In addition to the pains consequent upon love, the two most intelligent characters, Clym and Eustacia, feel the antilogy of making figments feel. Eustacia's view of life was begot by her situation on her nature. Partly because of the swift change from the gay society of Budmouth to the Egdon region, more importantly because of her innate tendency to seek the impossible, she is always yearning for what she cannot have. She is "eternally unreconciled" to Egdon Heath. She longs for a grand passion. She wishes to find a great hero to whom she can give her love wholeheartedly. She wants what is called "life": music, poetry, passion, war. Like so many Hardyan characters, she has unrealizable desires that she would realize. Inevitably she discovers none of the things she wants. In this "ill-conceived" world, "cruel" heaven makes sport with her, until, tired with its play, it kills her.[69]

Eustacia's predicament is an exaggerated form of the quandary in which Hardy believes intelligent human beings find themselves. Clym is in many respects like Hardy himself. He has reached the stage where the grimness of the general situation first becomes clear. He realizes the antilogy which exists between man's emotional longings and the possibility of their realization. Yet, just as Hardy did when he wrote *The Poor Man and the Lady*, he wants to make the world over so that it will suit him, and—again like Hardy—he hates to find finiteness in his Eden. Because of his knowledge that realization is impossible, he is discontented. Thought upon the "general situation" has even affected his physical appearance, for thought is a disease of the flesh, incompatible with emotional development and the perception of the evil in things. So Clym is, in the same limited sense that Hardy is, a pessimist. He would like to die and get rid of the horror of existence. It is better not to have been born; but, being born, one should strive to get out of life with as little shame as possible.[70]

This philosophy, however, does not keep Clym from having a distinct desire to ameliorate. He does not acquiesce any more than Eustacia. But, as he finds nothing very great in the highest walks of life or very low in the lowest, he is primarily interested in bettering the way of life of the peasants. He combats such superstitions as those of Susan Nonsuch. He is a moral preacher, an advocate of high thinking and plain living. He wishes to teach men that the knowledge of wisdom is more important than the knowledge of wealth. He hopes to raise the peasant class as a whole, not the individual at the expense of the class. He is not intent upon cramming unnecessary knowledge of any creed down the throats of the peasants. But he does hope to teach them an ethic, from which creeds and philosophies are omitted, that is based upon the Sermon on the Mount, the eleventh commandment, and those moral ideas that are common to all good men. Clym does not succeed any more than Hardy did with *The Poor Man and the Lady* and *The Hand of Ethelberta*, for, as the author comments, Clym is too far in advance of his age, and the peasants wish material before spiritual comfort.[71] Again, like Hardy, his failure to effect any notable change in social circumstance throws him back upon a pessimism as deep as that which pervades the novel in which he is a character. But his philosophy is never blankly pessimistic, for, while recognizing the defects in the general plan, he still continues to advocate the elimination of remediable ills. He is ahead of his time, not all times. Like his creator, he continues to see grounds for future hope even in moods of the most unrelieved depression.

Hardy, then, like his character, sees some hope in the future. But his perception of the consolation which may be found for evil times does not stop at the same point the perceptions of his chief character do, for he inserts in his story two illustrations of a way of life that makes living endurable even when it is faced by the worst contingencies. Neither Diggory Venn nor Thomasin Yeobright expects much of life. They lack both the infinite aspirations and the discontent of the major characters in the book. When Venn is disappointed a second time in his love for Thomasin, he suffers only a limited pain because he does not expect much. For him, disappointments seem the natural preface to realization.[72] Similarly Thomasin, though her circumstances cause her somewhat more unhappiness, is able to attain a measure of content because of her willingness to accept the inevitable. It is this quality in her, Hardy tells us, that accounts for her becoming reasonably happy, while Clym, Wildeve, and Eustacia find little but suffering during the course of their lives. These two characters who do not rebel unnecessarily achieve in the end a content impossible for those who refuse to accept their lot. Perhaps this new emphasis upon the virtues of renunciation is also a result of Hardy's own experience with *The Hand of Ethelberta*.

Even in *The Return of the Native*, then, one does see some basis for hope. Those who accept the inevitable are at least not *un*happy, and it is possible that efforts to change things will succeed eventually. But the book is in the main illustrative of the more somber side of Hardy's outlook. Tortured by natural law, unrealizable desires, Circumstance, and Chance, against a background inimical to

man, in a time out of joint, man is an unhappy creature. The reader
feels convinced that the author, in common with Clym and Sophocles, believes that not to be born is best. RUBBISH

*It's reason was against living but instinct +
emotion was for it .*   *12 He loved other people too much but
reason overwhelm him.*

What, then, of Hardy's philosophy as a whole? Our examination of *The Return of the Native* and its predecessors shows clearly
enough that there was variation from novel to novel in the details of
Hardy's outlook. But were there changes more fundamental that
justify our seeing an essential alteration in Hardy's Weltanschauung *(philosophy of
life)*
during the eight years that followed his thirtieth birthday?

There are still passages in Hardy's writing that suggest he often
felt Nature to be malign, but it has become perfectly clear that
Hardy regards Nature as entirely impersonal. As we have seen, it
is probable that he always considered Nature impersonal, but She
is personified in all his earlier poems. Although this metaphorical
practice still continues to a limited extent, the already quoted passage from *A Pair of Blue Eyes* and a note in his journal where he
speaks of Nature as "unconscious" show that it is now his reasoned
conviction that Nature is an impersonal force. There is even a passage in *The Return of the Native* where he speaks of a single spirit
moving all winds and sounds.[73] Since this passage is isolated and can
be interpreted most plausibly as a trope, it is dangerous to suggest
that Hardy is taking a step toward the idealistic pantheism of *The
Dynasts*—but it is unquestionable that he has already arrived at the
idea of Nature's unconscious impersonality which one later finds in
the Immanent Will.

The ideas that exist side by side with Hardy's belief in the impersonality of Nature show, however, that Hardy is still far from
the philosophy of *The Dynasts*. The "purblind Doomster," Time,
which appeared in the early poems as a separate force rather than as
an accomplice of an all-ruling Nature, is no longer referred to but is

replaced by another and equally powerful Doomster. Along with Nature and Chance, Circumstance, which roughly approximates environment, plays an apparently isolatable part in determining man's fate. There is no suggestion, as yet, of the co-ordinated working-together of everything in the universe under the domination of the Immanent Will.

Circumstance is less important in determining man's lot than the older Doomster, Chance. It is Circumstance that is responsible for Knight's inability to find a better friend than Smith, but it is Chance (what is incomprehensible) that accounts for the conception of love that causes his greatest unhappiness. Circumstance, along with Chance, accounts for the eventual misery of Elfride, but it is Chance, in the incomprehensible role of accident and coincidence, that most importantly affects her fate. Circumstance places Eustacia in an environment where her charms are a curse rather than a blessing, but it is Chance, as incomprehensible accident and as the incomprehensible force which allows unrealizable desires to become a part of human nature, that determines her failure to find happiness.

Evidently, one sees, Chance has become a more complicated and less consistently defined force than it was in Hardy's early verse. In his first poems Hardy regards Chance as a personification of the way almost all the laws of the universe impress man. If Hardy had always interpreted Chance in this fashion, it would not be inconsistent with the kind of scientific determinism one would expect of a believer in Darwinism, for this kind of Chance is really the inevitable sequence of natural law and appears to be Chance only because natural sequence cannot be totally understood by ethically minded man. But Hardy was not able to accept simple scientific determinism. Although he believes in evolution and shows the way life follows the laws of both natural and sexual selection, he never shows us the unassisted working of cause upon subsequent effect which would be expected of a scientist turned naturalistic novelist. A *deus ex machina* is continually appearing in his novels. "Crass Casualty," formerly a personification of man's view of law, so careful of the type, so careless of the individual, is replaced by a power that generally manifests itself as accident and coincidence. The Chance that determines Knight's reviewing of Elfride's novel and his acquaintance with her stepmother is altogether different from the "Doomster" of the poems. If another reviewer had been given her novel, if Knight had been unacquainted with the second Mrs. Swancourt, Smith would have probably married Elfride and been moderately happy despite cruel law. If Clym Yeobright had been awake when his mother came to his home, if Eustacia had received Clym's letter, their lives would have been far less troubled. It appears that there is a power altogether outside comprehensible natural law that continually interferes to make man unhappy.

Obviously, Hardy was far more conscious of accident than Darwin was. The scientist speaks of accidental variations and would undoubtedly have admitted the possibility of an accidentally destroyed variety and of the accidental destruction of members of a species, but Law, the explicable action of cause upon effect, is always primary in Darwin's explanation of development. When we look over Hardy's early novels, it often seems that the incomprehensible is more important than the comprehensible, that unaccountable accident is more important than natural or sexual selection. Here, certainly, Hardy diverges from Darwinism in his emphasis. Darwin emphasizes the known, the understandable working of comprehensible law; Hardy, though he is aware of the known, emphasizes the unknown far more than the scientist does. Accident assists natural law; it is equally careless of human values. Mrs. Yeobright is made unhappy both by the cruel law of sexual selection which draws Clym to Eustacia and by the cruel force of accident which causes her son to mutter her name in his sleep. If natural laws were less cruel, Eustacia, Clym, Mrs. Yeobright, and many others might have been more contented; if accident had not played so important a part in their lives, these characters might have been happier than they were, despite natural law. Hardy is not a strict scientific determinist with a cause-and-effect explanation for everything, and his pessimism is not altogether based upon the defects in the operation of natural law.

Where this extralegal element comes from one can say only conjecturally. Reared among a folk famous for their superstitious acceptance of an inexplicable force behind Nature, Hardy may have subconsciously believed that arms can be withered by spells or that men and women may be maimed by piercing wax images. At the least, the frequent notes on superstitions in his journals prove that he was greatly interested in such occurences. Religion, unless it happens to be a form of deism, fosters a belief in the miraculous powers of the Supreme Being. The boy who saw angels guarding his bed may have been sufficiently present in the mature man to keep him from giving up the miraculous altogether. Hardy, the artist, felt that the natural order confined and cribbed the imagination too greatly; he wanted another realm, above law, to expatiate in.[74] His desire may have been father to a belief in causes undreamed of in natural philosophy. But, whether it was one or all of these potential causes which developed Hardy's belief in accident, it is quite clear that Chance, as a personification of the incomprehensible, becomes as important as Chance, the personification of Nature's indifference, was in the early poems.

Aside from his amplification of the part Chance plays in the universe, his greater emphasis upon Circumstance, and his nearer approach to the conception of the Immanent Will in his treatment of Nature as impersonal and unconscious, there are no fundamental changes made in Hardy's earlier philosophy. The main importance, to us, of the expressions of Hardy's philosophy which now occur is that they have a more definite shape than they had hitherto. What it was necessary to half-conjecture from his poems can now be plainly deduced from statements he himself makes in his journal and in his novels.

The "intolerable antilogy of making figments feel," the result of the infrequency with which fulfilment follows desire, is plainly stated as well as illustrated in the novels. "And, once more in the history of human endeavor, a position which it was impossible to reach by any direct attempt, was come to by the seeker's swerving from the path, and regarding the original object as one of secondary importance.

"Renounce a desire for a long-contested position, and go on another tack, and after a while the prize is thrown at you, seemingly in disappointment that no more tantalizing is possible."[75]

The idea that the struggle for existence favors the bad as often as the good is implicit in several of Hardy's statements. He declares that Elfride's very devotion and lack of rebelliousness make it more difficult for her to win Knight. In his journal he suggests that works of art are frequently as successful for their faults as for their virtues.[76] The novels themselves show that the struggle for existence favors the bad rather than the good.

As in his earlier poems, Hardy's pessimism is most obvious in his treatment of love. The primarily sexual character of love is clearly demonstrated. Cytherea and Adelaide Hinton are "atoms of sex" when they realize that they are rivals. The women, by nature, cultivate the art of attracting men. The "instincts of her sex" show Cytherea her most attractive pose, and she cultivates it assiduously. Because women realize that the captivation of men is their chief aim in life, they are adept in the arts of coquetry. The lives of women in general are dominated by "woman's ruling passion—to fascinate and influence those more powerful than she." Similarly, man is dominated by sexual motives. In all Hardy's earlier novels, "love of the eye" is what attracts the men to the women. Idealization accompanies physical attraction, but it is, as often as not, an idealization that lacks a sound basis.[77] The most desirable moral qualities are inferred because the lover wishes to find them.

Since love is based upon the insecure foundation of sex, pain frequently results. Generally speaking, "love is a possible strength in an actual weakness." Fickleness is common among both men and women. Hardy's Ethelbertas, Elfrides, and Bathshebas err more in this respect than the men, but their faithlessness finds its counterpart in the actions of Troy and Manston. It is the exception rather than the rule when men and women form an enduring attachment, and, since this is true, marriage is nearly always a failure. To keep love unconsummated, Hardy remarks in *Desperate Remedies*, is with some people the only way to make it permanent. Thus, marriage is often a short cut to get over love, and one generally finds conjugal affection in early marriage only.[78]

But it is not only the fickleness of human beings that accounts for the pain that accompanies love. Reason is obscured by passion when either a man or a woman loves. When a man is young, he loves with his heart; as he grows older, his understanding participates, but his understanding might as well have been left out, since the brain is incapacitated when it comes into conflict with the emotions. For love, early or late, completely whirls away the reason. Because man is no longer a reasonable creature, idealization occurs. Although such idealization is justified in a few cases, more generally it is not. Most of Hardy's characters, like Boldwood, idealize with insufficient knowledge and suffer intense pain when they are disenchanted.[79]

Even when there is no fickleness and no false idealization, sexual selection necessarily involves pain to those not chosen. Sometimes choice falls upon the worst man, sometimes upon the best. When Elfride prefers Knight to Smith, unquestionably she chooses wisely. When Bathsheba prefers Troy to Oak and Boldwood, it is equally clear that she is making a mistake. But in both cases alike it is the wish for masterfulness in a lover that dictates the choice, and in both cases there are disappointed lovers who must suffer. The novels are full of illustrations of such cruel dilemmas, altogether similar to the dilemma Hardy blamed on Nature in one of his first poems.[80]

One should remember, however, that Hardy never believed there was a necessary connection between a belief in Nature's indifference and thoroughgoing pessimism and that he showed himself almost oversanguine in his first novel. Although a Chance-directed universe more often produces unhappiness than happiness, joy is far from an impossibility. So, in the novels as well as in the earlier poems and the earliest novel, many of Hardy's characters are left with a reasonable prospect of content. So, also, Hardy continued to see the possibility of making conditions more endurable. Although he makes no specific statement of faith in the future, his efforts to ameliorate through the medium of his novels indicate that he did have such a faith.[81] He did not, it is true, make an all-embracing effort to remedy conditions as he did in *The Poor Man and the Lady*. By now he has realized that discretion is necessary in what he prints—that he cannot revolutionize the world overnight with a socialistic novel. But he does make a definite attempt to point out remediable ills in man's relations with man.

His concern with social injustice, although it now becomes a more definitely minor note in his writing, continues. He deplores the manner in which town life submerges individuality, making the unit "self" a fraction of the unit "class." He speaks of the necessity of knowing how the poor live and regards frequent contact with their condition of life as a "wholesome though unpleasant social reminder." He comments upon unfair discrimination against the poor generally. He decries the senseless passion for position in society.[82]

As the novels clearly reveal, Hardy continued to be particularly concerned about the unfairness of class distinctions, one of the themes of his first novel. Although this theme is fairly important in *A Pair of Blue Eyes*, in which Hardy states plainly that the son of peasants, Stephen Smith, is the equal of the Swancourts for all their family tree, *The Hand of Ethelberta* is his most important protest against class snobbery. The heroine, Ethelberta, is shown to be infinitely superior to the upper-class characters who owe their position to "blood, not brain."[83]

But it is quite possible to overemphasize both the vigor and the specificness of Hardy's protest against society. For the most part he was concerned with clarifying and elaborating the outlook he had outlined earlier. To a slight extent he anticipates his later concept, the Immanent Will. Circumstance takes the place of the earlier Doomster, Time, and Chance becomes, for the most part, the power over accident and coincidence. Otherwise the major difference between Hardy's earlier reading of life and the one I have just discussed is one of clarity. His philosophy has been unmistakably formulated for the first time.

13

There were many factors in Hardy's life and in the life of the times that might have influenced his thinking between 1870 and 1878, but it does not seem likely that any of them had a great effect upon the form of his reading of life. His growing material prosperity, his popularity, and his happy marriage may have partly caused the conventionally optimistic tone of his first two novels. Since his continued personal happiness did not modify the somber tone of his later work, it seems more plausible to suppose that the propriety required of a popular novelist accounted for the "everyone lived happily" conclusion. But it is probable that the failure of his most positive attempt to alter abuses, *The Hand of Ethelberta*, accounts for the intensified pessimism of *The Return of the Native*.

No intellectual influence as important as that of Darwin affected the form of Hardy's thought. The philosophy of Leslie Stephen—perhaps to a lesser degree that of Herbert Spencer and J. S. Mill—helped him to co-ordinate his ideas and gave a greater clarity to his reading of life. Such ideas as he held in common with Schopenhauer were already part of his outlook. The only effect the spirit of the times generally had upon him was to confirm his adherence to ideas he had earlier accepted.

If one is looking for a thoroughly coherent philosophical system, Hardy's reading of life—though it resembles systematic philosophy more closely than the philosophy behind the poems that came earlier —offers more difficulty than the determination of influences. There is considerable variation in the use of terms. It is often difficult to tell when Hardy uses his terms metaphorically, when philosophically. Chance is sometimes a personification of the way the operation of the world appears to man. At other times it represents the power of coincidence and accident. Sex, most of the time, is the dominant factor in love, but there are occasions, as in *The Hand of Ethelberta*, when the sexual motive is comparatively unimportant. Love is almost always followed by disenchantment, but, in the case of Diggory Venn and Thomasin Yeobright and of Oak and Bathsheba, love ends happily. Hardy is an artist rather than a philosopher; his reading of life is far more consistent than that of the average novelist, but he does not try to form a hidebound system entirely free of inconsistency.

It is consequently difficult to say, as some have, that Hardy is either a determinist, a fatalist, an optimist, or a pessimist. If we consider the part accident plays in these early novels and forget the importance of the motives that impel the characters from within, we are likely to consider him a fatalist. If we reverse the process, we may call him a determinist. Actually, he is both and neither, for he believes that the lives of men are controlled from both within and without, by understandable and predictable urges as well as by incomprehensible and unpredictable forces which come like a god from a machine.

The altogether different question of whether Hardy was an optimist or a pessimist—for either a fatalist or a determinist can be optimistic or pessimistic, depending on how he interprets his explanation of the universe—can be answered more readily. When ,

Hardy is not making a forced bow to convention, he is never the optimist. His interpretation of life is usually somber. He clearly believes that there are important and irremediable cosmic ills; the struggle for existence favors the bad as well as the good; love, depending upon sexual emotion rather than reason, generally brings pain to both those who love and those who are not loved; man innately desires far more than he is capable of getting; chance happenings more often than not bring bad rather than good luck. So far Hardy is a pessimist. But he never feels that we live in the worst of all possible worlds. Even accident sometimes favors man. Sexual emotion is sometimes overcome by reason; sometimes sexual emotion leads to the right man or to the right woman. In the struggle for existence the good sometimes succeed as well as the bad. Most important of all, perhaps, Nature is not malign but indifferent. There are social injustices—poverty, class snobbery, hypocritical self-righteousness, unimaginativeness when considering the seemingly "wrong" actions of others—that man has caused and which the indifference of Nature makes it possible to alter.

There was even a time in this period when it seemed as though Hardy was moving toward a militant meliorism, when he directed most of his attack against remediable, social wrongs. From *A Pair of Blue Eyes* through *The Hand of Ethelberta*, there was a continuous intensification of Hardy's social criticism. Then, probably as a result of the reception of *The Hand of Ethelberta*, the lack of any important movement for social change with which he felt he could ally himself, and his loss of faith in his ability to effect social change through his books, his pessimism became more intense in *The Return of the Native*.

But there is not a single novel in which Hardy is consistently a fatalist, a determinist, an optimist, or a pessimist. In his explanation of the operation of the world he gives us a combination of fatalism and determinism which does not accord too badly with what the undogmatic scientist understands of the world about him. For, though science has explained much, it has not explained everything; there is still a great deal that is unaccountable and impossible to formulate into law. In his interpretation of the significance to man of the action of the universe, Hardy approaches most nearly the position of the meliorist. Believing that there is much irremediable evil in the world, he nevertheless believes in the possibility of a slow progress that will ultimately do away with those evils, mostly social, that do not inhere in the nature of things.

V

THE NATURE OF THE UNIVERSAL

Unadjusted impressions have their value, and the road to a true philosophy of life seems to lie in humbly recording diverse readings of its phenomena as they are forced upon us by chance and change.

—Preface, *Poems of the Past and the Present*

doctrine that the world
may be made better
by human effort

1

HARDY's personal life between 1878 and 1886 was not of a sort to change importantly the dubious meliorism that characterized his interpretation of the universe. Outwardly it was marked by his election to the Rabelais Club (1879), by a trip to the International Literary Congress (1879), by journeys to France (1880) and Scotland (1881), by the completion of his home at Max Gate (1885), by an increasing recognition of his literary ability, and by a severe illness (1880–81). With the possible exception of his illness, which actually coincided with the appearance of one of his least pessimistic novels, there is no apparent cause for a change in his outlook. Yet, despite this lack of any obvious cause for melancholy in his personal life, despite, also, a distinct increase in his hope for the future, Hardy's life was marked by an increasing tendency to moods of depression. Even among the virile Rabelaisians he succeeded poorly in his attempts to be gay. From 1879 onward he felt more strongly than ever before that "there had passed away a glory from the earth."[1]

If one looks, however, to Hardy's marriage for an explanation of these recurrent moods (as many have), he finds little illumination.

Emma Hardy may not have been the ideal wife for the novelist. She was a self-consciously devout Christian; she is reported to have taken credit for much of Hardy's work; to have said of London society women: "They are the poison; I am the antidote";[2] to have thought *The Trumpet Major* successful because it was "nice"; to have tried to get others to suppress *Jude* for her husband's sake;[3] to have been, most incredible of all, the amoral heroine of *Cakes and Ale*. Most of this, and certainly the last bit, sounds like the merest literary gossip, but there is, if one remembers the previously quoted passage of Emma Hardy's autobiography, a good deal of versimilitude about the remarks that stress her pious propriety. Certainly she did not sympathize with much that her agnostic husband wrote; certainly Hardy must have wished that she could see his point of view a little better.

But it is altogether stupid to hold, with T. P. O'Connor, that Emma Hardy accounts for the "pessimistic nature of the poor devil's work."[4] Granting that the first Mrs. Hardy did not seem, after the first very happy four years, all that one might wish in a wife, how can the woman to whom Hardy wrote more than fifty intensely sympathetic poems over a wide range of time* be considered the cause for a tendency to pessimism that appeared before he met Emma Hardy—a pessimism, moreover, that continued even during the "Sturminster Newton Idyll"? Hardy's pessimism can be accounted for better in other ways, as we have seen. But it is possible, though I should hestitate to put too much stress on such a conjecture, that Hardy's recurrent melancholy owed something to Mrs. Hardy's inability fully to appreciate him. Remembering, however, the very slight effect Hardy's personal life has had upon him in the past, it seems wise that one should also consider the possible effect of the spirit of the times upon him.

* After the first Mrs. Hardy's death, her husband wrote: "In spite of the differences between us, which it would be affectation to deny . . . . , my life is intensely sad to me now without her" (Rutland, *Thomas Hardy*, p. 108).

Even here, one does not at once hit upon an adequate reason for Hardy's increasing tendency to melancholy. The novels of the times—those of Meredith, Macdonald, Blackmore, Besant, Burnett, and Lyall especially—were optimistic enough. Although the positivists—Congreve, Brydges, and Beesley—have been accused of many un-Victorian activities, they have never been accused of a lack of optimism. Nor can one say, even, that the agnostic and naturalistic school inclined to pessimism. W. K. Clifford, Thomas Henry Huxley, Darwin, and Spencer, all of whom published frequently during this period, faced the future with both hope and courage. Certainly the idealists—John and Edward Caird, F. H. Bradley, T. H. Green, and J. H. Sterling—were sanguine enough to satisfy Browning's Pippa.

It is unquestionable, however, that the forces of doubt and pessimism were gaining a prestige they had never before enjoyed. Because they realized more clearly the implications of biblical criticism and naturalistic philosophy, many men commenced to feel the doubtful blessedness of existence: "Non seulement l'homme perdait son importance, son rang d'exception, et, par ses origines, rentrait dans la série animale, mais la psycho-physiologie, le déterminisme lui refusaient la liberté de ses actes et de ses pensées; en dépit de ses efforts, de ses illusions, de ses rêves, il était le jouet d'une inexorable nature, un mécanisme conscient, engrené dans celui de l'Univers."[5]

The growing importance of the "nightmare view" is unmistakable. Schopenhauer, previously the property of the esoteric, became almost well known. His *World as Will and Idea* was translated into English between 1883 and 1886. "By 1879," Goodale comments, "every person alive to the developments of the day must have heard of him; and by 1883 an educated man could not think of pessimism without thinking also of Schopenhauer."[6] Articles and books on pessimism and the value of life enjoyed an unprecedented vogue.[7] Even the poetry and fiction of the period bear witness. F. W. H.

Meyer's *The Renewal of Youth and Other Poems* (1882) and Amy
Levy's *A Minor Poet;* the novels of Olive Schreiner, George Gissing, and Grant Allen lament

> the pitiless order of things
> Whose laws we may change not nor break.[8]

Even Tennyson, as the reader of "Despair" and the second "Locksley Hall" realizes, felt the change.

However, we are confronted by an impasse, apparently, when
we turn to the records of Hardy's reading while the time was moving toward the position he had, with somewhat less consistency and
bitterness, held for a long time. Although Hardy was until 1885
constantly in London or its environs, although he was acquainted
with many of the most prominent figures of the time—John Morley, Richard Jefferies, Tennyson, Browning, Edmund Gosse—the
only contemporaries he mentions frequently are those whose influence was earlier: Swinburne, Huxley, and Darwin.[9] Still, it is
difficult to believe that Hardy was unaware of the changed spirit of
the time. He must have read reviews of many of the books I have
mentioned if he did not read the books themselves, or at the least
noticed that there were many, now, who felt as he did. Certainly
his knowledge of the spirit of the times must have fortified his own
convictions and deepened his melancholy.

As I have already suggested, I believe that the increasingly deterministic and pessimistic tone of the period did influence Hardy's
mood. I cannot understand how it could be otherwise with one who
moved in society and was alert to what was going on. But it does
not necessarily follow that the *substance* of Hardy's thought was
affected. It is not necessary to assume that Hardy would carefully
read books that would seem only to confirm his convictions. It is
not necessary to assume that he read even Schopenhauer, for, aside
from the questionable pleasure of reading a man whose thought presented undoubted similarities to the pessimistic side of his own

world view, what would it profit him? Certainly such a reading would not advance his search for some positive certainty to which he could hold or give him a firmer basis for his own very moderate meliorism. Certainly such a reading would alter only in its details, not in its conclusions or fundamentals, his own reading of life. Only after we have seen what the dialectic of Hardy's intellectual development was in this period, after we have seen what changes and modifications of his outlook appear in the novels and the journals, can we say definitely; but it seems an antecedent possibility that it was Hardy's mood—which we know became increasingly melancholic—rather than the substance of his thought that was affected by the time spirit.

2

The Trumpet Major (1880) does not indicate any considerable change in Hardy's point of view. It marks a return, although not a very rewarding one, to the pastoral novel. The interesting picture of Napoleonic times, dimly foreshadowing *The Dynasts*, is not accompanied by sufficiently moving characters or sufficiently serious treatment to interest either the student of Hardy's art or the student of Hardy's thought greatly. No doubt it is pleasant enough, even unusually good for a potboiler, but it is not for mere pleasantness that one comes to Hardy, nor to the potboilers of an author that one goes for serious revelation of his philosophy.

Nevertheless, like all Hardy's more conventional novels, *The Trumpet Major* contains unmistakable characteristics of its author's thinking. The plot centers about the love of two men for the same girl. Physical attraction accounts for the beginning of love. The girl, Anne, is coquettish; she tries equally hard to attract men whom she loves and men whom she does not love; her impulsive thoughtless actions often have disastrous effects upon those who are fond of her. Although the two brothers, John and Bob, contend for the girl's love amicably enough to fit in with the pastoral tone of the novel, their friendly battle ends quite as a more serious conflict might. Because a woman rarely chooses the worthier when she perversely desires the less worthy, Anne chooses the sailor Bob, who would have easily forgotten Anne if there were other girls about to make love to, and rejects the more steadfast John, whose reason is unable to convince him that he should not care. Because of the nature of the background and the author's tone throughout, this characteristic denouement does not strike the reader as particularly tragic, but Hardy's artistic judgment does not prevent his pointing out the unhappiness implicit in such an ending.[10]

Aside from this intrigue, the only portion of Hardy's outlook represented is the importance he attaches to accident and coincidence, and even this side of his philosophy is emphasized less than usual. A mediocre novel, it deserves only brief treatment.

3

In most respects *A Laodicean* (1881) is inferior, even, to *The Trumpet Major*. Perhaps because it was written when Hardy was seriously ill (1880–81), it is a book with many technical defects. As in his very early novels, Hardy overuses sensational devices. Although there are scenes throughout the book in which the characters show an almost unexpected lifelikeness, they never seem real for long. Accidental happenings that have little to do with the fate of the characters are imposed gratuitously upon the reader. The conventional ending is plausible but far from inevitable; another ending might well have captured what share of the reader's credence the book allows him to give.

But *A Laodicean* is a more important expression of Hardy's thought than *The Trumpet Major*. Side by side with the typical Hardyan treatment of love and of Chance, and the appearance of a typical Hardyan idealist who meets with disillusionment because his reach exceeds his grasp, one finds Hardy's most significant attempt to better the world since *The Hand of Ethelberta*. Again, as in that novel, he points to the incongruities caused by the fluctuation of classes and creeds. Again, in his account of the relationship between Somerset and Paula, he returns to the criticism of class snobbery which has so frequently occupied him since his first novel.[11] All these criticisms are voiced with a sharpness comparable to that one finds in *The Hand of Ethelberta*. It seems as though Hardy's meliorism, which was so muted as to be scarcely evident in *The Return of the Native*, is increasing in intensity again.

Certainly this seems to be true when we notice the new criticism which appears. He sympathizes with Paula's wish that higher education for women should be made possible. He derides the selfishness, based upon financial or social position, that one finds in most friendships and holds up, as an example to follow, the unselfish affection which exists between Charlotte De Stancey, the noblewoman, and Paula Power, the daughter of a man who has only recently become wealthy. Since Somerset is one of Hardy's characters who seem to be based upon the character of the author, it is even likely that Hardy shared Somerset's dream that human progress would eventually make such friendships as Paula's and Charlotte's more common.[12]

But one can exaggerate the degree of the book's meliorism. With the exception of the importance given the friendship of Paula and Charlotte, Hardy does not emphasize his criticism of society as much as he did in *The Hand of Ethelberta*. Both of his major characters are more passive than active; both of them, although they hope for a better future, do little but hope and criticize. Like Venn and Thomasin in *The Return of the Native*, they are inclined to believe that the best way of life is that which accepts the most and expects the least. Paula Power is a follower of the stoical philosophy of Marcus Aurelius. Somerset, although he starts out with all the unrealizable illusions of most Hardyan characters, learns before the close of the action that renunciation is the greatest wisdom. He learns the "sad science of renunciation, which everybody has to learn in his degree—either rebelling throughout the lesson, or, like Somerset, taking to it *kindly* by force of judgment."[13] Although it is certainly true that there is nothing in renunciation that is incompatible with meliorism—probably one who accepts the inevitable is better able to do away with remediable ills than one who does not—it is true that Hardy spends most of his time in the novel indicating why renunciation is forced upon his major characters rather than showing what they, once having renounced, can do to better things.

Nevertheless, the novel shows an increase of hope. Through his incidental criticisms and his portrayal of a relationship that strongly contrasts with the usual one between friends, Hardy shows that he himself is aware of evils that he may, through his novels, help to remedy. If he also feels, with Somerset and Paula, that renunciation is best, may that not be because his meliorism was always based upon a recognition of the worst? Everyone must reconcile himself to the evils that inhere in the universe before he can attempt to remedy what is remediable.

4

But it is with the evils that inhere in the universe that Hardy mainly concerns himself in his next novel. When he wrote *Two on a Tower* (1882), he intended to portray two infinitesimal lives against the stupendous stellar background, yet showing that the smaller magnitude is more important to man. With this purpose in mind, he tells of the fated love of the astronomer Swithin St. Cleve and Viviette in such a way that one often feels them to be literally star-crossed lovers. The solar background is emphasized throughout the story. Before the vastness of astronomical space, we are told, all terrestrial things seem reduced to atomic dimensions. About the "infinitely little" of humanity, the "beauty," the "frightfulness," and the "vastness" of the "infinitely great" stellar universe hangs like a nightmare vision. The "ghastly" and "horrible" size of the universe revealed by astronomy convinces the characters that nothing was made for man's pleasure; it sometimes even makes them feel that to live is entirely futile. The contemplation of these spaces and the realization of the littleness of humanity gives the characters a sense that all is predestined, that choice has nothing to do with life. Nor do the characters have any illusions about the kindliness of the force that controls their destinies.[14]

As in the novels that preceded, the characters contend against Chance and natural law and Circumstance, but there is now some difference in the importance Hardy attributes to each of these powers. Mainly because she is poor and marriage is the conventional thing for a woman, Viviette marries unhappily. When her husband does not return from an exploring trip, she feels that she is released from her obligation to him and turns her attention to the young Swithin St. Cleve. Because Viviette is in many ways a typical Hardyan woman—her impulses are stronger than her judgment, she is attracted chiefly by handsomeness, she is of an "emotional and yearning" temperament—she falls in love with the young astronomer. But here the similarity to the typical woman in the Wessex novels ends. She becomes more interested in Swithin's advancement than in his returning her love; she realizes that her greater age may make her an unsatisfactory wife for him; she feels that his career might be of more service to man if he were alone. At first her fight against the normal impulses of her sex is unsuccessful, and she secretly marries Swithin, but, when her discovery that her husband was actually alive when she married again coincides with the accidental discovery that Swithin must refuse a legacy if he marries her, she renounces her claim to him and urges him to carry out the plan he had previously conceived of charting the stars of the Southern Hemisphere. She is the first woman Hardy has presented in a serious novel who can conquer her natural impulses.[15]

But it is here that Hardy's peculiar sense of the irony and injustice of things enters in. Viviette's unusual reasonableness would have made Swithin's uncle change the terms of his will, Hardy tells us. Even though she is older than Swithin, she would have made him an exceptionally good wife. Yet her own good impulses and the power of Chance interfere to make her more unhappy than Hardy's less unselfish women. It is pure chance—the fact that her husband's death was reported inaccurately, the fact that she accidentally finds the letter that tells of the bequest—which gives her the opportunity to rise above normal sexual law and renounce her own happiness for Swithin's apparent good. But Hardy's ironic treatment goes still further. As soon as Swithin has left, leaving no address by Viviette's request, she discovers that she is pregnant and must, according to convention, marry. Her attempt to find Swithin comes tantalizingly close to success, but, as she drives up to the dock from which his boat leaves, the boat departs. Because convention makes it necessary, she marries a bishop she does not love. With an irony both peculiar and characteristic of the novel, Chance intervenes again. Her second husband dies just before Swithin returns to England, apparently making it possible for her to marry her lover. This time natural law prevents happiness, for she has aged rapidly, and Swithin, too much dominated by sexual law to see that *she* is the same in every important sense,[16] is shocked by her appearance into readily accepting her second renunciation. After he leaves Viviette and has considered the matter with a rationality her appearance had made impossible, he returns to reoffer his love. But Viviette's heart breaks from joy.

It can be seen that the ruling forces operate much as they have before. Natural law is responsible for their love, for Viviette's aging, for Swithin's repulsion when he sees that she has aged. Chance is, as usual, cruel—indeed unusually so. Accident and coincidence seem to be constantly working against the possibility of happiness. Yet we do see in the novel a ground for hope that has not been suggested before. Noble human impulses may conquer the seemingly insuperable force of sexual attraction. And, joined to this basis for hope, we have another attack upon the man-made cruelty of convention. Convention is responsible for Viviette's first unhappy marriage and for her equally unhappy second venture. Although the total effect of the book is to emphasize that which cannot be remedied, Hardy nevertheless shows that there is some basis for hope.[17]

Certainly, though, the ultimate effect of the book is to emphasize as never before those evils that are irremediable. As Swithin and Viviette sometimes imagine, there appears to be a malign force that is as unsympathetic to humanity's aspirations as is the stellar universe that predestines human activities. One has a sense, as one has not had before—even in *The Return of the Native*—of a co-ordinating power, above accident and natural law and Circumstance, that dictates the course of the universe. Even the noble impulses of the characters seem to be used by this power for ends the characters cannot understand. Even when this power allows man to transcend the sexual law that has always seemed unalterable in the past, it does not abrogate its laws for reasons that humanity can understand or for reasons with which man can sympathize. Although it may be merely indifferent and unaware of human aims, it seems malign, like the Spirit Sinister of *The Dynasts*. It indicates the "fatuousness of forethought," since events shape themselves regardless of us, in ways too mysterious for our understanding.[18] For the first time in the Wessex novels one has a sense, whether it was intended or not, of the co-ordinating, yet unconscious, Immanent Will of Hardy's epic drama. Although the artistic effectiveness of *Two on a Tower* is not comparable to that of either *The Return of the Native* or *Far from the Madding Crowd*, the novel approaches Hardy's later reading of life more closely than any work that has preceded it.

In *The Mayor of Casterbridge* (1886) the working of the Immanent Will is foreshadowed even more definitely. Nearly all the
characters know that the "iron hand of necessity" directs their actions. Because he is the protagonist and contends against Fate most
strongly and most frequently, Michael Henchard often expresses
this feeling. Once he believes himself in "Somebody's hand," again
he is convinced that a "power" is working against him, that the
tragic concatenation of events is the scheme of a "sinister intelligence." Hardy makes it clear that Henchard is mistaken in attrib-
uting malignity to Fate, that the events he believed the design of an
evil power developed without any consciously sinister motivation.
Yet there are times when even Hardy appears to feel a sinister intelligence in control, as when he comments that Henchard's newly
gained knowledge of how to live is useless because of God's "ingenious machinery" for "reducing human possibilities of amelioria-
tion to a minimum." Whether it is malign or not, it is clear throughout the story that a power which resembles remarkably the Immanent Will co-ordinates and controls the universe. There can be no
question of the cruelty of its operation, either, for it is responsible
for driving Henchard to the bitterness of his will and compels the
almost faultless Elizabeth Jane to feel "happiness an occasional episode in a general drama of pain."[19]

We are more clearly conscious of a directive power than in any
earlier novel, but this power uses much the same machinery it has
in the past. From the first pages of the book, where Hardy declares
that marriage alone could account for the stale familiarity between
Henchard and his wife, the law of sexual selection plays its part in
the action. Lucetta is the main cause of suffering as well as the chief
sufferer. A typical Hardyan woman, she is vain and coquettish; impulse rather than reason causes her to choose whom she will love.
Because her eye, like that of most women in the Wessex novels, is

ruled by the superficies of things,[20] she becomes indifferent to Henchard after she has made him love her and marries Farfrae, whom she attracts physically and who attracts her. Much of the unhappiness of both Henchard and herself is caused by her unreasonable action. As a further consequence, Elizabeth Jane, who loves Farfrae, is left without a lover.

Still, there are differences in the way in which love operates. Elizabeth Jane is hardly characteristic of woman in love. She is never more than modestly vain; sex never exerts itself strongly in her; she is too impersonally human to be vain, showy, or coquettish.[21] Like Viviette, she is not dominated by the generally insuperable power of sexual attraction. But there is this difference between the two: in Viviette, though there is a victory over natural law, there is also a struggle; in Elizabeth Jane sexual impulses are not sufficiently strong to require much resisting.

The struggle for existence in a more general sense affects the lives of the characters to a greater extent than in any earlier novel. Frequently this natural warfare is stressed by the phrasing of the author. Between Farfrae and Henchard, a "mortal commercial combat" takes place. Hardy speaks of the severity of the "battle of life." We are told that the group of people at the royal reception fall apart by a "process of natural selection." Man's "willful hostilities" are compared to the struggle that forever hides itself behind the peaceful face of Nature.[22] Throughout the novel this wilful and necessary hostility is one of the main themes. Henchard struggles for existence and happiness—at first against the town, later against Farfrae, still later against the town and Farfrae. Although we never feel that he deserves his fate, the relentless process of natural selection obviously dictates his defeat.

For there are reasons for Henchard's fall as understandable as Darwin's for the failure of single members of a species to survive. The responsibility of character in determining fate is stressed as Hardy has never stressed it before.[23] In other books the reader may

[[148]]

have felt that the unwillingness of the characters to accept the universe justified their failure to achieve happiness. But Hardy himself has never before emphasized the importance of character in bringing about catastrophe. Henchard's impulsiveness sometimes seems the primary cause for the disasters that overtake him. It is his impulsiveness, increased by drink, that makes him sell his first wife, Susan; his impulsiveness leads him to discharge Jopp and Farfrae, to sell out his corn at the worst possible time, to conceal Elizabeth Jane's whereabouts from her father, Newson. In fact, there are times when it appears that a just Power overcomes him. Especially in the return of Susan and in the retribution that results from his thoughtless cruelty to Newson and Jopp, a George Eliot–like nemesis seems to be pursuing Henchard.

But George Eliot would never have owned to the creation of the Chance-ridden universe in which Henchard lives. Chance, as accident, is as cruel as it is in other Hardy novels. Rain spoils Henchard's plans for a fete and makes Farfrae's closed carnival successful. It is Chance that causes Henchard to meet Lucetta, and Chance that makes him bring Farfrae to see her. Finally, it is the purest coincidence that Henchard should be in the magistrate's chair at the time the furmity woman, who had witnessed the sale of his first wife, came before him and revealed to the others present what he had thus far successfully concealed. All the forces of Fate are combined against him. With tragic irony even his knowledge of his errors comes too late, for, as Hardy comments, the "wisdom to do" comes after the "zest for doing" is past. After watching his suffering, the reader wonders with Elizabeth Jane "what that chaos called consciousness" began in and tends to.[24] For even the most severe judge must admit that Henchard is more sinned against than sinning. Whatever punishment he does deserve, the agony that comes upon him is excessive rather than just. We feel that even his character is not his fault. The seemingly sinister power that designed the cruel process of sexual selection and the law of battle by which men live, which controls even accident, also dictated Henchard's impulses.

Still, despite the harrowing nature of the tragedy, we do not feel that the world of *The Mayor of Casterbridge* is altogether depressing. One speaks properly of the pathetic fate of most of Hardy's early heroes and heroines. With equal propriety one can speak of the tragedy of Michael Henchard. Whereas in a pathetic tale one sees the victim slowly worn down by repeated blows which he neither can, nor will, resist, in tragedy there is a sharp conflict between two forces. Although a seemingly sinister Fate opposes him, Henchard always struggles on. There is a strong unyieldingness about him that makes him rise even after many misfortunes come upon him. He rarely considers whether destiny is hard; he only knows that he must endure. Misery only teaches him a "defiant endurance" before fortune's buffetings. He extenuates nothing and is always his own worst accuser. Even when his misfortunes have piled up to where most men would give up entirely, he declares, "But my punishment is *not* greater than I can bear."[25] We may be struck by terror at his fate, but we are also aroused to admiration by his dogged courage. We feel that it is an honor to belong to the same race with a man who so courageously resists an implacable and sinister Fate. This is the purgation of our emotions that tragedy produces, not the helpless feeling that comes after reading a pessimistic tale of the futile and petty lives of futile and petty people.

Moreover, Hardy offers the same consolation for the worst possible contingencies of existence which he offered in *A Laodicean*. If one does not choose to battle heroically with destiny as Henchard does, he may find a reasonable degree of content in a stoical philosophy such as Somerset, Paula, and, now, Elizabeth Jane embrace. Although her negative excellences do not win for her as much admiration as Henchard's positive virtues and vices, Elizabeth Jane unquestionably illustrates a practical way of making the best of things as they are. When the one she loves gravitates toward Lucetta, she looks on stoically because she has long since cultivated the art of renunciation. As a reward, perhaps, she finally marries Farfrae and seems likely to make a reasonable success of her life. For, whatever may be the consequences of her marriage, we know that she is one of those who make "limited opportunities endurable" by a "cunning enlargement" of those "minute forms of satisfaction" offered to anyone not in positive pain.[26]

Still more importantly, although Hardy again emphasizes the evils that seem inevitably consequent upon the fact of existence, he protests with unusual strength against the evils he believes to be man-made. Acknowledging God's "ingenious machinery" for "reducing human possibilities of amelioration to a minimum," he nevertheless tries to point out what can and should be altered. He says that it is civilization, which has subjected Susan to the evil of poverty, rather than Nature that accounts for the hard, apathetic expression of her face. Society is sometimes less just than Nature. By natural law Elizabeth Jane is a "flower of nature" despite the fact that she was the result of Henchard's tampering with the edicts of society; society, measuring her altogether by the social fact of her illegitimate birth, wrongly considers her an outcast. Again, in the portion of the story devoted to Lucetta, Hardy attacks the injustice of convention. Although Lucetta has never done anything to justify society's suspicion, she is considered compromised by Henchard and suffers as a consequence. Though Lucetta's laxity had been of inadvertence rather than intention, her careless behavior with Henchard was no less likely to operate fatally between her and her future husband. Hardy's sympathy with her plight is clearly shown in his protest aganst the injustice of the "skimmity ride," perhaps symbolic of the characteristic attitude of all society to one like "poor Lucetta."[27] There may be philosophic inconsistency in Hardy's attitude, for if human nature is determined, so is society—but there can be no doubt that he joins to his indictment of the cruelty of the universe an indictment of social evils that he feels to be remediable.

Taken as a whole, *The Mayor of Casterbridge* shows a greater modification in Hardy's ideology than any novel that has preceded it. Although the old forces, natural law and Chance, importantly affect the fate of the characters, sexual law does not seem as improbably all-inclusive as it has before, for Elizabeth Jane never feels its compulsion strongly. It seems, as in *Two on a Tower*, that there is a controlling and co-ordinating force that is above or works through everything else, but Hardy nevertheless shows us a character with the courage and the strength to resist the inevitable. It seems, as never before, that the Power that dominates the universe is an inevitable determiner, but Hardy at the same time tries to demonstrate the remediable injustice of social bigotry. Despite the fact that he appears to see the worst contingencies man can meet more clearly than ever, he still insists upon the possibility of amelioration. Recognizing the inevitable, believing that "if way to the Better there be, it exacts a full look at the Worst," he still sees that the future is not entirely hopeless, and concerns himself with remediable ills. A strange amalgam, perhaps, but effective. For, whether this outlook satisfies the strict canons of philosophic consistency or not, Hardy's reading of life has produced in *The Mayor of Casterbridge* a convincing and moving tragedy. The Shakespeare who wrote *King Lear* would honor it.[28]

6

As one would suspect from the greater emphasis upon Fate and the more obvious co-operation of Chance and natural law in *Two on a Tower* and *The Mayor of Casterbridge*, Hardy's journals show that he is approaching the concept of the Immanent Will. For the first time we begin to see the emergence of that Willer, dumb and blind, who

works unconsciously, as heretofore,
Eternal artistries in Circumstance,
Whose patterns, wrought by rapt aesthetic rote,
Seem in themselves Its single listless aim.[29]

Early in 1880 Hardy speaks of London as "a monster whose body [has] four million heads and eight million eyes." It is possible that this is no more than description by personification, but there is a striking similarity between this many-limbed animal and Hardy's description of the anatomy of the Immanent Will: "The controlling Immanent Will appears . . . . as a brain-like network of currents and ejections, twitching, interpenetrating, entangling, and thrusting hither and thither the human forms." Late in the same year Hardy speaks of a dressmaker who acts "as by clockwork; she puts each cloak on herself, turns round, makes a remark, puts on the next cloak, and the next, and so on, like an automaton."[30] Again, this may be nothing more than description, but one remembers that Hardy later viewed all human beings as automatons moved by clockwork. Both these passages appear to be vague gropings for the concept of the Willer and his mode of operation.

Early in the year in which he was writing *Two on a Tower*, Hardy's visualization of this power seems to become still clearer. On March 27, 1881, in one of his frequent notes that look forward to *The Dynasts*, we have automatism definitely considered with relation to the actions of human beings: "Mode for a historical Drama. Action mostly automatic; reflex movement, etc. Not the result of what is called *motive*, though always ostensibly so, even to the actors' own consciousness."[31] In addition to helping us understand why the characters in *Two on a Tower* and *The Mayor of Casterbridge* frequently feel themselves to be puppets in the power of an unknowable force, this statement shows us that Hardy has already come very close indeed to the principle of automatic determinism which *The Dynasts* illustrates. Similar notes, developing the idea of human automatism, occur in his journal throughout these years. But there is, at first, no indication that Hardy's view that human actions are automatic is for other than artistic purposes. The following entry, of October 20, 1884, clearly presents Hardy's own speculations about the nature of reality: "Query: Is not the present quasi-scientific system of writing history mere charlatanism? Events and tendencies are traced as if they were rivers of voluntary activity, and courses reasoned out from the circumstances in which natures, religions, or what-not, have found themselves. But are they not in the main the outcome of *passivity*—acted upon by unconscious propensity?"[32]

Besides the implication that Hardy at least tentatively believes in this interpretation of history, we have the first mention of the Willer of *The Dynasts*. The name is different, but the "unconscious propensity" which acts upon history is Hardy's later unconscious Immanent Will—without benefit of Schopenhauer. A journal entry of March 4, 1886, completes this early outline of the metaphysic of *The Dynasts:* "The human race to be shown as one great network or tissue which quivers in every part when one point is shaken, like a spider's web if touched."[33] In its main essentials these journal notes outline the philosophic basis of *The Dynasts*.

This deterministic philosophy explains why the reader of *Two on a Tower* and *The Mayor of Casterbridge* feels that there is a power controlling and co-ordinating the force of Chance and natural law to a greater degree than ever before, but it makes other portions of Hardy's outlook even less comprehensible. If human beings are automatons, how can they, like Viviette, successfully combat sexual law? How can predetermined mankind possibly repress the desires that are natural and learn, with Elizabeth Jane and Somerset, the sad science of renunciation? How is it possible to alter and ameliorate social conditions that conditioned man has conditioned? In a certain sense these contradictions cannot be resolved. Logically, these concepts do not fit together. But we should again recall the nature of Hardy's reading of life. He is an artist rather than a systematic philosopher. He always maintained that his artistic work possessed "little cohesion of thought or harmony of colouring."[34] He was never certain that he had arrived at absolute truth. Although he believed his interpretation of the universe more probable than the others with which he was familiar, at bottom he was frankly agnostic. In his poem "To the Unknown God" he declares

> Long have I framed weak phantasies of Thee,
> O Willer masked and dumb![35]

Here he acknowledges what it is easy to forget—his inability to attain to ultimate metaphysical knowledge. Similarly, speaking of the philosophic basis of *The Dynasts*, he remarks that the "doctrines are but tentative, and are advanced with little eye to a systematized philosophy warranted to lift 'the burthen of the mystery' of this unintelligible world."[36] The inconsistencies of his "readings"—perhaps he would call them inconsistencies inherent in the nature both of language and of reality—Hardy frankly recognized. We must do the same, all the more gladly, perhaps, if we think what *The Mayor of Casterbridge* would have been without any relief for its somberness or *Two on a Tower* with the tentacles of the Will still more obviously controlling the characters.

This inconsistency is not an inconsistency adopted by Hardy to make his novels more palatable to readers who would accept human automatism less readily than he. It is to be found in his journals as often as in his novels. So, in the same years in which he tentatively adopted a deterministic philosophy, he also expressed a hope parallel to that we have found in the novels. Although he feels that man's is indeed a sorry plight—the emotions are not realizable in a world of defect; as human beings have become more intelligent than Nature intended, there is no adequate satisfaction for this intelligence; there is a painful disproportion between the desire for serenity and the power of obtaining it—he still believes civilization to be partly responsible for this state and thinks gradual progress possible. Al-

[155]

though he recognizes that history is not an organic and systematic development, that there are upright, oblique, prostrate, and inverted periods in the world's life, he still takes an interest in the truth embodied in the positivist's idea of progress. When he hears of a "wronged" woman who refuses to marry her seducer, he declares her action one of the first glimmers of woman's enfranchisement. He maintains that we should conserve the good, discard the bad; he resolves never to praise or blame merely because of accepted opinions; he interests himself in a project to have art studied in the national schools; he sympathizes with the activities of the social evolutionist, Joseph Arch, among the rural poor.[37]

And, at the worst, he recognizes, with some of the most intelligent characters in his novels, that there is a consolation for Nature's arch deceit, for experience's unteaching, for the fact that nothing bears out in practice what it promises incipiently. One can, with Marcus Aurelius, endure bravely and renounce stoically: "This is the chief thing: Be not perturbed; for all things are according to the nature of the Universal."[38]

Philosophic consistency eludes us in the journals as well as in the novels, but we are able to see that the contradictions in Hardy's illustrations of his reading of life are at least consistent with his own inconsistencies. An artist and an agnostic before he is a dogmatic philosopher, Hardy honestly shows us life as, with its mysteries and contradictions, it impresses him.

7

As one watches the development of that part of Hardy's thinking which approaches the condition of systematic philosophy, it becomes increasingly obvious that there is a sense in which his philosophy may be called either deterministic or fatalistic. Both determinism and fatalism include the central doctrine of man's powerlessness to control his own destiny. This, by implication, has been

Hardy's belief since the writing of his first metaphysical poem, "Hap." Few of his more seriously conceived characters are masters of their fate; their own will is powerless before the play of forces that determines events. That Hardy is, in this limited sense, a determinist becomes increasingly clear in the years between 1878 and 1885. In his journals he speaks of human automatism. In his novels we sense, as never before, the presence of a power which makes the efforts of the individual will all but impotent.

But it still remains important that we remember the sense in which Hardy was not a determinist. Explicable moral or natural law accounts for the fate of the characters in the novels of George Eliot, Grant Allen, and George Gissing. Explicable forces only partly account for the fate of Hardy's characters; the unexplainable is also important. Hence those critics who hold that his outlook becomes deterministic after the writing of *Two on a Tower*, if they mean that he became a determinist in the more limited sense, are mistaken. For the external force that ostensibly guides accident and coincidence is still important in *The Mayor of Casterbridge*. More, it is true, is explained by the forces that act from within personality and by natural law than previously, but the inexplicable still remains important. Although Hardy is more a determinist in every sense at the close of this period than he ever was before, he remains a fatalist in so far as he attributes to a transcendent and mysterious Chance the ability to alter man's fate.

Hardy's interpretation of this predetermined universe, although the scales still incline toward pessimism rather than toward optimism, is more melioristic than in the preceding period. His belief in the slow but real course of progress is plainly indicated. Even in the unequal struggle of Michael Henchard against his destiny, we see that there is something in human nature worthy of honor. Even if we are terrified by the inequality of the struggle, we are proud to belong to the race of man. In the ability of Elizabeth Jane and Viviette to subdue some of the streams of tendency that oppose them, we see human nature's capacity to become contented. In Hardy's attacks upon foolish or cruel conventions we find support for a belief that social conditions can be changed for the better. Although it is still impossible to fit Hardy neatly into any philosophic category, it is possible to distinguish the counterpoise of the elements that make up his reading of life and to see that he is tending to become more deterministic and, inconsistently, more of a meliorist during this period.

Why this change in Hardy's outlook occurred can be explained in part by the greater prevalence of determinism in the literature of the period. We know that Leslie Stephen, whose determinist views are clearly expressed in *The Science of Ethics* (1882), was still Hardy's close friend. This tendency in the literature of the time and his frequent contact with Stephen probably affected Hardy's thinking, whether he was fully aware of it or not. But we need not suppose this was necessarily true. The tendency of science generally, in which Hardy's continued interest is manifest,[39] had been since 1860 in the direction of determinism. It is quite likely that the action of Hardy's mind upon the scientific knowledge he had previously assimilated largely accounts for the more definitely deterministic aspect of his outlook. Remembering, however, that Hardy was much in society and that he had every opportunity to become familiar with the thought of the period, I am inclined to believe that the tendency of the time accelerated or accentuated the natural direction of his own thinking.

But we are confronted by a more difficult problem when we try to account for the shift in the optimism-pessimism balance. The thought of the time tended more toward pessimism than it had before, and Hardy himself was more continually subject to moods of melancholy. Schopenhauer's name and the general nature of his thought were becoming well known in England. Hence, there is a more considerable presumption that Hardy became acquainted with his system. Indeed, there is a poem referring to the year 1883 in which Schopenhauer is mentioned.[40] Of course, Hardy's pessimism about love, his stressing of the antilogy of consciousness, of the unrealizability of legitimate human desires, his generally somber view of existence, can hardly be accounted for by the influence of Schopenhauer, for they were part of Hardy's thought before he knew of the philosopher. But the belief in an "unconscious propensity" that impels all things and the belief that one may escape from the service of the Will through renunciation are typical Schopenhauerian ideas that have never been stated before in the work of Hardy.

Nevertheless, I can see no adequate reason for supposing that the German philosopher did have an important influence. The naming of Schopenhauer only proves that Hardy, in common with most educated men of his time, was familiar with the name and its generally pessimistic significance. When the doctrine of renunciation and stoical acceptance is spoken of, Marcus Aurelius, an adequate source for such an attitude, is almost invariably referred to. Hardy does not, in either his journals or his novels, use any characteristic Schopenhauerian phraseology. He never refers to the "Will" or to the fluctuation between pain and boredom. He does not acknowledge that Schopenhauer has influenced him, although he admits readily enough, later, the effect of Von Hartmann. When he refers to human automatism, it is an "unconscious propensity," not a Will, which he sees guiding the process. Unless we are to suppose that Hardy cleverly concealed the truth, I can see no reason for believing that the German philosopher was influential during this period.*

* W. R. Rutland gives Hardy's ownership of a copy of the Haldane-Kemp translation as evidence of Schopenhauer's influence. But he is mistaken in dating the translation 1883, when only the first volume appeared. Hardy, who did not know German, certainly could not have had any thorough knowledge of Schopenhauer's entire system until 1886, when the last two volumes of the translation were issued. Moreover, Schopenhauer does not introduce his concept of the "Will" until the second volume.

To explain Hardy's becoming more melioristic while the thought of the time became more pessimistic, one must point to the virtual independence of Hardy's intellectual development in all but the early periods of his life. Perhaps, too, his study of Comte, his friendship with Stephen, and his frequent association with such determined optimists as Besant, Browning, and Rhoda Broughton, were partially responsible for his increased hopefulness. Perhaps, the wave of pessimism that affected the previously undisturbed had less effect upon one whose somber view of life was first developed two decades before. One is not likely to be too much disturbed by a reiteration of what one already knows.

VI

TO THE BETTER

If way to the Better there be, it exacts a full look at the Worst.

—*Poems of the Past and the Present*

1

Hardy spent most of his time at Max Gate after it was finished in 1885, but he continued to keep in touch with the world outside during the years that preceded the publication of *Jude*. He took numerous trips to the Continent and spent at least a quarter of each year in London, attending receptions and dinners, visiting the art galleries and theaters, reading in the British Museum. There were but few of the important people of his day that he did not know at least casually. To name people at random, he was often with Lady Portsmouth, Mrs. Jeune, Mrs. Cragie, Sir George Douglas, Edmund Gosse, Charles Wyndham, Lady Carnarvon, Grant Allen, Edward Clodd. His literary reputation—despite, perhaps in part because of, the frequent attacks upon his last two novels —continued to grow. In 1891 he was admitted to the exclusive Athenaeum Club. By 1895 *Tess* had been published in German, French, Russian, Dutch, and Italian. Except for the attacks upon *Tess* and *Jude*, nothing happened to him personally that was likely to affect the development of his thought. Actually, even these attacks did not change the direction of his thinking; what they did do was to prepare him to leave prose and its enormous, undiscriminating public for poetry—where he hoped to write to a smaller but more intelligent audience.

There was one characteristic of the period that may have impressed Hardy greatly. As we have seen, there was little more than sporadic support for social protest during the years that followed the writing of *The Poor Man and the Lady*. Hardy's quest for positive certainties was rarely rewarded by the discovery of thinkers who recognized the worst and strove for the better. Now, for the first time, Hardy began to see all about him sincere and earnest men seriously engaged in a relatively unfettered examination of individual and social problems.

For its new direction, literature was unquestionably indebted to life. Throughout England there was a growing consciousness of the gravity of the social problems that accompanied industrial progress. Truly enough, this was not a consciousness that had been but a short time growing or a movement which discovered for the first time its literary prophets. Carlyle and Ruskin, both of whom Hardy had read, had agitated against the consequences of a purely material civilization long before 1886. Maurice and the Christian Socialists had been responsible for the founding of the Working Man's College as far back as 1854. In 1873 Cambridge had inaugurated a series of extension lectures for the workingman; in 1885 Oxford had done the same. But it was only during the years from 1885 to 1895 that the tendency toward sociological reform became a movement strong enough to inspire hope that it might effect changes in the status quo.

This effort to right admittedly unjust social conditions was importantly affected by the Settlement Movement, with which Hardy came into direct contact through his friendship with the Jeunes.[1] These settlements, homes where members of the upper classes lived among the working classes in order better to understand and educate them, were based upon a conviction that only when the actual conditions of the people are understood can they be ameliorated. They had first appeared in England in 1884, when the Ratliff settlement was founded in London. By 1895 there were sixteen similar organizations throughout Great Britain, striving, all of them, to understand what was wrong with the condition of the working class and to do away with the greatest evils of the industrial system.

How far a still more general movement for sociological reform had permeated English society, even by 1885, can be gathered from the Radical Programme, sponsored in that year by Joseph Chamberlain and John Morley. The Radicals favored "the intervention of the State on behalf of the weak against the strong, in the interests of labour against capital, of want and suffering against luxury and ease."[2] During the time of the Unionist Parliament, from 1886 to 1892, and the succeeding administration, this socialistic movement gathered still greater strength. Impressed by the gravity of the social conditions disclosed by the research of the Settlement Movement and by the alarming revelations of such books as Booth's *Labour and Life of the People* (1893–97), encouraged by the relative strength of the labor movement and the relative liberality of those in power, socialism properly so called had its first considerable success. William Morris, Clifford Bax, and the Fabians published a number of books, which, although they revealed somewhat varying interpretations of socialism, were united in a common concern about the deplorable conditions forced upon the poor by the course of capitalistic development. In 1886 Bax's *Religion of Socialism* appeared; in 1889 he published *The Ethics of Socialism;* in 1894 Morris and he published *Socialism: Its Growth and Outcome.* Alone, Morris published the socialistic *A Dream of John Ball* (1888) and *News from Nowhere* (1891). Under the editorship of George Bernard Shaw, *Fabian Essays* (1889), containing articles by Sidney Webb, William Clarke, Annie Besant, Graham Wallas, and Herbert Bland, made an appearance. Moreover, it was not only in books that the strength of the socialist movement showed itself. In 1884 the Social Democratic Federation was founded; in 1893 the Independent Labour party was formed.

In the years that elapsed between the foundation of the Ratliff settlement and the formation of the Labour party, the hope for social justice assumed an importance without precedent in nineteenth-century England. Whether they were socialist, advocates of the single tax, or simply friends of the working class, the people of England were conscious of the problems inherent in the system of capitalism. Apathy disappeared. A desire to know the worst about the way things are, so that conditions could be bettered, became a much more prevalent attitude: "In 1886, Socialism was the creed of a few revolutionary enthusiasts; in 1892 it was being discussed in every intelligent household, and in hundreds of debating societies throughout the land. . . . . At the opening of the [Unionist] Parliament, Socialism had hardly any English literature; at its close, *Looking Backward* and *Fabian Essays* were selling by thousands, and Sir William Harcourt had proclaimed that "we are all Socialists now."[3] In supposing all Englishman to be socialists, Harcourt was undoubtedly mistaken, but he was without question correct in the feeling that inspired the remark. Most intelligent Englishmen of the period felt that there was something very wrong about the system of society that prevailed. And they wished to make things better.

This concern for social justice, more manifest than ever before in the actions of the English people, is naturally revealed in literature. But it was not altogether a growth indigenous to England, although the critical thinking of men like Arnold and Mill and the scientific spirit of many Englishmen must have prepared the soil. Zola, especially as he was followed by Gissing, Moore, and Crackanthorpe, was undoubtedly a great stimulant to candor in English fiction and helped to regain for writers some of the freedom Thackeray had envied Fielding.[4] Ibsen was probably even more of an influence upon the social seriousness of English letters. Although he had been translated as early as 1876 and had been written of enthusiastically by Gosse and Archer in the late seventies and early eighties, he did not become popular until 1893. But the more intelligent had been conscious of him for some time before and had unquestionably felt his influence almost a decade earlier.[5]

The fiction of the period reflects the growing seriousness. Even such a book as *Robert Elsmere* (1888), primarily devoted to an advocacy of Broad Churchmanship, deals with the state of the poor and the place of women, perhaps the two problems before which writers most frequently became vocal. George Gissing, Hubert Crackanthorpe, William Morris, and Arthur Morrison were primarily concerned with the condition of the poor and of the working class, while Grant Allen and George Meredith were as much interested as Jones, Pinero, and Shaw in criticizing conventional notions about women and in attacking prejudiced views of personal relationships in general. A reading of such a novel as Allen's *The British Barbarians* (1895) or of such a play as Shaw's *Mrs. Warren's Profession* (1898) indicates that there were few conventions that still received unstinted homage. It was a period of storm and stress: not only a time in which aesthetes, Irishmen, imperialists, and determined optimists flourished, but an era in which the accepted moral ideas were subjected to more thoroughgoing critical examination than had been dreamed of in the middle of Victoria's reign.

It was, moreover, a comparatively hopeful time. Some writers of the period, such as Crackanthorpe, were extremely pessimistic, to be sure. None of them shared Pippa's feeling about the rightness of the world. Not a few of them would agree with Grant Allen's peroration in *The Woman Who Did:* "Blank pessimism is the one creed possible for all save fools. To hold any other is to curl yourself up selfishly in your own easy chair, and say to your soul, 'O soul, eat and drink: O soul, make merry, Carouse thy fill. Ignore the maimed lives, the stricken heads and seared hearts, the reddened fangs and ravening claws of nature all around thee.' Pessimism is sympathy. Optimism is selfishness. . . . . The pessimist knows well self-deception like that is either a fraud or a blind, and recognizing the seething mass of misery at his door gives what he can,—his pity, or, where possible, his faint aid in redressing the crying inequalities and injustices of man or nature."[6]

But this is not "blank pessimism." At least the latter part of this quotation shows a belief in the possibility of ameliorating conditions. Most of these writers look frankly upon the miseries of life, realizing that "if way to the Better there be, it exacts a full look at the Worst." But they are all—either in their objective portrayal of conditions, as in the books of George Moore and Arthur Morrison, or in their attacks upon what they think meretricious or cruel, as in the case of Allen and Shaw—they are all soldiers in the war for the liberation of humanity, contending for a cause they think it possible to win. Perhaps they felt themselves inhabitants of a nether world as dark as Gissing's. Still they could say: "Where they abode it was not all dark. Sorrow certainly awaited them, perchance defeat in even the humble aims that they had set themselves; but at least their lives would remain a protest against those brute forces of society which fill with wreck the abysses of the nether world."[7]

Encouraged by others who attacked more vehemently than he had dared since *The Poor Man and the Lady*, might not one expect Hardy to become more strongly protestant?

2

But, when we turn to *The Woodlanders* (1887), we are at first more impressed by "blank pessimism" than by any sign of kinship to the militants of the period. Hardy approaches consistent determinism even more closely than he did in *The Mayor of Casterbridge*. As in that novel, the characters are generally aware how little they have power to direct events. Fitzpiers feels that all is determined as by the hands of a clock. Creedle is a fatalist. Giles Winterbourne believes that the fates are against him. What the characters feel Hardy emphasizes by his own statements. He remarks that Grace

Melbury moves as by clockwork. Destiny, he says, is responsible for Marty's laborer's hand. Giles could not prevent Fitzpiers' coming to know Grace. It was "doomed" to happen. All the characters are part of the "great web of human doings," compelled by the "Unfulfilled Intention" which makes life what it is, a struggle in accordance with natural laws that take no care of human sentiments. In such a predetermined universe it is true that we blame offenders, the human beings who ostensibly cause our sorrow, but we are mistaken. Our petulance should be directed against the Cause which shaped the situation for both the offenders and the offended.[8]

In the struggle "the Cause" has ordained, man and the sentient and insentient beings of the woodland follow the same law. Owls, mice, stoats, rabbits, wintergreens, all acknowledge the law of battle. Birds quarrel; trees rub each other into wounds and wrestle for existence. Félice fights the "battle of life." Marty South "struggles bravely" against conditions. All life is mortal combat for survival. Because she realizes this, Marty imagines that both trees and men are sorry to begin life, and certainly Marty's conjecture is confirmed by the characters in the book. Fitzpiers' face says he has suffered wrong in being born, and Grace wonders if there is one world in the universe where the fruit has no worm.[9] No human villain appears upon the scene; still, life is tragic. The conditions and the laws of man's being are responsible.

One of these laws, the law that governs sexual selection, is particularly important in this novel. But it is not a woman, as it usually has been before, who is the focal point for the law's action. Fitzpiers, who is "handsome, coercive, irresistible," is unable to subordinate his impulses to his reason. He is able to love several women at the same time with equal sincerity. Like many of Hardy's women, he either does not foresee or does not care about the consequences of his entanglements. Although he has won the love of Grace Melbury, attractive as well as a good "marriage bargain," he by no means contents himself with her alone. Before he marries

Grace, he seduces Suke Damson. After he is married, his impulses so coincide with those of Félice Charmond that they run away and leave Grace. Naturally, both Grace and Suke are made unhappy, but the consequences, as usual, do not stop with those most immediately concerned. Tim, Suke's lover; Giles Winterbourne, who loves Grace; and the gentleman from South Carolina, Félice's former sweetheart, are also caused pain by the way sexual law manifests itself in Fitzpiers. Through Grace, another of this law's instruments, sorrow is brought to Marty South, who is in love with Giles. In fact, all the major characters suffer, for Félice is killed by a disappointed lover, and, even when Fitzpiers returns to Grace, we know that he will continue to be tormented by the daemon that continually sets him after new conquests.[10]

Yet no one is held responsible for this chain of tragic incidents. Grace could not help preferring Fitzpiers until it was too late. Félice and Fitzpiers' impulses are to be deplored but they cannot be blamed for following the laws of their own natures. Hardy is altogether sympathetic in his treatment of Félice; he gives admirable qualities to Fitzpiers. Even some of the characters perceive the blamelessness of those who hurt them. Grace's conventional bitterness disappears when she realizes that both Suke and Félice love Fitzpiers. It is the situation and the shaper of the situation that are to be blamed.

From the above it would appear that Hardy no longer sees the possibility of escape from sexual law that he saw when he wrote *The Mayor of Casterbridge* and *Two on a Tower*. This, however, is not the case. Grace partially escapes from the imperatives of sex when she treats Suke and Félice kindly after she knows of their love for Fitzpiers. Giles is completely free from "grosser passions"; his wish to marry Grace is based upon loving-kindness rather than desire. He is even able to look upon Grace critically, a trait Hardy seems to approve because it marks how far Giles had escaped from the generally inescapable tendency to overidealize. Marty South eventually escapes sexual law entirely. She is one who deserts sex "for the loftier quality of abstract humanism,"[11] like Viviette and Elizabeth Jane. The consequences of escape from its dominion are far from overwhelming happiness, but it is nonetheless true that Hardy again shows the human intelligence able to resist the law of sex that seemed irresistible in his novels published before 1882.

Joined with the play of sexual law and almost inseparably connected with its operation are the action of natural selection and the power of Chance. Both Marty and Giles suffer from the struggle for existence. In both cases the failure to succeed in practical life importantly affects the failure in love. Marty is compelled to sell her hair to keep alive, and it is this hair that helps to make Félice attractive, assists in bringing Fitzpiers to her, and causes Grace and Giles to resume their old affection for each other. Giles's loss of his lifehold makes him feel it necessary that he withdraw his offer for Grace's hand. For this important economic setback, Chance is mainly responsible. Giles's cart makes Félice's carriage turn aside, causes her to become angry with him, and finally prevents her from renewing the lifehold which passes back to her when his father dies. Just as Fitzpiers is about to buy a Budmouth practice which will take him and Grace away from Félice, Félice becomes ill and calls him to her. A heavy fall of rain when Grace is fleeing from her husband causes her to take refuge with the sick Giles. His generous surrender of his shack to her is the reason for the exposure to the storm that finally brings on a fatal sickness. The determiners, Chance and natural law, work together against man's opportunity for joy. In their operation we feel the presence of the "Unfulfilled Intention," indifferent in its aim but cruel in its effects.

But society is also to be blamed. The lower social and cultural station of Giles is in a sense his tragic flaw. Because of this "flaw," Melbury, who has a wrongheaded faith in aristocratic connections irrespective of the individual's merit, prefers Fitzpiers for his daughter's husband. It is the wish of her father as well as Fitzpiers' attractiveness that cause Grace to desert Giles and marry unhappily. Further, it is society that is to blame for the continuation of Grace's unhappy marriage. Indeed, the law of the land is more to blame than the natural law which directs man's actions. When he kisses Grace after her marriage to Fitzpiers, Giles is committing the "wrong, the social sin," no more. It was "social law [that] negatived forever their opening paradise." Had Grace and Giles been like the animals about the hut, who "knew neither law nor sin," it would have been better, Hardy declares.[12] Where natural law and Chance for once allow the possibility of happiness, society prevents such a consummation.

If this were all there were to *The Woodlanders*, one would have a remarkable singleness of effect. The antagonist, the "Unfulfilled Intention," controlling both Chance and natural law, would be logically predestined to victory; the protagonists, all the human beings involved, would be predestined to defeat. It would be an example of what Hardy once spoke of as the highest tragedy—"the WORTHY encompassed by the INEVITABLE." But the novel does not achieve such singleness of effect, for the reader becomes too aware of Hardy's philosophic inconsistencies. Although consistency would have compelled Hardy to consider society, the product of man, to be determined by the "Unfulfilled Intention" as well as the play of Chance and natural law, he does not carry his premise to its logical conclusion. He does not carry it to its logical conclusion, moreover, because he himself did not realize his inconsistency. Tragedy may be created, he says, "by an opposing environment either of things inherent in the universe, or of human institutions." Again he says that high tragedy can be built around "Nature's unconsciousness not of essential law, but of those laws framed merely as social expedients by humanity, without a basis in the heart of things."[13] Apparently Hardy did not realize that if man is "inherent in the universe," so are his institutions, that the laws framed as "social expedients," since they are made by man, have an equal, if more indirect, "basis in the heart of things."

But Hardy always had hoped for—one might even say had faith in—the possibility of ultimate amelioration and preferred inconsistency to a denial of his insight. Even in the days in which he first lost his early theistic faith, he retained hope, believing that 1967 would show a "scope above our blinkered time." In all his novels, to a degree which fluctuates with both the circumstances of his life and the spirit of his times, he shows his belief in the possibility of social change by his protests against "man's inhumanity to man." This belief, which he does not always seem fully conscious of himself, which he was not able to reconcile with the rest of his system until he wrote *The Dynasts*, is important even in those novels which are otherwise most strongly pessimistic and deterministic. It appears, as we have seen, in *The Return of the Native* and *The Mayor of Casterbridge* as well as in *Far from the Madding Crowd* and *The Hand of Ethelberta*, often to the consternation of the philosophically minded reader. For Hardy's social protests, based upon a hope for ultimate amelioration, are as much, though inconsistently, a part of his reading of life as his emphasis upon the tragedy he regards to be inherent in the nature of things. In *The Woodlanders*, *Tess*, and *Jude*, particularly, he is writing at the same time of two tragedies: that "created by an opposing environment . . . . of things inherent in the universe" and that "created by an opposing environment . . . . of human institutions."[14] And, since he considers some of the human institutions without "a basis in the heart of things," he tries to show through his novels both the necessity and the possibility of amelioration.

Probably because there were now many others who were concerned with changing social conditions while he had previously been only one of a few who dared to criticize, Hardy's social protest is much stronger in *The Woodlanders* than it has been in his past work. By pointing out the importance of Giles's social position in bringing about his own and Grace's unhappiness, and by Grace's frequent remark that she now sees how little acquirement and culture weigh beside "sterling character," he again shows his conviction that class distinctions are baseless. But it is a plea which has only been hinted at earlier that Hardy most plainly emphasizes—a protest against the rigorous unfairness of the marriage laws of England. For the most part Hardy criticizes indirectly. He shows that Fitzpiers fails to become a husband who forms a "sympathetic interdependence" where "mutual weaknesses are . . . . grounds of . . . . defensive alliance."[15] He clearly portrays Grace's consequent pain and her gradual recognition of the worthiness of Giles. Then he shows the pathetic failure of Melbury to secure a divorce that would enable her to marry more happily, and the evil effects of this failure upon all concerned. In the mere telling of the story, there is a moving plea against the prevailing marriage code.

This plea is emphasized by the conversations of the characters and by the author's direct statements. Melbury wonders why there should be no external interference with unhappy marriages. Giles thinks of Grace as a "defenceless creature conditioned by such harsh circumstances." Grace herself argues against such marriages as hers with Fitzpiers. She feels revolted by social laws when she walks with Giles, the one she really loves. She can see no "moral wrong" in her love for Giles. From her own experience she refutes the logic of a double standard of morals. When she thinks over her marriage vows, she cannot help wondering if God could possibly have joined her to Fitzpiers. Hardy's pitying comment that " 'Whom God hath joined' " was a "staggerer for a gentle woman of strong devotional sentiment" shows both that he agrees with Grace and that he inclines to go still further to agree with Fitzpiers' view of marriage as a "mere civil contract." Aside from the just-quoted statement and Hardy's admission in the Preface that a purpose of the book was to contest the undue rigor of the marriage law, he generally allows the characters to point the situation by their remarks and by their actions. But he forgets his position as impartial creator long enough to speak of the "dangerous structure of imperial law" and to stress the wider applicability of this single instance of marital unhappiness. Grace's domestic disasters, he says, are exactly like those of a thousand others, like Ariadne's, Vashti's, Amy Dudley's.[16] Certainly the creator of this situation and the maker of these criticisms is exerting himself very foolishly if he has no hope.

3

Hardy's avowed intention in *Tess of the D'Urbervilles* (1891) was to present a story in which the conventions would be so reversed that a seduced girl becomes the heroine. If this true sequence of events should offend some, he asks that they remember that it is better that an offense should come out of the truth than that the truth should not be told.[17] From Hardy's defensive attitude in this Preface to the work, one assumes that he is about to attack society more wholeheartedly than he has done before—an assumption that the book as a whole confirms. But *Tess* nonetheless illustrates the "pessimistic" view of the world that has frequently been assumed to be *the* philosophy of the Wessex novels.

The characters and the author stress the magnipotence of Fate. Izzy, Marion, and Retty do not blame Tess for winning the man they love. 'Twas to be. Although she was at first inclined to believe herself mistress of her fate, Tess soon begins to admit the fatalistic convictions of the neighboring field folk, who associate more with natural phenomena than with man. One of these field folk, her mother, looks upon Tess's seduction with a fatalism similar to that with which she regards the weather. Sometimes the characters are still more specific in their statements of belief. Tess refuses to pray for Alec because she realizes that the great Power would not alter his plans on her account. She feels that the universe is an "immense sad soul, coterminous with the universe in space, with history in time." Angel Clare speaks of Tess's life as the only chance given her by an "unsympathetic First Cause."[18] But it is Hardy himself who most clearly and often specifies the nature of the controlling power.

The most memorable of these specifications is, of course, the ironical sentence, " 'Justice' was done, and the President of the Immortals, in Aeschylean phrase, had ended his sport with Tess." But this is really no more than a trope, indicative of the way the fate of Tess impresses unreasoning humanity. Hardy's more seriously intended statements are frequently addressed against conceptions that are conventional rather than statements of a new force such as we know he had conceived of. Where, Hardy asks, was the providence of Tess's simple faith when she was seduced? What justice satisfactory to man can be found in the retribution that offers up Tess as a sacrifice for the sins of her ancestors? After he had described the utter dependence of the D'Urbeyfield children upon their improvident parents, he says: "Some people would like to know whence the poet whose philosophy is in these days deemed as profound and trustworthy as his song is breezy and pure gets his authority for speaking of 'Nature's holy plan.' " More positively, Hardy speaks of his sympathy with the fatalism of the peasants, the unalterable truth of their " 'twas to be." He agrees with Angel Clare's denomination of "It" as unsympathetic. He believes that even so fine a woman as Tess is of no more consequence than a fly before the universe, that she is caught like a "bird in a springe." No character, not even Alec, is truly responsible for his fate. When Angel has been cruelly intolerant of Tess, Hardy asks what this harshness is, compared to the "universal harshness out of which they grow; the harshness of the position towards the temperament, of the means towards the aims, of today towards yesterday, of hereafter towards today." But he never denominates this harshness as active or conscious. He does not even give It a name in the novel. He merely states, "So do flux and reflux—the rhythm of change—

alternate and persist in everything under the sky." This rhythm of change, before which human beings must willy-nilly bow, operates as relentlessly as it has in earlier novels, in such a way that birth often seems something which may be palliated, never justified.[19]

The "intolerable antilogy of making figments feel" is emphasized as it has not been since *The Return of the Native*. Consciousness is a veiled damnation, for it makes us realize our true situation. It has caused a "decline of belief in a beneficent Power," making melancholy chronic. The necessity of taking thought has made the heavens gray. More importantly, consciousness has made us aware of desires that cannot be satisfied. Even starving hopes persist; there is an "irresistible, universal, automatic tendency to find sweet pleasure somewhere," an "invincible instinct towards self-delight." But there is unfortunately another force which works against this instinct. At work everywhere is "the inherent will to enjoy, and the circumstantial will against enjoyment." Those characters who understand their situation feel with Tess, even in happy times, that all good fortune will be scourged out of them later in heaven's usual way. The gods are persistent ironists. By the time we learn, our experience has incapacitated us for doing. "In the ill-judged execution of a well-judged plan," "the call seldom produces the comer." Nature infrequently says "See" when the saying leads to happiness; It only allows clear vision when the body's hide-and-seek has become an outworn game.[20] So, when Tess is ready for love, she meets Alec rather than Angel. So, when Angel learns how he has misjudged Tess, it is too late, and Angel and Tess can be happy together for only a short time, for the eternal flux and reflux dictate that their inherent will to enjoy be counterbalanced by the circumstantial will against enjoyment.

One of the laws by which this circumstantial will operates is emphasized for the first time. Although Hardy's notions of heredity have previously seemed both vague and incredible, in *Tess* heredity is an important and credible factor in the heroine's development.

From her mother Tess inherits her prettiness and her early womanly fulness. The race from which she is descended transmitted to her a slight incautiousness of character.[21] The latter quality partially accounts for her seduction. The former qualities account for the seducer's interest. These inherited traits help to account for the unhappiness for which the general principles of sexual selection are even more responsible.

Tess is both the victim and the cause of most of the evils that result from love in the book. She is not, however, as dominated by sexual law as most of Hardy's earlier heroines. She is not a coquette; she pities sincerely Izz, Marion, and Retty for the sorrow Angel's love of her causes; although sexual impulse is unquestionably responsible for the beginning of her love for Angel, her later affection becomes almost asexual. But this does not mean that sex is not importantly responsible for her sorrow and for the sorrow of the other characters in the novel.

Because she is physically attractive, Alec seduces her. As Joan D'Urbeyfield comments, " 'Tis nater, after all, and what do please God!" Because of physical attraction, she and Angel converge as if subjected to an irresistible law. They gravitate into one. Angel is driven toward her "by every heave of his pulse," and the same might equally well be said of Tess. As usual, the consequences of this convergence extend much farther than the principal parties involved. Although they regret loving him, Izz, Retty, and Marion love Angel Clare. They become each but a portion of "one organism called sex," writhing under Nature's law. No one but Angel will satisfy their longing, so, despite the fact that Angel's conscience saves them from a seduction similar to Tess's, they are inconsolable. Marion refuses to marry the dairyman who loves her, and takes to drink; Izz no longer sings; Retty attempts to drown herself. One thinks of Troy's speech about sexual selection after reading of all this misery, yet there is no human villain blamed, for even Alec acts according to his predetermined nature. Because she sees the results of sexual selection more plainly than most women, Tess feels that she does wrong in inhabiting the fleshly tabernacle Nature gave her. Still the "vulpine slyness of Dame Nature" makes her forget that children would be an infliction upon others of what she bewailed for herself, birth.[22]

In addition to the play of sexual selection and heredity, the harshness of the struggle for existence contributes to the tragic nature of the action. This is particularly obvious in the desperate poverty of the D'Urbeyfields and in Tess's pathetic attempt to make a living after Angel deserts her. But it was also the poverty of the D'Urbeyfields that made Tess go to the D'Urberville estate in the first place.

Chance, too, plays a significant part in bringing about Tess's seduction and subsequent misery. Alec chances to make his attempt to seduce her just after she has become tired and discouraged from a fight with some other workers on the estate who resented her favored position. At almost any other moment, Hardy comments, she would have refused to accompany Alec.[23] Later on in the novel, it is Chance that keeps Angel from reading Tess's letter of confession. If he had read this letter, he might have forgiven her. Certainly there would not have been the terrible alternation of extreme joy and extreme pain that actually occurred. Finally, when Tess makes her weary journey to Angel's home, instead of meeting the kindly father, she sees and hears the narrow-minded brothers, is discouraged, and returns to her lonely battle for a living without having made any appeal for assistance.

Still, in spite of the forces that oppose her—and these forces seem as malign as they did in *The Mayor of Casterbridge*—Tess is no more easily conquered than Michael Henchard. Although she is helped by no one, she bravely resists what seems to be her fate. She refuses Alec's offers of money and clothes. She will not lie about her love. She refuses to try to make her seducer marry her for the sake of social appearances. Even when Angel renounces her, she does not give in. Accepting no one's help, despite the fact that she knows Angel's parents will give her money if she appeals to them, she struggles on at Flintcombe-Ashe, working long after the others have finished their tiresome day. Finally, when the police find her and take her from Angel, after their reconciliation has brought momentary happiness, she still seems undefeated. When the officers are about to take her away, she says: "It is as it should be. . . . . I am almost glad—yes, glad! This happiness could not have lasted. . . . . I have had enough."[24] Her courage gains the reader's respect and admiration. After watching her struggle for content, life does not seem contemptible or the struggle futile. Her fight seems to have value in itself because of the nobility of her nature. Like Michael Henchard, she is a tragic character in the truest sense of the word.

But there are other reasons, as well, why life does not appear worthless to the reader of *Tess*. Hardy, it is true, makes no attempt to gloss over the irremediable ills man must face, but he also emphasizes, as he never has before, the remediable ills that society rather than the inherent nature of things has caused. Indeed, in many portions of the book, it seems that the law of Nature is preferable to the law of society and contradicts it. Walking about in the quiet of nature after her seduction, Tess thinks of herself as "Guilt intruding into the haunts of Innocence. But all the while she was making a distinction where there was no difference. Feeling herself in antagonism, she was quite in accord. She had been made to break an accepted social law, but no law known to the environment in which she fancied herself such an anomaly." It is the false standard of society that makes her feel herself a sinner. On a desert island Tess would have quite properly felt no shame. "Most of the misery had been generated by her conventional aspect, and not by her innate sensations." After a time, Tess herself becomes unable to understand why she is condemned. She cannot understand in what sense her child, Sorrow, has offended against society. Yet, this bastard gift of senseless Nature, must suffer through no fault of its own. Nor can she understand why, since she is worthier than her companions—Marion, Izz, and Retty—in all other respects, the eyes of propriety believe her less worthy because of her "sin." Eventually she realizes that her sense of guilt is based on nothing more tangible than condemnation by an arbitrary law with no foundation in Nature. If she could rise above opinion (or opinion be changed), her sorrow would be at least tolerable.[25]

Indeed, though Hardy himself tends to confuse the reader by shifting the blame back and forth between inevitable and evitable causes, it might even be contended that Tess's life would not have been tragic at all if it had not been for society's cruel conventions. After her seduction, it is the social chasm which opens before her that hurts. If Tess could have avoided mankind, "that cold accretion called the world," neither her child nor her loss of maidenhood would have been cause for unhappiness, and the undying appetite for joy might have asserted itself freely again. But it seems that society believes maidenhood the only thing in Nature denied recuperative powers; so Tess suffers. Had it not been for the world's opinion, her experiences would have been simply a liberal education, Hardy tells us. It is, moreover, society, or its sacred book, convention, that is largely responsible for Tess's unhappiness after she meets Angel. He is too much bound by convention: he does not realize that Tess deserves King Lemuel's praise for virtue, that moral value should be reckoned by tendency, not by achievement. Angel has too little "nature" in him. His love is more ideal, fanciful—less thoroughgoing than that of Tess. His affection is "ethereal to a fault, imaginative to impracticability." And it is this conventional standard of judgment, adhered to by Clare, that is responsible for Tess's later unhappiness.[26] Natural law—sex and heredity—can be held responsible for Tess's seduction; but the consequence of her seduction would have been only to teach Tess better judgment if social law were not so harsh. Once Tess's fortune is declining, Chance seemingly delights in furthering her decline; but there might

[[179]]

not have been any decline if Angel had not been so dominated by convention.

Since, then, society is so largely responsible for the unhappiness of Tess, we see better ground for hope than we have found in any preceding novel. Always before, society has been a definitely subordinated factor in tragedy: causes against which man could not contend with success were primarily responsible for the catastrophes of Hardy's earlier books. In this novel Hardy does not stop with a mere picture of the way social forces increase or create unhappiness. Through the mouth of Angel Clare, now repentant, Hardy preaches a superior moral law to society: "Having long discredited the old systems of mysticism, he now began to discredit the old appraisements of morality. He thought they wanted readjusting. Who was the moral man? Still more pertinently, who was the moral woman? The beauty or ugliness of a character lay not only in its achievements, but in its aims and impulses; its true history lay, not among things done, but among things willed."[27] To show the truth of this moral standard, which Hardy shared with Clare, was one of the main purposes behind the writing of *Tess*. Because this is true, *Tess* is more than a "pessimistic" novel. It is a fine contribution to the war against "man's inhumanity to man" which so importantly characterized the last decade of Hardy's career as a novelist.[28]

4

The Well-beloved (1892) is a not very successful or very important attempt to illustrate two characteristic Hardyan themes. The first of these notions is expressed in Hardy's journal for 1884: "Write a novel entitled *Time against Two*, in which the antagonism of the parents of a Romeo and Juliet *does* succeed in separating the couple and stamping out their love,—alas, a more probable development than the other!"[29] In germinal form the second idea appears in Hardy's notebook for 1889: "The story of a face which goes through three generations or more, would make a fine novel or poem of the passage of Time. The differences in personality to be ignored."[30]

With the first of these themes Hardy deals but briefly. Jocelyn Pierston falls in love with Marcia Bencomb, whom he accidentally encounters when she is in distress. It is a typical case of love at first sight, but it does not result in the usual Hardyan conclusion. Instead of marrying and suffering, or not marrying and suffering, the lovers separate when their parents oppose the match and forget about each other. Long afterward, when both of them have passed through many years of life and a great number of love affairs, they meet again, and a practical, unloving, unromantic marriage takes place. It is with the years between that Hardy is more importantly concerned rather than with the unusual parting and coming-together of his *fin de siècle* Romeo and Juliet.

Between the time of Pierston's first and last meeting with Marcia, he falls in love with Avice Caro, Avice's daughter, and Avice's granddaughter, all of whom strikingly resemble one another, who have the "family face," in fact. Although Avice the first loved him while she lived, Pierston does not love her until she dies; after her death, he falls in love with her laundress daughter who lacks all but the physical attractiveness of the mother—but this Avice does not care for him. Finally, it appears that he will be successful in wooing Avice the third, the most recent reproduction of the family face. But, on the literal eve of his success, she marries a man who is more nearly her own age. In themselves these experiences (especially since they are set on the Isle of Slingers, where such reproductions of a face are said to occur frequently) are not altogether improbable. It is the way in which Hardy treats this pursuit of the well-beloved that makes the tale strange to the point of incredibility.

Pierston is not a particularly sensual man; despite the fact that he falls in love with many women besides the Avices and Marcia, sex is never the primary reason for his attraction to these women. None-theless, the attraction of the women is neither rationally explicable nor satisfying in the results it produces. It is "the traction of some mystic magnet which has nothing to do with reason." Each Avice is "the exponent of the Long-pursued—as one who, by no initiative of his own, had been chosen by some superior Power as the vehicle of *her* next début."[31] It is possible that Hardy believed this "mystic magnet" to be sex, that this superior Power works through the laws of Nature as it has done before. But it is certainly true that the natural explanation of this traction is not stressed by the author. The successive passages of the well-beloved from woman to woman are surrounded with an air of mystery unprecedented in Hardy's previous treatment of love.

Yet there is a characteristic idea embodied in the prolonged pursuit the book portrays. Essentially, Pierston appears to be seeking his alter ego, an ideal woman, who temporarily appears in the form of some one woman. The qualities he attaches to the actual woman exist only in his brain; some mystic power makes him feel for a time that he has found the embodiment of his ideal, but this feeling is always an illusion. Like Shelley, he is in pursuit of "one shape in many names,"[32] and, in this respect, he is characteristic of most Hardyan lovers. Like Knight, Eustacia, Clym, Springrove—in fact, most of Hardy's men—Pierston pursues an unattainable ideal that always eludes him.

It seems probable, in fact, that Hardy is giving us in *The Well-beloved* an unsuccessful technical exercise that foreshadows, never-theless, what he later did in *The Dynasts*. As early as 1886, he had declared: "Novel-writing as an art cannot go backward. Having reached the analytic stage it must transcend it by going still further in the same direction. Why not by rendering as visible essences, spectres, etc. the abstract thoughts of the analytic school?"[33]

It is true that Hardy does not carry out this intention fully in this novel, but we certainly get in Pierston more a visible essence, a symbol for the abstraction that man always pursues the unattainable, than a realistic character. And the novel as a whole symbolizes, rather than realistically presents, a characteristic part of Hardy's reading of life, as Hardy himself recognized. The book illustrates "the theory of the transmigration of the ideal beloved one, who only exists in the lover, from material woman to material woman. . . . . There is, of course, underlying the fantasy followed by the visionary artist, the truth that all men are pursuing a shadow, the Unattainable."[34]

As an illustration of Hardy's belief in the unrealizability of man's higher desires, one of the primary reasons why he lamented the antilogy involved in giving man consciousness, the book is important, for it is the fullest expression of this aspect of Hardy's thought. But it is also a rather tedious and long-drawn-out illustration of ideas Hardy handled more artistically and credibly, if less extensively, in other portions of the Wessex novels.

5

JUDE

Paradoxically, *Jude the Obscure* (1895) is at once the most outspoken expression of Hardy's "pessimism" and his most significant attempt to make the future a time in which man's life will be more endurable. It is pessimistic in its emphasis upon the relentless way in which destiny prevents happiness; melioristic in its contradictory emphasis upon the social causes which contribute, but may not always contribute, to man's failure to find a satisfactory life.

Jude is "predestinate Jude."[35] From the start Hardy predicts the catastrophe to come. Nature's scorn for man's finer emotions and her lack of interest in his aspirations are obvious throughout. Although Hardy does not use the name he borrowed from Schopenhauer, the world of *Jude* is guided by the same Willer, dumb and blind, of whom he later wrote in poetry and drama. For the first time in the novels, there is an extended exposition of the metaphysical conditions in which his characters are placed: "The world resembled a stanza or melody composed in a dream; it was wonderfully excellent to the half-aroused intelligence, but hopelessly absurd at the full waking; . . . . the First Cause worked automatically like a somnambulist, and not reflectively like a sage . . . . at the framing of the terrestrial conditions there seemed never to have been contemplated such a development of emotional perceptiveness among the creatures subject to these conditions as that reached by thinking and educated humanity."[36]

In such a tragically misplanned universe, where every man or woman is unconsciously but inevitably guided to his or her destiny, no human villain appears. Neither Phillotson nor Arabella is responsible for his or her actions, although both of them fulfil the conventional function of the villain. Only the universe can be blamed legitimately, and to do that is futile.

One can see the work of this First Cause most clearly in the tragedy of Jude. It has given him desires and aspirations that he cannot satisfy. At first he wishes to become a scholar. Because social and natural law combine to make this impossible, he decides to live the "ecclesiastical and altruistic" life. Again circumstances are against him. Finally, he decides to follow "inclinations which do [him] and nobody else any harm and actually give pleasure to those [he loves] best."[37] In even this modest aim he fails.

In making his life a failure, Fate makes use of all the powers we have seen acting before. Jude hopes to satisfy his thirst for knowledge at Christminster. But he is poor and belongs to a class that is beneath Christminster's limits of condescension; his mental aptitude seems irrelevant to the university authorities. So society becomes his first stumbling block. He is also ignorant, and subject to sexual law.[38] So, when Arabella takes a fancy to have him for her husband, Jude is an easy victim. His marriage and his poverty effectually silence his aspirations for a while. When, after Arabella's desertion, he again tries to get to Christminster, a combination of

Social laws condemn with
their nature, again
malice

natural and social circumstances cause him to abandon altogether the intellectual life. But, having renounced his first ideal, he is no more successful in his pursuit of the second best, for his wish to serve mankind as a preacher is made unrealizable by his love for Sue Bridehead. Before he had been able to prevent it, Sue had married Phillotson. When she discovers that physical and intellectual incompatibility makes her marriage with Phillotson impossible, she goes away with Jude. Society's discovery of their anomalous relationship makes it necessary that Jude give up his second conception of the way life should be lived and brings him to the still more limited aim of making Sue happy.

Society, natural law, and accident again prevent realization. By heredity, both Jude and Sue belong to a family that does not live freely and happily in marriage bonds. Sue, who is at first less bound by convention than Jude, knows this and begs him not to force her to marry him.[39] Although Jude continues to insist, they are never married, but if this slightly helps their personal relationship, it makes their relationship to society more difficult. They become permanently stigmatized, and the cruel mass that constitutes the world of people adds to their already difficult struggle for existence. As if this were not bad enough, Chance intervenes to make matters still worse. Jude's child by Arabella, Father Time, is returned at the least propitious moment possible. Taking literally Sue's statement that it is a pity to enter a world so ill-conditioned, Father Time kills himself and the children of Jude and Sue.

Unbalanced by this disaster, Sue returns to the conventional ideas that have always retained their force subconsciously and feels herself to be a sinner pursued by a just God. She leaves Jude, goes back to Phillotson, and destroys forever the possibility of happiness for either herself or her lover. Chance and natural law work together, once Sue is gone, to precipitate the final catastrophe. Jude is plagued by a hereditary tendency toward drunkenness. Chance throws Arabella in his path when he is intoxicated, and he returns

not quite;
she is instrumental

[185]

to her. So it is Arabella, the least admirable and least sympathetic character in the book, who carelessly watches over him in the fatal illness that ends his lonely struggle for a satisfactory existence.

The course of the story and the nature of the First Cause specified in the story are sufficient indications of the somberness of Hardy's outlook, but he is not willing that his somber view go before the world without further emphasis. Jude frequently feels that it would be better had he not been born. He attempts to kill himself. Father Time is an embodiment of the "coming universal wish not to live." All the important characters are convinced of the cruelty of life. Nature's law is mutual butchery, Sue declares. Phillotson thinks of cruelty as the law pervading all nature and society.[40] Jude believes that he has all along been struggling against malignant stars. When the action closes, there are few readers whose immediate reaction is not sympathetic with Jude's bitter quotation from Job:

"Let the day perish wherein I was born, and the night in which it was said, 'There is a man child conceived.' " . . . .
"Wherefore is light given to him that is in misery, and life unto the bitter in soul?"[41]

Yet it cannot be maintained that the ultimate intention of the author or the ultimate effect upon the reader is blankly pessimistic. The case of Jude and Sue can undoubtedly be paralleled, but it is not representative of normal human characters in a normal human situation. As Hardy later explained, the book is "concerned first with the labours of a poor student to get a University degree, and secondly with the tragic issues of two bad marriages, owing in the main to a doom or curse of hereditary temperament peculiar to the family of the parties."[42] As the limiting conditions of the book are adequately clear to the disinterested reader, it is evident that neither the author nor the reader could claim *Jude* to have a universal representative value. Hence, the most that we may properly say is that Hardy was blankly pessimistic about the fate of such characters at such a time. It is, moreover, worth our while to consider the last qualification more closely. *Jude* was in some ways representative of conditions that might arise at the time of the book's publication, but the novel actually portrays conditions in the middle of the last century and certainly makes no claim to being an interpretation of conditions that will always exist.

Indeed, there are frequent expressions of hope for the future. Sue, remarking upon the situation in which she and Jude find themselves, declares: "When people of a later age look back upon the barbarous customs and superstitions of the times that we have the unhappiness to live in, what *will* they say!"[43] And Jude, after he and Sue have finally decided they must separate, says: "Perhaps the world is not illuminated enough for such experiments as ours! Who were we, to think we could act as pioneers!"[44] Even later, while Jude is lying on his deathbed, he does not give up hope for the future: "As for Sue and me, when we were at our own best, long ago—when our minds were clear, and our love of truth fearless—the time was not ripe for us! Our ideas were fifty years too soon to be any good to us."[45]

These passages clearly point to the possibility of happiness in the future for even such persons as Jude and Sue.

In fact, I believe that Hardy's hopefulness for the future—which he could never divorce, one remembers, from a clear vision of the worst contingencies man may meet—was in large measure responsible for the writing of the book. Certainly, as we know from Hardy's journal, he felt that there was something he could *show* the world in *Jude*. Originally, the novel was to be "a short story of a young man—'who could not go to Oxford'—His struggles and ultimate failure. . . . . There is something [in this] the world ought to be shown, and I am the one to show it to them."[46] Although the novel which grew out of the short story became immensely more complex than the original plan (the university theme is definitely subordinated to the complication of social and personal difficulties encountered by an underprivileged intellectual), Hardy does succeed in showing his readers the injustice, some of it remediable, met by one who is at the same time poor and deserving. Oppressed by forces from within and without, Jude remains an admirable figure. Except at the last, when his illness deprives him of all hope, he struggles bravely even when the odds against him are overwhelmingly great. Though his hopes and his desires are never more than partially realized, he always appears to be a moral pioneer, striking out for the light, suffering more, perhaps, because he is conscious that he is preparing a better lot for similar unfortunates in the future. Even when he is drunk, baffled, and confused, he does not despair altogether: "I am in a chaos of principles—groping in the dark—acting by instinct and not after example. Eight or nine years ago, when I came here [Oxford] first, I had a neat stock of fixed opinions, but they dropped away one by one. . . . . I perceive there is something wrong somewhere in our social formulas: what it is can only be discovered by men or women with greater insight than mine."[47]

At the darkest, Jude is resolved to look eventualities in the face, and, confused, almost blinded though he may be, he concentrates all his efforts upon trying to see the light. Though he sometimes regrets his position—"Who were we, to think we could act as pioneers?"—he remains throughout most of the course of the story a courageous contender against social intolerance, a fighter in a struggle that will some day be of service to humanity. His value to humanity and the desirability of society's preserving and fostering such characters are made more emphatic by the tragedy of the ending.

The more direct social criticism in *Jude* reinforces the conviction that Hardy is trying to correct, as well as to warn against, what cannot be avoided. The novel does not, as some contemporary critics believed, attack the status of marriage as a whole, but it does criticize the irrevocable character of the marriage contract more strongly than does any previous work of Hardy. Describing the marriage of Jude and Arabella, he writes: "And so, standing before the aforesaid officiator, the two swore that at every other time of their lives they would assuredly believe, feel, and desire precisely as they had believed, felt, and desired during the few preceding weeks. What was as remarkable as the undertaking itself was the fact that nobody seemed at all surprised at what they swore."[48]

As a careful reading of this passage shows, the real criticism is directed against the social necessity of marriage *in every case*, even when people are as ill fitted for marriage as Arabella and Jude, or Sue and Jude.[49] The reader also perceives that it is society which has ordained the marriage contract to be all but irrevocable, which is mainly responsible for condemning Jude and Sue to a fate much worse than they deserve. If Jude had not been bound by his tie to Arabella when he and Sue first met, Sue might have married him rather than Phillotson and overcome her repugnance for the irrevocableness of marriage that was later accentuated by her marriage with Phillotson. If Jude and Sue had been accepted by society, or even just tolerated by society, without the sanction of a license for their living together, their peculiar hereditary repugnance for the strongly tied bonds of marriage would never have spoiled their life together.

In *Jude* Hardy not only shows us the worst contingencies that a man may be called upon to meet; he also shows us that much of the misery man suffers is remediable by greater social enlightenment. Much of the evil against which man must contend is due not to the relentless and unconscious action of natural forces but to the conscious actions of man, who, because of this very consciousness, may change those things that are shaken and of ill repute. Although the idea is not given formal expression, and the artistic effect of the book is again reduced by the reader's inability to distinguish clearly what Hardy considers remediable and what irremediable, we see here again the germ of his later belief that the unconscious Immanent Will may become conscious and beneficent through the conscious efforts of the conscious creatures It has unknowingly produced.

6

When we examine sources other than the novels[50] for further developments in Hardy's reading of life, [we find more explicit statements of the deterministic philosophy that increasingly manifested itself in the period that culminated with the appearance of *The Mayor of Casterbridge*. In his journal for 1886, Hardy remarks that he has come to think of society gatherings as a collection of people in a somnambulistic state, people acting automatically, not knowing what they mean. In 1890 he makes a similar statement about people seen in art galleries.[51] Once again, Hardy remarks, in true determinist fashion, that people are blameless for their actions: "He, she, had blundered; but not as the Prime Cause had blundered. He, she, had sinned; but not as the Prime Cause had sinned. He, she, was ashamed and sorry; but not as the Prime Cause would be ashamed and sorry if it knew."[52] In 1890 he decides that the First Cause must be called "It," as in the passage above, because of its unconscious impersonality. He declares that even Nature is blameless for the way in which she acts, for she, too, is controlled by a higher force.[53] All these definitions of the deterministic side of Hardy's outlook are clarifications of an earlier point of view rather than evidences of a further development, but there are other, very important, aspects of Hardy's thought that appear for the first time in these years.

From his direct statements of the past, we know that the First Cause is one, immanent in the universe, and unconscious. But there have been no statements that proved that this Prime Mover was immaterial rather than material. Indeed, excepting the fact that Chance did not work in accordance with any known law, the insistence upon the part natural law plays in human and subhuman life might logically lead us to believe that the "unconscious propensity" of which he speaks is no more than a personification of material forces. But it becomes clear now that such, if it ever was the case, is true no longer.

8

In 1886 Hardy wrote concerning *The Dynasts:* "The human race to be shown as one great network or tissue which quivers in every part when one point is shaken, like a spider's web if touched. Abstract realisms to be in the form of Spirits, Spectral figures, etc."[54] The pantheistic and monistic portions of this statement are not new to Hardy's thought, but the tendency toward transcendental idealism is new. Throughout the remainder of this period frequent notes recur to this view. In the same year Hardy declares that novel-writing must advance still further toward abstraction—a view he himself illustrates in *The Well-beloved*. In 1887 he remarks: "I was thinking a night or two ago that people are somnambulists—that the material is not the real—only the visible, the real being invisible optically. That it is because we are in a somnambulistic hallucination that we think the real to be what we see as real."[55] In the same year he speaks of seeing souls outside bodies at a concert. In 1889, after reading Plato's *Cratylus*, he writes: "A very good way of looking at things would be to regard everything as having an actual or false name, and an intrinsic or true name, to ascertain which all endeavor should be made."[56] And, finally, in 1892, he says: "We don't always remember as we should that in getting at the truth, we get only at the true nature of the impression that an object, etc., produces on us, the true thing in itself being still, as Kant shows, beyond out knowledge."[57]

This idea that the real is not the material object that meets the eye, that the essential reality is not the apparent reality, is, of course, basic in *The Dynasts*, where the immaterial Spirits, themselves directed by the invisible Will, are more important than the human actors or actions. But such a development in Hardy's philosophy, although he certainly made no definite statement of belief in idealism before 1886, does not come altogether unexpectedly. As early as *The Return of the Native* (1878), one finds approximations of the transcendental point of view. Clym Yeobright is an enthusiast of ideas, careless toward outward things. A poem of 187–, "She," emphasizes the impossibility of detecting actual feelings by appearances.[58] Hardy's frequent use of Chance in his novels indicates that he does not feel natural law to be, by itself, an adequate explanation of reality. The continual emphasis upon the impossibility of judging fairly by externals such as class distinctions and wealth demonstrates that he was not satisfied with the material appearance of things. Hardy was always careful to probe beneath the surface for truth, and this inclination to emphasize the fundamental rather than the apparent reality helps to explain why he ultimately became an idealist.

But it is difficult to say with absolute precision what precipitated the change in Hardy's outlook. In May, 1886, it is true, only two months after his first profession of agreement with idealism, he was reading Hegel. But his remarks upon the German philosopher do not indicate any marked sympathy: "Have been thinking over the dictum of Hegel—that the real is the rational and the rational the real—that real pain is compatible with a formal pleasure—that the idea is all, etc. but it doesn't help much. These venerable philosophers seem to start wrong; they cannot get away from a prepossession that the world must somehow have been made to be a comfortable place for man. If I remember, it was Comte who said that metaphysics was a mere sorry attempt to reconcile theology and physics."[59]

It is possible, however, that an earlier reading of Hegel caused him to think more intensively about the unreality of the apparent, upon the elusiveness of the thing-in-itself. It is possible that a reading of Schopenhauer, whose *World as Will and Idea* became available in English translation in 1886, was responsible for leading him into the idealist camp. I am inclined, however, to doubt this. Hardy first agreed with the idealists in March, 1886. If a reading of Schopenhauer inspired this agreement, why did Hardy not mention Schopenhauer as an exception to the idealists who have pretty preconceptions in his note on Hegel in May of the same year? It is also possible that his re-reading of Carlyle, of whom he speaks in his journal for 1891, his reading of Plato, whom he was studying in 1889, or his reading of Kant, mentioned in 1892,[60] took place earlier and affected the course of his thought.

Such tenuous threads of evidence cannot be woven together into a thoroughly convincing pattern. The most that we can say with positiveness is that Hardy, at a time when he was undoubtedly reading the idealistic philosophers more assiduously than he ever had before, came to believe in the probability of the idealist position; that the idealism with which he agreed was not an optimistic idealism similar to that of the philosophers he admits he read or to that of his English contemporaries in philosophy; that his idealism, if one excepts *The Well-beloved*, did not materially affect the reading of life exemplified in the novels or his usual explanation of the way in which the world operates. Further, perhaps, one should make the necessary qualification that Hardy still does not embrace idealism with dogmatic confidence. As the quotation about Kant—"the true thing-in-itself being still . . . . beyond our knowledge"—shows, Hardy's belief in the probability of idealism does not contradict his fundamental agnosticism.

A practical meliorism is not necessarily incompatible with the metaphysic Hardy has tentatively adopted. It is not, therefore, surprising to find that the journal notes are often emphatically melioristic. Hardy favored Irish separation at a time when many Englishmen indignantly repulsed such a suggestion. He maintained that it was unjust to make marriage the only career open to women and favored women's suffrage when suffragettes were generally viewed as annoying oddities. He complained of the unrealistically sheltered education young girls received at teacher's training colleges. He as-

serted that the peculiarity of the conditions of life of actresses justified their being judged by a separate code of morals. He approved a
woman's resolve to go by her own rather than her husband's name.
He declared himself an intrinsicalist in politics, against all accidental privileges.[61] But these scattered protests against the status
quo are not so important as his more broadly social criticism.

As one would assume from reading the novels, Hardy does not
believe that it is always a suprahuman power that causes unhappiness. The guilt of society is implicit in his statement of a further
truth with which "modern" tragedy may concern itself. It can treat
Nature's "unconsciousness not of essential laws, but of those laws
framed merely as social expedients by humanity, without a basis
in the heart of things." This belief is the basis for his pleas against
social injustice, for

> Why should Man add to Nature's quandary,
>   And worsen ill?[62]

It accounts for the more positive attempt to remedy injustice
through the medium of the novels.

Moreover, these attempts to lessen ill are motivated by a belief
in eventual amelioration. Progress may be a "looped orbit," he
says, and this age is certainly not the climax of human history, but
it is nonetheless true that in the "lapse of countless ages . . . . improved systems of moral education will considerably and appreci-
ably elevate even the involuntary instincts of human nature." He
even goes so far as to maintain that the Golden Rule will become
practicable when we realize that we are all parts of one organism
and that pain to one member of humanity actually reacts upon ourselves.[63]

There is one other important statement of Hardy's during this
period, which I have taken out of its chronological place because it
shows that he has finally found a philosophic basis for the seemingly
inconsistent belief that man can change a universe which an "un-

conscious propensity" has called into being. In the poem "He Wonders about Himself" (dated November, 1893), he not only uses the
term "Will" for the first time but also suggests a logical foundation
for a belief in progress:

> Part is mine of the general Will,
> Cannot my share in the sum of sources
> Bend a digit the poise of forces,
> And a fair desire fulfil?[64]

This is the earliest statement of what Hardy later regarded as an
original solution to the problem of free will and determinism. To
quote from a letter of 1902 to Edward Wright, he came to believe
that "the Unconscious Will of the Universe is growing aware of
Itself . . . . [for] what has already taken place in a fraction of the
whole (i.e. so much of the world as has become conscious) is likely
to take place in the mass; and there being no Will outside the mass
—that is, the Universe—the whole Will becomes conscious there-
by: and ultimately, it is to be hoped, sympathetic."[65]

Although the isolation of this passage (no repetition of the
reasoning occurs until the years in which he was actually writing
The Dynasts) causes one to assume that Hardy had not yet firmly
grasped the significance of this solution to his logical dilemma, it is
nevertheless clear that the major contradiction in his thinking has
disappeared. The universe is constantly in the process of change;
hence the Immanent Will, which is identical with the universe, also
changes. As a result of an almost infinite process of change, as an
unconscious and undesired result of the Immanent Will's dialectic,
consciousness emerged in man. Through man's conscious awareness he can control and change those parts of the universe which
are the products of his consciousness (i.e., society) even if he cannot overcome or change for the present the unconscious portions of
the universe or the unconscious (i.e., emotional) parts of himself.
Ultimately, perhaps, consciousness will inform the entire Will,
and all things will be fashioned closer to even the heart's desire. The

novels, where one still fluctuates with frequent perplexity between an arraignment of the universe and of society without understanding their precise interconnection, show that Hardy has not yet assimilated his solution fully enough to present it in artistic form; but this poem of 1893 does show that the entire Weltanschauung of *The Dynasts* has been tentatively conceived.

7

For the first time, I believe, we have found trustworthy evidence that Hardy has been influenced by German pessimism. Although it is still possible that Hardy adopted the term "Will" independently of Schopenhauer, the fact that his library contained a first edition of the Haldane-Kemp translation of *The World as Will and Idea* (completed in 1886), and his reference to the renunciative side of Schopenhauer's philosophy in *Tess* (1891),[66] inclines me to believe that Hardy adopted the term "Will" for his First Cause because he was impressed, sometime between May, 1886, and 1893, by the arguments contained in Schopenhauer's great work. But there is little else, if anything, that Hardy owes to the German thinker. As I have already shown, everything else in Hardy's reading of life can be traced more convincingly to other sources.

Another German philosopher, and a follower of Schopenhauer, was more influential in determining the final shape of Hardy's philosophic thinking. As Rutland has shown in his recent study, Hardy erred in thinking that his explanation of the way consciousness might inform the Unconscious Will was original. Indeed, Hardy had himself admitted in an interview with William Archer that he was much impressed by the arguments of Von Hartmann that parallel precisely his own.[67] As Von Hartmann's *Philosophy of the Unconscious* first appeared in English in 1886 and the poem in which Hardy first makes use of this idea was written in 1893, it seems likely that the influence of Von Hartmann was active at about the same time as that of Schopenhauer.

It is doubtful if the greater intensity of Hardy's meliorism can be accounted for by Von Hartmann's helping him out of a logical dilemma (for it was already more intense before Hardy wrote "He Wonders about Himself" in 1893), but it is probable that the growing social seriousness of the time had an important effect upon his greater hopefulness. We cannot, however, narrow this influence down to any single writer. Since Hardy's familiarity with Ibsen dates from a period later than the writing of *The Woodlanders* and *Tess*, it is not likely that Ibsen influenced even the direction of his thinking. Zola, whom he had read by 1891, may have given him more courage to treat social problems frankly, but we cannot say that Ibsen, Zola, or any of his English contemporaries exercised a specific influence upon him.[68] It was the spirit of the time, the increasing tendency to subject prevalent moral and social ideas to criticism, and not the work of any one man, that gave Hardy an incentive to attack convention in a manner unparalleled in his earlier work.

Contradictions such as one would expect in the work of a novelist who insists that he does not particularly strive for philosophic coherence still appear, but Hardy's tentative explanation of the universe is much more consistent than it has ever been before. Chance still exerts an important influence upon the lives of his characters, but there is nothing in this belief in Chance that contradicts his idealistic determinism. For Hardy now maintains—he had felt this long before as the importance of Chance in all the novels indicates—that there is an immaterial and unconscious First Cause that determines and contains everything. Unlike the scientific determinist and like the fatalist, he does not claim that the First Cause works in such a way that its operation is always capable of comprehension by man; nevertheless, his immaterial First Cause works for the most part in a manner that the scientific determinist would approve.

Although Chance continues to play a part in determining man's fate as late as *The Dynasts*, its part is much less important in his later novels than it was in *Two on a Tower* or even in *The Mayor of Casterbridge*.

For Hardy's interpretation of the universe, although there can be no doubt that he continues to emphasize the irremediable ills in life, there can be no better term than "meliorism." With the help of Von Hartmann, Hardy has finally reconciled his belief that man's actions are determined and his belief that man can change his world. Despite the fact that Hardy often interprets the world pessimistically and rarely emphasizes the fact that the Will operates dialectically, he is still a believer in progress and a meliorist. Hardy believed that there was more evil that was irremediable than the English positivists did; the positivists believed that there were more things susceptible to change than Hardy did. But they were at one in a belief that the world is getting better and will continue to do so.

Indeed, if we can forgive him for the straightforward English that replaces the logical jargon of the philosophers, there is more truth to life and a more dependable tonic quality to Hardy's most forceful statement of his own interpretation of life than there is in all the literature of positivism: "People call me a pessimist; and if it is pessimism to think, with Sophocles, that 'not to have been born is best,' then I do not reject the designation. I never could understand why the word 'pessimism' should be such a red flag to many worthy people; and I believe, indeed, that a good deal of the robustious, swaggering optimism of recent literature is at bottom cowardly and insincere. I do not see that we are likely to improve the world by asseverating, however loudly, that black is white, or at least that black is but a necessary contrast and foil, without which white would be white no longer. That is mere juggling with a metaphor. But my pessimism, if pessimism it be, does not involve the assumption that the world is going to the dogs, and that Ahriman is winning all along the line. On the contrary, my practical philosophy is distinctly melioristic. What are my books but one plea against 'man's inhumanity to man,' woman, and to the lower animals? . . . . Whatever may be the inherent good or evil of life, it is certain that men make it much worse than it need be. When we have got rid of a thousand remediable ills, it will be time enough to determine whether the ill that is irremediable outweighs the good."[69]

As Hardy recognized, and as too many dogmatic philosophers have not recognized, idealism, naturalism, pessimism, meliorism, fatalism, and determinism are no more than categories into which man tries to press the nature of ultimate reality. In each of these concepts, at least a residuum of truth is to be found. Absolute or final truth is not discoverable in any of them—witness the succession of philosophers through the ages. Perhaps Hardy, who always remained enough of an agnostic to welcome an apparent truth even when it did not square beautifully with his entire outlook, approaches the nature of the universe more nearly than those who hold to a more rigid system.

VII

ANOTHER STARTING-POINT

Much is there waits you we have missed;
Much lore we leave you worth the knowing,
Much, much has lain outside our ken:
Nay, rush not: time serves: we are going,
        Gentlemen.

—*Late Lyrics and Earlier*

1

A s HARDY himself recognized better than most of his critics, it is easier to exaggerate his consistency than his inconsistency. When I speak of his solving the inconsistency of his world view in the poem "He Wonders about Himself," I attribute an importance to this solution Hardy would have perhaps smiled at. Perhaps, too, he would have been surprised to discover that he had advanced, though hesitantly, a clarification of the problem of change in a determined universe as early as he did. Indeed, it is altogether possible that this poem represents only the germinal phase of a later solution, that it did not assume major importance in his philosophic thinking until after he abandoned the writing of prose. The unresolved inconsistency of arraigning the universe and society as separate causes for the same offense and the irreconcilable views of tragedy as either man against the universe or man against society exemplified in the novels from *The Woodlanders* to *Jude* would lead one to think so—as would the isolation of the passage itself.

Hardy did not mind his own inconsistencies. Although he often thought as a philosopher, he did not pretend to be one. "Unadjusted impressions," he wrote, "have their value, and the road to a true philosophy of life seems to lie in humbly recording diverse readings of its phenomena as they are forced upon us by chance and change." Perhaps his strenuous insistence upon his right to incongruous interpretations of life resulted from his distaste for most philosophers: "These venerable philosophers seem to start wrong; they cannot get away from a prepossession that the world must somehow have been made to be a comfortable place for man."[1] It is not unlikely that the strength of his insistence was due to his own resolve to avoid similar prepossessions. At any rate, Hardy's devotion to his right to be inconsistent made him angry with those who called him a pessimist, with those, indeed, who fitted his thought into any philosophical category whatsoever.

In one sense, at least, he was justified. He was primarily an artist, and he was wise in insisting upon his right to explore new manifestations of reality, whether they accorded or did not accord with previous preconceptions. But it is unwise for an artist to occupy himself with slices of life without thinking of the relation of the part to the whole. Unless an artist has thought out a philosophy that organizes his universe, his work will have only the value of the part that may be fitted into the whole, never the greater value of a part that is fitted into a whole. One may go even further. If the philosophy of the artist is meretricious or false, it is no good, finally, whatever its temporary appeal to people similarly addicted to turning their backs upon things as they are. Further still, if the philosophy of the artist is inconsistent with itself, his work loses aesthetic value because of this inconsistency.

Whatever Hardy may have thought about the desirability of having a namable philosophy, it is obvious that he had one; indeed, it is obvious that he for a time had several. Because mechanistic determinism (at least so it seems to most modern thinkers) is no more a satisfactory philosophy than fatalism or blank pessimism, it is probably fortunate that Hardy was an inconsistent philosopher during the fifty-five years it took him to arrive at consistency. Without the touch of the inexplicable Hardy introduces into *The Return of the Native*, without the intimations of hope one finds in the same book, the novel would be inferior to what it is. A rigid conformity to mechanistic determinism would have made *The Return of the Native* a mere illustration of a philosophy that does not conform to man's deepest insight into reality.

But it is nonetheless true that the inconsistencies of Hardy's philosophy do hurt the totality of effect of many of his novels. I cannot share some critics' belief that *The Return of the Native* is a perfect novel. It is one of the best novels of the nineteenth century because it artistically embodies a reading of life that approximates the nature of ultimate reality, but it is imperfect because it embodies a philosophy inconsistent with itself. If I had to choose, I should say that the later novels, from *The Mayor of Casterbridge* to *Jude* (excepting *The Well-beloved*) approach perfection more nearly, because the philosophy that dictated them comes closer to striking a mean between what is comprehensible (natural law) and what is incomprehensible ("Chance"), because the philosophy that dictates them approaches more nearly a balance between the equally absurd extremes of absolute optimism and absolute pessimism. But this does not mean that even the later novels approach perfection too closely for comfort. As I have already pointed out, Hardy's failure to resolve the contradiction involved in his belief that society has been determined, and yet can be changed, detracts from the effectiveness of the later novels. The best of Hardy's novels are very good indeed; they are always honest embodiments of his best insight and products of good craftsmanship; they are based upon a reading of life that lacks the speciousness one frequently finds in the philosophies of George Eliot, Thackeray, Dickens, Trollope— even sometimes (remember *Richard Feverel*) in the philosophy of

Meredith. The best of Hardy's novels compare very favorably with the best of more modern novels. But they are all quite a distance this side perfection and less satisfactory, as wholes, than the best of the poems and *The Dynasts*, where one always finds a philosophy congruous with itself.

2

During the first fifty-five years of his life, Hardy was continually in search of philosophical congruity. Until he reached this age, his world view was in a process of such constant alteration that it would be difficult to say with precision what his essential philosophy was at any strictly delimited moment. But from that year onward—whether it was age or the satisfaction that comes once one has reconciled all discords that account for the constancy—his essential philosophy remained the same.

At bottom agnostic (for he could never elevate a hypothesis to the dignity of an absolute truth), nevertheless he held it highly probable that the primal "stuff" is Will, that the Will is unconscious, that the unconsciously produced by-product of the Will's operation, consciousness, may ultimately inform the whole until all things are fashioned more fairly. In his interpretation of life he introduced minor deviations from this central theory: in moods of despair he even goes so far as to deny the possibility of consciousness informing the Will. But if frequency of repetition is any criterion for the constancy of his belief, there were no fundamental variations from the philosophy he had accepted by 1895.

It must be admitted, however, that there are certain superficial indications that Hardy was inconsistent. Immediately setting aside such poems as "The Mother Mourns" and "The To-Be-Forgotten" as poetic metaphors Hardy did not intend to be judged by any canons more strict than those of the imagination, one still comes upon a number of passages in prose and verse that appear to contradict my contention that Hardy was fundamentally consistent. For the most part these passages follow the outbreak of World War I, which upset Hardy tremendously. Evidently he was beginning, in the years that preceded the war, to believe that consciousness already had informed the Will sufficiently to make such a catastrophe impossible. Because he believed "altruism . . . . will ultimately be brought about . . . . by the pain we see in others reacting on ourselves, as if we and they were a part of one body," he also hoped strongly that "The Sick Battle-God," "who rarely gladdens champions now," would die. "If I had been told three months ago," he wrote, reviewing his earlier feelings after the war had broken out, "that any inhabitants of Europe would wilfully damage such a masterpiece as Rheims in any circumstance whatever, I should have thought it an incredible statement."[2]

The war did not cause Hardy to alter permanently the shape of his philosophy, but it did produce *moods* in which he was more blankly pessimistic than he had ever been before. In August, 1914, he wrote Sir Sydney Cockerell: "As for myself the recognition that we are living in a more brutal age than that, say, of Elizabeth or of the chivalry which would cry: 'Gentlemen of the Guard, fire first' (far more brutal, indeed; no chivalry now) does not inspire one to write hopeful poetry, or even conjectural prose, but simply makes one sit still in an apathy, and watch the clock spinning backwards. . . . . " As late as 1925 he told Monsieur Lefèvre that he thought "we are entering on a dark age whose port of entry was the abominable war we have just lived through." At one time, at least, he became so despondent that he told the second Mrs. Hardy that the war had "led him to despair of the world's history," that it had "destroyed all [his] belief in the gradual ennoblement of man," that he "would probably not have ended *The Dynasts* as he [had] if he could have foreseen what was going to happen within a few years."[3]

Such passages as these, however, do not represent his reasoned conviction. Although the war increased both the frequency and the intensity of his recurrent moods of blank pessimism, he still maintained the probability of consciousness ultimately informing the Will. There is little difference between the following passages, despite the fact that the last two came after the outbreak of World War I:

That the Unconscious Will of the Universe is growing aware of Itself I believe I may claim as my own idea solely—at which I arrived by reflecting that what has already taken place in a fraction of the whole (i.e. so much of the world as has become conscious) is likely to take place in the mass [June 2, 1907].

I think the view of the unconscious force as gradually *becoming* conscious: i.e. that consciousness is creeping further and further back toward the origin of force, had never (so far as I know) been advanced before *The Dynasts* appeared [December 21, 1914].

> The Will speaking:
> "Though, viewing the world in *my* mode,
> I fail to see it in *thy* mode,
> As 'unfulfilled intention,'
> Which is past my comprehension
> Being unconscious in my doings
> So largely, (whence thy rueings);—
> Aye, to human tribes nor kindlessness
> Nor love I've given, but mindlessness,
> Which state, though far from ending,
> May nevertheless be mending."[4]
> [Written in 1920 and 1926.]

Hardy never renounced permanently his melioristic interpretation of the universe or the determinism, at once idealistic and evolutionary, he considered to be the most probable explanation of the universe.

3

It would be foolish, of course, to claim that all Hardy's poems are better than all Hardy's novels because, by the time he turned to poetry, he had arrived at a consistent philosophy that does little violence to the deepest insight of modern man. Many of the poems are altogether without the benefit of his philosophy: tedious journalistic pieces that reflect the blurred insight of England during the first World War; trivial retailings of incidents that have a significance too personal to be communicable. Many of the poems that are, directly or indirectly, philosophical, fail because, as Lascelles Abercrombie once said, there is a "lack of that wedding of form and sense which constitutes greatest poetry." The portions of "A Philosophical Fantasy" quoted at the end of the preceding section illustrate sufficiently Hardy's occasional inability to make form and content bed together happily.

Moreover, it would be equally foolish to claim that only those poems that are permeated by Hardy's conscious philosophy succeed. The charming little poem "Weathers" might have been written by any true poet of any philosophical school at any time:

> This is the weather the cuckoo likes,
>   And so do I;
> When showers betumble the chestnut spikes,
>   And nestlings fly:
> And the little brown nightingale bills his best,
> And they sit outside at "The Travellers' Rest,"
> And maids come forth sprig-muslin drest,
> And citizens dream of the south and west,
>   And so do I.

The same might be said of many of Hardy's best poems. "I Found Her Out There," which was written shortly after his first wife's death, could have been written by any poetic husband to his dead wife:

I found her out there
On a slope few see
That falls westwardly
To the salt-edged air,
Where the ocean breaks
On the purple strand,
And the hurricane shakes
The solid land.

I brought her here,
And have laid her to rest
In a noiseless nest
No sea beats near.
She will never be stirred
In her loamy cell
By the waves long heard
And loved so well.

There is a neutral region in poetry—of sensation, of love, and of death—that is affected greatly by the author's ability to communicate what he sees and feels beautifully, often not at all by his philosophy. And, however delightful it might be to explore such neutral territory, it is not the province of a critic who is writing of Hardy's philosophic thinking.

Those poems, however, which represent in poetic form Hardy's central philosophy do seem to me to be more successful wholes than any of the novels produced during the years in which Hardy groped for consistency. Where there is a marriage of form and sense, as in "To the Unknown God," one finds in Hardy a great philosophical poet:

Long have I framed weak phantasies of Thee,
    O Willer masked and dumb!
    Who makest Life become,—
As though by labouring all-unknowingly,
    Like one whom reveries numb.

How much of consicousness informs Thy will,
Thy biddings, as if blind,
Of death-inducing kind,
Nought shows to us ephemeral ones who fill
But moments in Thy mind.

Perhaps Thy ancient rote-restricted ways
Thy ripening rule transcends;
That listless effort tends
To grow percipient with advance of days,
And with percipience mends.

For, in unwonted purlieus, far and nigh,
At whiles or short or long,
May be discerned a wrong
Dying as of self-slaughter; whereat I
Would raise my voice in song.

Even here (and this is true of most of Hardy's best poems) the marriage is not absolute. If one must search for minor flaws, there is an awkwardness about the use of "kind" in the second stanza. But the imperfections of the poem do not appear unless one is straining to show himself a discerningly severe critic. What is most notable, and rightly so, is the compression of broad philosophic scope into an effective pattern. For it is the philosophy itself, ultimately, that makes this a great poem. Whether one is a dialectical materialist, a follower of Dewey or Whitehead, or a modern realist, the Weltanschauung here expressed approaches what we suspect to be the ultimate nature of reality sufficiently closely for us to suspend disbelief about any points of disagreement.

What applies to those poems in which Hardy compresses his central philosophy applies equally to other poems which are conditioned by his world view but do not express it completely. There is nothing, for example, in "The Darkling Thrush" with which any intelligent modern cannot poetically agree. Who is there, who has lived through two world wars and their awful consequence of years, who has not felt some barren landscape to be -

> The Century's corpse outleant,
> His crypt the cloudy canopy,
> The wind his death-lament?

Who has not, a little tremulously, seized upon some actual equivalent of the darkling thrush as a symbol of

> Some blessed Hope, whereof he knew
> And I was unaware?

Similarly, one might run through the gamut of Hardy's philosophic themes. One might greet such a poem as "The Man He Killed"—

> "Yes; quaint and curious war is!
> You shoot a fellow down
> You'd treat if met where any bar is,
> Or help to half-a-crown"—

with much the same rational emotion one feels after seeing the magnificent close of Renoir's recent cinema, *La grande illusion*, or Hardy's better-known "In Time of 'The Breaking of Nations.'" Of naming and quoting, always excluding the poems where form too obviously nullifies content and the poems in which the philosophy is caricatured beyond all possibility of rational acceptance, there might be a continuation far beyond the limits of this study. . . . . But it is to *The Dynasts*, finally, that one must turn as a testing ground for the value of Hardy's philosophy to Hardy's art.

4

So much has been written of *The Dynasts* (and so much of what has been written has been very good) that I do not propose to give Hardy's epic full treatment. It has been recognized by almost every commentator worth his critical salt to be among the greatest long poems of modern times. There have been excellent studies of its fidelity to its sources, of the accuracy of its historical characterizations, of the frequent magnificence of its description, of the machinery of Spirits that forms its superstructure, and of its basic philosophy. What I should like to do is to suggest how much its greatness owes to the consistency and relative accuracy of the philosophy it illustrates.

The philosophy, obviously enough, is the same that appears in the shorter philosophic poems, the same world view Hardy had arrived at in the year in which *Jude* was published. All of us, Napoleons or humble peasants, are parts of the anatomy of the mindlessly slumbering Immanent Will,

> Which thinking on, yet weighing not Its thought,
> Unchecks Its clock-like laws.

By these "clock-like laws" man and the universe have evolved to the point where man became conscious, to the point where the Unconscious Will compelled man to the catastrophe of the Napoleonic Wars. Even in these century-old times, however, this intolerable conflict is not seen as the best end to which the passage of time may lead. Early in the first part of the drama, the Spirit of Rumour predicts

> "There may react on things
> Some influence from these [who are conscious and men
>   of good will], indefinitely,
> And even on That, whose outcome we all are."

At significant points in the drama, notably at the end of the second part and at the conclusion, this logical hope is reiterated, as if it were an adjuration to the conscious reader to direct his part of the sum of forces toward the abolition of such monstrous conflicts:

> "Men gained cognition with the flux of time,
>   And wherefore not the Force informing them,
>   When far-ranged aions past all fathoming
>   Shall have swung by, and stand as backward years?"

The war itself is not presented mystically as an incomprehensible and eternally necessary product of the Will. The clocklike laws, which take us back to the years in which Hardy was studying the *Origin of Species*, are represented in a form comprehensible to the understanding. As the complex end product of the struggle for existence, the lust for empire, now still further complicated by a lust for gold, has come into being. So we have the Dynasts—Napoleon in France, Alexander in Russia, Francis in Austria, Pitt and his successors in England—carrying the laws of the jungle into international affairs. By economic and military means they contend for prizes they desire, in part for the economic supremacy that will accompany them, in part for the satisfaction that it gives their lust for power. Behind them and led by them are what Marx called the *Lumpenproletariat*, men and women in the mass who have neither power nor ill-will, intelligence nor overweening selfishness.

Such a portrayal of the Napoleonic Wars as this, presented almost invariably with an artistry that meets the demands of the difficult material with which it works, does not affront the modern intelligence. Even if one believes, with the dialectical materialist, that there is no immaterial force behind and controlling phenomena, the Immanent Will and its machinery fit Napoleonic times closely enough to win poetic faith. Even if one believes the basic cause of all historical phenomena is economic, he will find satisfaction in Hardy's persistent emphasis upon the importance of English gold, which is busy buying back Napoleon's confederates from Ulm to Waterloo. And the hater of war will have to look far and wide, farther even than *All Quiet on the Western Front*, before he finds a more quietly emphatic indictment of war than this typically Hardyan description of the field of Albuera: "Hot corpses, their mouths blackened by cartridge-biting, and surrounded by castaway knapsacks, firelocks, hats, stocks, flint-boxes, and priming-horns, together with red and blue rags of clothing, gaiters, epaulettes, limbs, and viscera, accumulate on the slopes, increasing from twos and threes to half-dozens, and from half-dozens to heaps, which steam with their own warmth as the spring rain falls gently upon them."

It may very well be that there will come a time when the more thinking among mankind, blessed almost beyond the limits of modern imagination with economic and political democracy, will look upon *The Dynasts* much as we look upon the *Iliad* and *Paradise Lost* today. Then, perhaps, they will admire *The Dynasts* as a magnificent proof of the powers of human imagination, as an epic whole that can be appreciated by a strenuous suspension of disbelief. It may even happen that it will be remembered, as we remember Keats's *Endymion*, mostly for separate lines—for the apt characterization of Mother Nature as "that lay shape we use to hang phenomena upon," for the epigrammatic succinctness of "Great men are meteors that consume themselves to light the earth"—as many people today remember the "rosy-fingered Dawn" and "darkness visible" better than the epics of Homer and Milton. But that day is yet some time removed from us. Men now read and admire *The Dynasts* because, with consummate art, it represents man's insight into his place in the universe as no other modern epic does; because it is the consummation of more than fifty years of honest and intelligent thought about the nature of the universal by a great thinker and poet.

5

Nevertheless, it would be foolish to think of Hardy's philosophy or *The Dynasts* as a stopping-place for modern man. It is Hardy's peculiar advantage over most nineteenth-century writers that he precapitulates—to a point—the history of most intelligent and sensitive men today. He started life a believer in divine Providence. He was disillusioned by scientific thought and the exigencies of a social world that seemed to reproduce the heartlessness of the struggle for existence one found below the level of human nature. By almost infinite striving, because of an unlimited capacity for honesty and a ceaseless hatred of those who mimicked Pangloss' attitude toward the Lisbon earthquakes, he arrived at a conception of the world which is, at any rate, the starting-point for most of those who have reached intellectual maturity in our day. Although most of us would not put as much emphasis upon the need for the agnostic and the supernaturalist to kneel in the same pew, there is little with which we should disagree in the fundamental thought of Hardy's "Apology":

What is to-day, in allusions to the present author's pages, alleged to be "pessimism" is, in truth, only such "[obstinate] questionings" in the exploration of reality, ... [as] is the first step towards the soul's betterment, and the body's also.

If I may be forgiven for quoting my own old words, let me repeat . . . .
    If way to the Better there be, it exacts a full look at the Worst:
that is to say, by the exploration of reality and its frank recognition stage by stage along the survey, with an eye to the best consummation possible: briefly, evolutionary meliorism. But it is called pessimism nevertheless; . . . . and the subject is charitably left to decent silence, as if further comment were needless.

Happily there are some who feel such Levitical passing-by to be, alas, by no means a permanent dismissal of the matter; that comment on where the world stands is very much the reverse of needless in these disordered years of our prematurely afflicted century: that amendment and not madness lies that way. And looking down the future these few hold fast to the same: that whether the human and kindred animal races survive till the exhaustion or destruction of the globe, or whether these races perish and are succeeded by others before that conclusion comes, pain to all upon it, tongued or dumb, shall be kept down to a minimum by loving-kindness, operating through scientific knowledge, and actuated by the modicum of free will conjecturally possessed by organic life when the mighty necessitating forces—unconscious or other—that have "the balancings of the clouds," happen to be in equilibrium, which may or may not be often.

Here most of us can find, if not a common faith, at least a common hope.

But Hardy also suffered from disadvantages which modern man does not have to face. Coming from a yeoman's family, socially isolated in an age when there were few social thinkers at once humane and practical, Hardy took fifty-five years to realize that the direction of the mass may be affected by the direction of a part of the mass. And, although this gave him a basis for hope reasonable enough to appeal to modern man, Hardy placed, as modern man need not, too much emphasis upon the single part and neglected the parts which are made up of combinations of men of good will. In all his novels, it is the single and unassisted individual who strives to bring about change: Clym preaching on Rainbarrow to lackadaisical peasants; Jude retailing the wisdom of a life unusually rich in experience to workingmen who are more certain that he is intoxicated than that his intoxication has released him from inhibitions and enabled him to speak wisely. A similar view of the course of human history appears in *The Dynasts*. History is not to Hardy, as it is to Tolstoy in *War and Peace*, a process whereby leaders draw sustenance from the mass. Rather it is the old Carlylean march of great men: Napoleon, Fox, Pitt, Wellington. People in the mass, people in groups, are the sort who stupidly tear up the famous paintings they find, who love drinking and carousing above all other pleasures in life.

This limitation upon Hardy's thought was, of course, partially justified by history itself. In the nineteenth century many of those who worked for social betterment worked alone, as both Hardy and his characters did; in the Napoleonic Wars the *Lumpenproletariat* was more evident than it is today, and it is still with us. If one remembers the lonely struggle of Shelley for social change (and recalls his final retirement to a Platonic universe); if one remembers Swinburne's failure to find allies in his effort to advance mild republicanism; if one recollects that even professed socialists such as Morris and Shaw were strongly individualistic in their approach to the problem of change, there is nothing remarkable about Hardy's failure to recognize the importance of group action. This limitation upon his thought was indigenous to his period. It is hardly generous to demand that one who transcended the limitation of his century in so much should have transcended it altogether.

And it is remarkable how much Hardy transcends his period, how relevant the art that represents his thought remains today. Hardy may have longed, like Keats, for a life of sensation rather than of thought, but he never sought refuge in a world of the senses. Though he became, like Shelley, an idealist, his idealism was patterned after the world as it exists, not after the world as he would have liked to have it. He never committed an Amelia Sedley or a Little Nell. He gave us a Tess instead of a Hetty Sorrel. And who would trade either *In Memoriam* or *The Ring and the Book*, good as they both are in a more limited way, for *The Dynasts?*

Hardy is not the greatest thinker of modern times or the greatest artist. But no man of letters of our period, with the exception of Thomas Mann, has so well combined the function of the thinker with the function of the artist. As a thinker, Hardy had a scrupulous regard for the philosopher's obligation to face both the pleasant and the unpleasant, a consciousness of the philosopher's duty to attempt coherence without excluding ideas that do not immediately fit into his established categories, and a breadth of vision that included as much of the configuration of the universe as the limitations of his time would allow. As an artist, he was equally scrupulous in his regard for accurate and vivid representation. What he saw he has made others see.

Among the many men of talent or genius still writing today there will be, one hopes, some who will transcend Hardy's representation, as they have already transcended his vision. Hardy was a man of sixty when the twentieth century began, and our century's emphasis upon the collective nature of the problems of the individual was alien to him. But if someone alive today writes an epic drama greater than *The Dynasts*, or a philosophical poem better than "Long Have I Framed Weak Fantasies of Thee," he will be greatly indebted to the philosophic structure Hardy has erected. Hardy hoped that he would have successors who would surpass both his philosophy and his artistry, for he wrote:

> Much is there waits you we have missed;
> Much lore we leave you worth the knowing,
> Much, much has lain outside our ken:
> Nay, rush not: time serves: we are going,
>> Gentlemen.

Notes

NOTES TO CHAPTER I

1. Arthur McDowall, *Thomas Hardy* (London, 1931), p. 18.

2. *Jude the Obscure* (New York: Book League of America, 1930), p. 400.

3. See Carl J. Weber, "Chronology in Hardy's Novels," *PMLA*, LIII (March, 1938), 319.

4. "In Tenebris," *Collected Poems of Thomas Hardy* (New York, 1931), p. 155; "I Was the Midmost," *ibid.*, p. 630.

5. "The Unborn," *ibid.*, p. 268. Similar views of childhood are expressed in "In a Waiting Room," "At the Entering of the New Year," "Yuletide in a Younger World," "Boys Then and Now" (*ibid.*, pp. 487, 605; *Winter Words* [New York, 1929], pp. 53, 107).

6. "To Outer Nature," *Collected Poems*, p. 54.

7. "Memory and I," *ibid.*, pp. 170–71. See also "He Revisits His First School," *ibid.*, p. 481.

8. Samuel Chew, *Thomas Hardy: Poet and Novelist* (rev. ed.; New York, 1928), p. 15.

9. F. A. Hedgcock, *Thomas Hardy: penseur et artiste* (University of Paris doctoral dissertation [Paris, (1911)]), pp. 26–27. See also Pierre d'Exideuil, *Le Couple humain dans l'œuvre de Thomas Hardy* (Paris, 1928), pp. 44–45; Louise de Ridder-Barzin, *Le Pesimisme de Thomas Hardy* ("Travaux de la Faculté de Philosophie et Lettres de l'Université de Bruxelles" [Bruxelles, 1932]), p. 7.

10. G. R. Elliot "Spectral Etchings in the Poetry of Thomas Hardy," *PMLA*, XLIII (1928), 1189.

11. My primary source is, of course, Florence E. Hardy, *The Early Life of Thomas Hardy* (New York, 1928) and *The Later Years of Thomas Hardy* (New York, 1930). Unless otherwise indicated, all the facts about Hardy's life come from either *Early Life* or *Later Years*. Exact sources of information are indicated only when it is a source other than the official biography or when the information appears in an unexpected position in Mrs. Hardy's volumes (i.e., when information about Hardy's youth appears in *Later Years*).

12. S. M. Ellis, "Thomas Hardy: Some Personal Recollections," *Fortnightly Review*, CXXIX (March, 1928), 396.

13. *Early Life*, p. 35.

14. *Ibid.*, p. 32.

15. Ellis, *op. cit.*, p. 400.

16. *Early Life*, p. 18.

17. *Ibid.*, p. 19.

18. *Later Years*, p. 263.

19. *Ibid.*, p. 93.

20. "To Outer Nature," *Collected Poems*, p. 54.

21. "In Tenebris," *ibid.*, p. 155. A similar attitude toward his mother is expressed in "The Roman Road" (*ibid.*, p. 248) and in "After the Last Breath" (*ibid.*, p. 253).

22. His reverence for his father, to whom he addressed but one poem—"To My Father's Violin" (*ibid.*, p. 423)—is evidenced by the fact that he went to see him nearly every Sunday as long as he lived (*Later Years*, p. 261).

23. "Midnight on Beechen, 187–," *Collected Poems*, p. 735.

24. *Early Life*, p. 5.

25. *Ibid.*, p. 27.

26. Hedgcock, *op. cit.*, p. 3.

27. *Early Life*, p. 9.

28. Ellis, *op. cit.*, p. 395.

29. Ernest Brennecke, *The Life of Thomas Hardy* (New York, 1925), p. 77.

30. *Tess of the D'Urbervilles: A Pure Woman* ("Harper's Modern Classics" [New York and London, 1920]), p. 133.

31. *Under the Greenwood Tree* ("Anniversary Edition," Vol. VII [New York, 1920]), p. 193.

32. "Domicilium," *Early Life*, pp. 4–5.

33. C. G. Harper, *The Hardy Country* (3d ed.; London, 1925), p. v.

34. *Desperate Remedies* ("Anniversary Edition," Vol. XIV [New York, 1920]).

35. Ruth M. Firor, *Folkways in Thomas Hardy* (Philadelphia, 1931), p. 305.

36. W. R. Rutland, *Thomas Hardy: A Study of His Writings and Their Background* (Oxford, 1938), pp. 8–9.

37. Brennecke, *op. cit.*, p. 78.

38. Ridder-Barzin, *op. cit.*, pp. 175–76.

39. Madeleine L. Cazamian, *Le Roman et les idées en Angleterre* ("Publications de la Faculté des Lettres de l'Université de Strasbourg" [Strasbourg, 1923]), pp. 19–24.

40. John Hunt, *Religious Thought in England in the Nineteenth Century* (London, 1896), *passim*.

41. Clement Webb, *A Study of Religious Thought in England from 1850* (Oxford, 1933), p. 9.

42. Hugh Walker, *The Literature of the Victorian Era* (Cambridge [England], 1921), p. 82.

43. Hunt, *op. cit.*, p. 333.

44. J. H. Newman, *Apologia pro vita sua* ("Everyman's Library" [London, 1927]), p. 64.

45. *Ibid.*, p. 109.

46. Quoted from a letter to his mother by George Saintsbury in *A Consideration of Thackeray* (London, n.d.), p. 168.

47. In *Old Curiosity Shop* (New York: American Book Co., n.d.), p. 534.

48. "The Two Voices," *Poems of Tennyson* ("Oxford Poets" [London, 1926]), p. 191.

49. Walker, *op. cit.*, p. 81.

50. *Ibid.*

51. *Ibid.*

52. *Dorset County Chronicle*, March 12, 1840.

53. *Ibid.*

54. *Ibid.*, July 30, 1840.

55. *The Victoria History of the County of Dorset*, ed. William Page (2 vols.; London, 1908), II, 43–44.

56. *Dorset County Chronicle*, February 13, 1840.

57. *Ibid.*, July 26, 1855.

58. *Early Life*, p. 15.

59. If he had, he surely would have been able to have helped Hardy better in his controversy over pedobaptism (see *Early Life*, p. 38).

60. *Collected Poems*, p. 309.

61. *Ibid.*, p. 60. Regret for a lost faith is also expressed in the poems found on pp. 413, 490, 565, 680, 689, and 439. Even in *The Dynasts* (London, 1921) (p. 306) and in his prose "Apology," *Collected Poems* (p. 531), this regret is to be found.

62. *Later Years*, p. 225. (My italics.)

63. *Ibid.*, p. 176. (My italics.)

64. *Collected Poems*, p. 254.

65. *Ibid.*, p. 268. A similar view of childhood is expressed in "In a Waiting Room," "At the Entering of the New Year," "Yuletide in a Younger World," and "Boys Then and Now" (*ibid.*, pp. 487, 605; *Winter Words*, pp. 53, 107).

66. "In Tenebris," *Collected Poems*, p. 155.

67. "I Was the Midmost," *ibid.*, p. 630.

68. "Memory and I," *ibid.*, pp. 170–71. See also "He Revisits His First School," *ibid.*, p. 481.

69. *Tess*, p. 155.

70. *Op. cit.*, p. 1189.

71. "Barrie Reviews Hardy," *Literary Digest*, C (February 2, 1929), 22.

72. See Rutland, *op. cit.*, pp. 14–15, for evidence of this.

73. *The "Iliad" of Homer*, trans. Andrew Lang, etc. (New York, 1915), Book xxiv, ll. 23–24, p. 494.

74. This list is to be found in Hardy's copy of Samuel Clarke's edition of the *Iliad*. Hardy purchased the edition in 1858 and abandoned study in it in 1860, according to Rutland (*op. cit.*, pp. 21–22).

75. *A Laodicean* "(Anniversary Edition," Vol. XVI [New York, 1920]), p. 240.

76. *Tess*, p. 312; in *An Indiscretion in the Life of an Heiress*, ed. Carl J. Weber (Baltimore, 1935); *A Pair of Blue Eyes* ("Anniversary Edition," Vol. X [New York, 1920]).

77. Springrove senior makes this comment to his son (*Desperate Remedies*, p. 147). The search for the ideal in things in general is not uncommon in the novels. Somerset (*A Laodicean*, p. 6) and Clym Yeobright (*The Return of the Native* ["Modern Student's Library" (New York, Chicago, Boston, 1917)], p. 241) are good examples of this tendency.

78. "Midnight on Beechen, 187–," *Collected Poems*, p. 736; "The Minute before Meeting," *ibid*., p. 219; "A Confession to a Friend in Trouble," *ibid*., p. 9; "Love the Monopolist," *ibid*., p. 450.

79. This idea is notably expressed in Hardy's journal for 1881 and 1883 (see *Early Life*, pp. 192, 213).

NOTES TO CHAPTER II

1. Henry H. Milman, *The History of Christianity under the Empire* (1840).

2. Connop Thirlwall's translations of Schleiermacher's *A Critical Essay on the Gospel of St. Luke* and Niebuhr's *History of Rome* in 1825 and 1828–32, respectively.

3. James Martineau's position approached very closely that of Feuerbach and Strauss: "What is properly Revelation is God's work in nature and humanity, and it is carried on in a way that is natural and human" (quoted in John Hunt, *Religious Thought in England in the Nineteenth Century* [London, 1896], p. 250).

4. George Eliot translated Strauss's *Life of Jesus* in 1846.

5. Notably in *Empedocles: The Poems of Matthew Arnold*, ed. Sir A. T. Quiller-Couch ("The World's Classics" [Oxford, 1926]), pp. 88–98. As Benn points out, these views are not dramatically or historically appropriate to Empedocles (A. W. Benn, *The History of English Rationalism in the Nineteenth Century* [2 vols.; London, 1906], II, 52).

6. In addition to the *Biographical History*, significantly subtitled *A History of Philosophy from Thales to Auguste Comte* in its third edition, Lewes published in 1853 *Comte's Philosophy of the Positive Sciences*.

7. The *Westminster Review* reviewed George Eliot's translation of Strauss sympathetically in April, 1847; defended Chambers' *Vestiges of Creation* in October, 1847; published the first English review of Schopenhauer in April, 1853; and frequently defended Comte (notably in the issues for July, 1854, and April, 1858).

8. See especially "The Development Hypothesis," *The Leader*, March 20, 1852.

9. Robert Chambers, *Vestiges of Creation* (1844).

10. *Saturday Review*, VIII (December 24, 1859), 775.

11. In *Man's Place in Nature and Other Essays* ("Everyman's Library" [London, 1933]), p. 350. Reprinted from the London *Times* of December 26, 1859.

12. *British Quarterly*, XXXI (April, 1860), 399.

13. *Edinburgh Review*, CXI (April, 1860), 251–75.

14. *Westminster Review*, LXXIII, 295.

15. *Saturday Review*, IX (May 5, 1860), 573.

16. C. Henshaw Ward, *Charles Darwin* (Indianapolis, 1927), pp. 313–15.

17. *Quarterly Review*, CVIII, 134–35.

18. *Blackwood's Magazine*, LXXXIX, 165–83, 614–17.

19. *Saturday Review*, XI, 632.

20. *Origin of Species*, p. 1.

21. *Saturday Review*, XIV, 486.

22. Edward Clodd, *Thomas Henry Huxley* ("Modern English Writers Series" [Edinburgh and London, 1905]), p. 112.

23. Sir Charles Lyell, *The Geological Evidence of the Antiquity of Man* ("Everyman's Library" [London, 1914]), pp. 389–94.

24. *Saturday Review*, XVI (November 14, 1864), 636. The first article is a review of Lyell's *Antiquity of Man*: XV (March 7), 311–12. The second article is "Men and Brutes": XVI (November 7), 606–7.

25. *Origin of Species*, p. xiv.

26. Ward, *op. cit.*, chap. xii, *passim*.

27. Evelyn Abbott and Lewis Campbell, *Life and Letters of Benjamin Jowett* (2 vols.; London, 1897), I, 291.

28. *Westminster Review*, LXXXIV, 177.

29. *Quarterly Review*, CIX, 150–51.

30. *Edinburgh Review*, CXIII (April, 1861), 235–36. The *Saturday Review* was perhaps the most frequent recorder of the progress of the case for and against the Essayists (see XI, 113–15, 211, 233–34, 285, 439–40).

31. Advertisement in *Saturday Review*, XI (March 23, 1861), end pages.

32. *Ibid.*, p. 285.

33. Abbott and Campbell, *op. cit.*, I, 292–93.

34. "A Clerical Strike," *Saturday Review*, XVI (December 5, 1863), 725.

35. *Fraser's Magazine*, LXII (1860), 242.

36. *Man's Place in Nature*, p. 103.

37. As reported by a letter of John Addington Symonds of February 4, 1861, in Horatio Brown, *John Addington Symonds: A Biography* (London, 1903), p. 90.

38. *Ibid.*, pp. 86–90.

39. *Letters of John Richard Green*, ed. Leslie Stephen (London, 1901), p. 17.

40. Richard Jefferies, *The Story of My Heart* (London, 1883), pp. 59–60.

41. Ward, *op. cit.*, p. 304.

42. *Chambers' Journal*, XLII (March 18, 1865), 161–64.

43. *Quarterly Review*, CIX, 150–51.

44. Moule's *Christian Oratory: An Inquiry into Its History during the First Five Christian Centuries* (London and Cambridge, 1859) was lengthily discussed in the *Saturday Review*, VIII (September 10, 1859), 316–18. According to Mrs. Hardy, Moule was just starting as a reviewer when he first met Hardy (*Early Life*, p. 43). As he was certainly writing for the *Saturday Review* later (*Early Life*, p. 120), and as his own book received such rapid and flattering attention in its columns, I assume that he was writing for the *Saturday* from the start.

45. References to Gibbon appear on pp. 3, 42, 79, etc.; to Niebuhr on pp. 19, 194, 197; to Bunsen (extensively) on p. 40; to Milman on pp. 4, 14, 19, etc.; to Grote on pp. 9, 184, 192.

46. See esp. pp. 41, 191, 205.

47. Hardy read the book before he went up to London. Moule is the only friend of Hardy who would have been likely to recommend the book to him. *Early Life* (p. 43) states that Moule introduced *Essays and Reviews* to Hardy.

48. Frederick Temple, "The Education of the World," in *Essays and Reviews*, ed. Frederick H. Hedges (American ed. from the second London impression; Boston, 1862), pp. 22, 50. (My italics.)

49. Rowland Williams, "Bunsen's Biblical Researches," in *Essays and Reviews*, pp. 87, 103.

50. H. B. Wilson, "Séances historique de Genève—the National Church," in *Essays and Reviews*, pp. 169, 182–83, 172, 226, 224–25. Here is perhaps the first germ of a proposal Hardy himself made in the twentieth century with no more success.

51. C. W. Goodwin, "The Mosaic Cosmogony," in *Essays and Reviews*, p. 271.

52. Baden Powell, "Evidences of Christianity," in *Essays and Reviews*, pp. 160, 157.

53. *Origin of Species*, p. 458.

54. *Ibid.*, pp. 76–77, 67.

55. *Ibid.*, p. 84. Darwin italicizes the words "whenever and wherever opportunity offers." The other italicizing is mine.

56. *Ibid.*, p. 185.

57. *Ibid.*, p. 455.

58. *A Pair of Blue Eyes*, p. 243.

59. Vere H. Collins, *Talks with Thomas Hardy at Max Gate: 1920–1922* (London, 1928), p. 37.

60. R. H. Goodale, "Schopenhauer and Pessimism in Nineteenth Century English Literature," *PMLA*, XLVII, 260–61.

61. *Early Life*, pp. 198, 43.

62. Sir George Douglas, "Thomas Hardy," *Hibbert Journal*, XXVI (April, 1928), 387.

63. *Later Years*, pp. 118–19.

64. J. S. Mill, *On Liberty, Etc.* ("The World's Classics" [London, 1924]), p. 43.

65. W. R. Rutland, *Thomas Hardy: A Study of His Writings and Their Background* (Oxford, 1938), pp. 56–64.

66. The first evidence we have of Hardy's assimilation of Spencer's thought occurs in a note of 1888 (*Early Life*, p. 269).

67. *Two on a Tower* ("Anniversary Edition," Vol. XII [New York, 1920]), p. vii.

68. Henry Moule, *Good Out of Evil* (London, 1863).

69. *Saturday Review*, Vols. XV–XVI, *passim*. Reviews of Renan's work appeared in *ibid.*, VII (September 3, 1859), 282–83, and *ibid.*, X (November 3, 1860), 549–50.

70. Quoted in *ibid.*, XVI (December 12, 1863), 750.

71. Schopenhauer is mentioned in *ibid.*: XIII, 310; XIV, 146; XVI, 323–25.

72. Of the other books mentioned by Mrs. Florence Hardy, Walter Bagehot's *Estimates* (later included in *Literary Studies*, ed. R. H. Hutton [2 vols.; London, 1891]) may have had an influence upon him. Bagehot's essay on Gibbon, combined with Moule's conversation, may have caused Hardy to read the *Decline and Fall*. (His reading of the fifteenth chapter may have still further in-

clined him to discard Christianity. It seems to me, however, that a definite claim that Gibbon influenced Hardy's anticlericalism, such as is made by Pierre d'Exideuil [*Le Couple humain dans l'œuvre de Thomas Hardy* (Paris, 1928), p. 45], is unjustified by available evidence.) Likewise, Bagehot's essay on Bishop Butler suggests the insensibility of Nature to our human difficulties and the hopelessness of man's state if Revelation is not believed (*Literary Studies*, II, 88). In this same essay Bagehot declares: "The condition of men here does seem to be in a considerable measure the result not of what they do, or of what their characters are, but of the mere circumstances in which they are placed, over which they have no control, choice, or power" (*ibid.*, p. 92). The essay as a whole, and this passage in particular, reminds us of Hardy's later interpretation of Nature and suggests that the reading of Bagehot *may* have influenced the development of this point of view. There can be no doubt that Hardy's later reading of Sophocles confirmed his own view of existence. But, inasmuch as Hardy, in his most formative years, gave up Sophocles and Aeschylus before he had done more than start the *Agamemnon* and *Oedipus Rex*, there seems to be insufficient reason for finding the Greek dramatists a substantial influence upon his thinking. The only contemporary poets who might have influenced the direction of Hardy's thought are Swinburne, Clough, and Arnold. (As we have already seen, Hardy always read much of his near-contemporary Shelley, but there seems to me inadequate reason to suppose his influence was substantial. Most of Hardy's allusions to Shelley are either to the unhappiness of his life— where he perhaps saw a parallel to his own—or to the poems written in a dejected mood. These stanzas written in dejection undoubtedly had a peculiar appeal for Hardy because he, too, often had such moods. But that is altogether different from saying that Shelley helped shape the form or content of Hardy's thought.) Hardy did not read Swinburne until the publication of the first series of *Poems and Ballads* in 1866. Hardy's writings do not contain a single allusion to Clough, and there are no references in his work to the *poetry* of Arnold. Ruskin's *Modern Painters* and Newman's *Apologia*, if they had an influence, would have counteracted the intellectual forces that finally prevailed in his thought. The scanty religion which Trollope attributes to the highest dignitaries in *Barchester Towers* may have further disposed Hardy against modern Christianity. That some of Thackeray's satirical portraits may have contributed to Hardy's disillusion, and consequently to his eventually gloomy view of life, is suggested by his remark on Thackeray in 1863: "Because his novels stand so high as works of Art or Truth, they often have anything but an elevating tendency . . . . " (*Early Life*, p. 53). Bulwer-Lytton's occasional cynicism in *Pelham* and Byron's frequent cynicism in *Childe Harold* may have increased his disillusionment similarly.

73. *Early Life*, p. 66.

74. *Collected Poems*, p. 7.

75. D'Exideuil (*op. cit.*, pp. 44–45), who believes Hardy to have lost his faith about 1860; Hedgcock (*Thomas Hardy: penseur et artiste* [Paris, 1911]), who puts the date between 1860 and 1870; and Lionel Stevenson (*Darwin among the Poets* [Chicago, 1932], pp. 238–39), who rightly states that Hardy first definitely broke with Christianity in 1865—all believe that *Essays and Reviews* had an important destructive effect upon Hardy's religious convictions.

76. D'Exideuil, Hedgcock, and Stevenson all agree that Darwin's influence upon Hardy's philosophy was important. D'Exideuil believes that Hardy's learning of the struggle for existence in Darwin and his personal contact with this struggle account for the novelist's early pessimism (*op. cit.*, pp. 47, 49–50, 67). He also conjectures that the works of Arnold, Thomson, Clough, Fitzgerald, Le Lisle, and Baudelaire may have had an effect upon Hardy's philosophy (*ibid.*, p. 48). All the evidence points against this last conjecture. Hedgcock attributes Hardy's early pessimism to *Essays and Reviews*, the *Origin of Species*, and the general spirit of the time (*op. cit.*, pp. 20–25). Stevenson adds Hardy's temperamental tendency toward despondency to the factors Hedgcock suggests (*op. cit.*, pp. 238–39, 244). I do not believe that Stevenson has sufficient reason for this assumption, as I have shown already.

77. *Early Life*, pp. 65, 63–64.

78. *Ibid.*, p. 63.

NOTES TO CHAPTER III

1. William Whewell, *History of the Inductive Sciences* (2 vols.; New York, 1858), I, 41.

2. The title of his survey of the development of nineteenth-century science (Alfred Russell Wallace, *The Wonderful Century* [New York, 1898]).

3. A. K. Rogers, *English and American Philosophy since 1800* (New York, 1922), pp. 113–14.

4. Hardy's first poem is obviously an imitation of Wordsworth's style (see "Domicilium"); Wordsworth's "Resolution and Independence" is one of the cures for despair Hardy listed in the 1860's.

5. *Early Life*, p. 76.

6. J. S. Mill, *On Liberty, etc.* (1859), p. 73.

7. Frederick Harrison, *The Philosophy of Common Sense* (New York, 1907), pp. 59–60.

8. The first phrase is Benjamin Constant's (quoted in George Brandes, *Main Currents in Nineteenth Century Literature* [6 vols.; London, 1901], I, 65). The second quotation is from Byron, "Cain: A Mystery," *The Poetical Works of Lord Byron* ("The Oxford Poets" [London, 1923]), p. 514.

9. *Early Life*, p. 63.

10. *The Letters of Alexander Macmillan*, ed. George A. Macmillan (Glasgow, 1908), pp. 245–47.

11. "Rebecca West Proves a Beatitude," *Literary Digest*, CVIII (February 21, 1931), 18.

12. Granville Hicks, "Was Thomas Hardy a Pessimist?" *Educational Forum*, II, 64.

13. *Early Life*, pp. 65, 63.

14. *Collected Poems*, p. 9.

15. "San Sebastian," *ibid.*, p. 17; "The Memorial Brass," *ibid.*, pp. 474–75.

16. *Ibid.*, pp. 6, 8, 11–13, 10–11, 11.

17. *Ibid.*, pp. 598–602.

18. *Ibid.*, pp. 188–91.

19. *Early Life*, pp. 78–79.

20. *Ibid.*, pp. 81–82; *The Letters of Alexander Macmillan*, p. 245.

21. "A Singer Asleep," *Collected Poems*, p. 304.

22. W. R. Rutland, *Thomas Hardy: A Study of His Writings and Their Background* (Oxford, 1938), p. 73.

23. *Selections from Swinburne*, ed. William Raymond (New York, 1925), pp. 58–59.

24. *Atalanta in Calydon* (London, 1896), p. 48.

25. *Early Life*, p. 73.

26. *Collected Poems*, p. 281.

27. *Early Life*, p. 73.

28. *Collected Poems*, pp. 67–68; 569.

29. *Early Life*, p. 79.

30. *Jude*, p. ii.

31. *Collected Poems*, p. 75.

32. Of those who deal with Thomas Hardy's early philosophy, the briefest but most accurate account comes from Samuel Chew, who considers "Heiress and Architect" symbolic of the young man's outlook: "The heiress being a representative of humanity, full of hopes and ideals, and confronted by the architect, [an archdesigner,] who typifies the rigor and indifference of the universe" (*Thomas Hardy: Poet and Novelist* [rev. ed.; New York, 1928], pp. 16–17).

33. *The Dynasts*, I, 100.

34. *Collected Poems*, pp. 8, 12, 68–70, 13–14.

35. Journal note for May 9, 1881 (*Early Life*, p. 192).

36. "A Confession to a Friend in Trouble" (1866), "From Her in the Country" (1866), "Dream of the City Shopwoman" (1866), "Heiress and Architect" (1867), "To an Actress" (1867), *Collected Poems*, pp. 9, 217, 576–77, 67–68, 219.

37. *Ibid.*, p. 577.

38. *Ibid.*, p. 6.

39. "At a Bridal" (1866), *ibid.*, p. 8. This poem is significantly subtitled "Nature's Indifference."

40. "The Two Men," *ibid.*, pp. 68–70.

41. *Origin of Species*, p. 87.

42. *Collected Poems*, pp. 6, 10–11, 11–12, 214. As Hardy himself admitted, the lines "That which makes man's love the lighter and woman's love no brighter" refers to the decrease of love subsequent to intercourse (Vere H. Collins, *Talks with Thomas Hardy at Max Gate: 1920–1922* [London, 1928], p. 23).

43. *Collected Poems*, pp. 16, 10, 208–9, 214.

44. *Ibid.*, pp. 9, 11–13.

45. *Ibid.*, pp. 8, 759–60.

46. "At Waking" (1869), *ibid.*, p. 209.

47. Pierre d'Exideuil, *Le Couple humain dans l'œuvre de Thomas Hardy* (Paris, 1928), pp. 102–4.

48. *Collected Poems*, pp. 68–70, 63–66, 13–14.

49. *Early Life*, p. 73.

50. *Collected Poems*, p. 204.

51. "Her Dilemma," "To an Actress," "To an Impersonator of Rosalind," *ibid.*, pp. 10–11, 218, 219. See, in addition to "Ditty" (1870), "Poems of 1912–1913" in *Satires of Circumstance*.

52. The two critics differ only on matters of minor detail.

53. *Early Life*, p. 81.

54. G. M. Young, *Victorian England* (London, 1937), pp. 169–70.

55. Rutland, *op. cit.*, pp. 117–20.

56. A. L. Morton, *A People's History of England* (London, 1937), pp. 395–406.

57. "A Song in Time of Revolution," in Raymond, *op. cit.*, p. 93.

58. Particularly Alexander Macmillan and Meredith (see the account of their reactions in *Early Life*, chap. iv).

NOTES TO CHAPTER IV

1. *A Pair of Blue Eyes*, p. viii.

2. "The poem entitled 'At the Word "Farewell," ' seems to refer either to this or the following visit" (*Early Life*, p. 99).

3. "At the Word 'Farewell,' " *Collected Poems*, pp. 405–6.

4. "When I Set Out for Lyonnesse," *ibid.*, p. 294. " 'When I set out for Lyonnesse' refers certainly to this first visit" (*Early Life*, p. 99).

5. *Early Life*, p. 90.

6. *Ibid.*, p. 91.

7. *Ibid.*, p. 96.

8. *Ibid.*, p. 156.

9. "Midnight on Beechen, 187–," *Collected Poems*, p. 736.

10. "Revulsion," *ibid.*, p. 11.

11. *Early Life*, pp. 129–31. There were two exceptions: *Nation* (New York), XIX (December 24, 1874), 423–24, and *The Athenaeum*, No. 2458 (December 5, 1874), pp. 747–48.

12. Coventry Patmore (*Early Life*, p. 138); Mrs. Proctor (*ibid.*, p. 132).

13. *Ibid.*, p. 127.

14. *Far from the Madding Crowd* ("Harper's Modern Classics" [New York and London, 1918]), p. 9.

15. *Early Life*, p. 161.

16. *The Return of the Native*, p. 169. The novel was appearing serially in *Belgravia* during the year (1878) in which the incident occurred (see A. F. Webb, *A Bibliography of Thomas Hardy* [London, 1916], p. 57).

17. This quotation from Keats appears on the title-page of *The Return of the Native*.

18. F. A. Hedgcock, *Thomas Hardy: penseur et artiste* (Paris, 1911), pp. 392, 397–98, 483–84.

19. Vere H. Collins, *Talks with Thomas Hardy at Max Gate: 1920–1922* [London, 1928], p. 74.

20. Hedgcock, *op. cit.*, p. 364.

21. *Early Life*, p. 149.

22. *Ibid.*, p. 148.

23. "In Tenebris" (1896), *Collected Poems*, p. 154.

24. Journal entry for November 28, 1878 (*Early Life*, p. 162).

25. *The Return of the Native*, p. 5.

26. *Journal of Anthropology*, I, 312–32; *Contemporary Review*, XVIII, 67–86; four other essays: *Contemporary Review*, XIX (May, 1872), 775–88; *ibid.*, XXI (February, 1873), 440–63; *Journal of Speculative Philosophy*, IX (1875), 113–38; *Westminster Review*, CV (April, 1876), 246 ff.

27. Hedgcock, *op. cit.*, p. 499.

28. W. R. Rutland, *Thomas Hardy: A Study of His Writings and Their Background* (Oxford, 1928), pp. 56–58, 67–70.

29. *Early Life*, p. 132.

30. Leslie Stephen, *An Agnostic's Apology, and Other Essays* (London, 1893), pp. 28–29; *The Science of Ethics* (London, 1882), pp. 123–31, 42–58, 444–47.

31. *The Science of Ethics*, pp. 9–10. I assume that the ideas in this book came up in conversation during this period.

32. E.g., *Desperate Remedies*, pp. 7, 11, 27, 270; *A Pair of Blue Eyes*, pp. 237, 241–42; *The Hand of Ethelberta* ("Anniversary Edition," Vol. XV (New York, 1920]), p. 254; journal entry of 1876 (*Early Life*, pp. 146–47); *The Return of the Native*, p. 9.

33. *A Pair of Blue Eyes*, p. 243.

34. *The Return of the Native*, p. 169.

35. Joseph Warren Beach, *The Technique of Thomas Hardy* (Chicago, 1922), p. 23.

36. Cytherea Graye remarks that, when three coincidences fall together, it appears that there are "invisible means at work" (*Desperate Remedies*, pp. 168–69).

37. God will soon be abolished (*ibid.*, p. 358); children to another (*ibid.*, p. 273); similar heterodox statements (ibid., pp. 68, 175); ". . . . bide where we be" (*ibid.*, pp. 430–31).

38. Search for his "alter ego" (*ibid.*, pp. 200–201); perfection when there isn't any (*ibid.*, p. 147); later becomes disillusioned (*ibid.*, p. 25).

39. *Ibid.*, pp. 163, 166.

40. "In his power" (*ibid.*, pp. 154, 155, 161, 234); "natural selection" (*ibid.*, p. 182); physical attractiveness of Springrove (*ibid.*, pp. 23–25, 130, 159).

41. *Ibid.*, p. vii.

42. Perhaps the visit to Elizabeth the witch should be excepted. The witch, however, turns out to be only a woman with unusual common sense.

43. There is no suggestion of other than physical qualities which accounts for these loves (see *Under the Greenwood Tree*, pp. 18–21, 29–35, 53–54, 135, 183–84, 187).

44. ". . . . Once more a free man" (*ibid.*, p. 151); ". . . . dying for thee just the same" (*ibid.*, pp. 115–16).

45. *Ibid.*, p. 61.

46. *Ibid.*, p. x.

47. *A Pair of Blue Eyes*, pp. 8, 25.

48. Inevitably disappointed (*ibid.*, pp. 227–28); love with Elfride (*ibid.*, p. 56); to the workhouse (*ibid.*, p. 209); suit his happiness (*ibid.*, p. 64); whomever he may love (*ibid.*, pp. 213, 361); physical attractiveness (*ibid.*, pp. 179, 249);

incarnate in Elfride (*ibid.*, p. 380); Smith (*ibid.*, pp. 146–47; hurrying world) (*ibid.*, p. 207); ". . . . frail casket of a body "(*ibid.*, p. 299).

49. Greater masculinity (*ibid.*, pp. 299, 300, 315); Hardy tells us (*ibid.*, p. 216).

50. *Ibid.*, pp. 146–47, 177, 430.

51. See *ibid.*, esp. p. 160.

52. Preoccupation with abstractions (*ibid.*, p. 390); suspicious in love (*ibid.*, p. 382); ". . . . true in heart" (*ibid.*, p. 430).

53. *Ibid.*, p. viii.

54. Beginning of love (*Far from the Madding Crowd*, pp. 18, 19, 30, 112–13, 202, 245); subject men to her (*ibid.*, pp. 26, 33); physical force (*ibid.*, p. 188).

55. *Ibid.*, p. 148.

56. *Ibid.*, p. 198.

57. *Ibid.*, pp. 456–57.

58. *Ibid.*, p. 295.

59. *The Hand of Ethelberta*, p. vii.

60. *Ibid.*, pp. 391, 132, 131.

61. *Ibid.*, pp. 224, 188.

62. *Ibid.*, pp. 364, 215, 191, 110–11, 184, 102.

63. Half-knowledge of a life misjudges (*ibid.*, p. 11); useless aristocracy (*ibid.*, p. 224); ". . . . congenial regard" (*ibid.*, p. viii).

64. *Early Life*, pp. 142–43.

65. *The Return of the Native*, pp. 4–5, 279.

66. *Ibid.*, pp. 169, 219.

67. *Ibid.*, p. 260.

68. *Ibid.*, pp. 119, 125, 198–99, 51, 62, 64–65, 202.

69. *Ibid.*, pp. 70, 67, 69, 132, 284, 359, 344.

70. *Ibid.*, pp. 190–91, 208, 241, 138–39, 382, 386–87.

71. *Ibid.*, pp. 257, 174–75, 204, 398, 411–12.

72. *Ibid.*, p. 81.

73. Journal note in 1877 (*Early Life*, p. 153); *The Return of the Native*, p. 53.

74. By spells, in "The Withered Arm," *Wessex Tales*; wax images, *The Return of the Native*; interested in such occurrences, *Early Life*, pp. 140, 147, 148, 165, 220; a realm above law, Archer, *Real Conversations* (London, 1904), p. 45.

75. ". . . . of secondary importance" (*Desperate Remedies*, p. 109); ". . . . no more tantalizing is possible" (*A Pair of Blue Eyes*, p. 245).

76. *A Pair of Blue Eyes*, pp. 64, 349; journal entry for 1877 (*Early Life*, p. 150).

77. Sexual character of love (*A Pair of Blue Eyes*, p. 249; *The Return of the Native*, p. 241; *Early Life*, p. 151); "atoms of sex" (*Desperate Remedies*, p. 137) "more powerful than she" (*A Pair of Blue Eyes*, p. 215); "love of the eye" (*Desperate Remedies*, p. 2); "lacks a sound basis" (*ibid.*, pp. 2, 43).

78. ". . . . An actual weakness" (*Far from the Madding Crowd*, p. 27); to make it permanent (*ibid.*, p. 5); to get over love (*ibid.*, p. 37); early marriage only (*The Hand of Ethelberta*, p. 417).

79. Reason is obscured by passion (*A Pair of Blue Eyes*, p. 316); conflict with the emotions (*ibid.*, p. 213); whirls away the reason (*Desperate Remedies*, p. 105); like Boldwood (*Far from the Madding Crowd*, p. 134); when they are disenchanted—even Eustacia (*The Return of the Native*, p. 102).

80. "Her Dilemma," *Collected Poems*, pp. 10–11.

81. Two of his journal notes imply such a faith (*Early Life*, pp. 146, 150–51).

82. *A Pair of Blue Eyes*, pp. 96, 141; *The Hand of Ethelberta*, pp. 22–23, 197.

83. *A Pair of Blue Eyes*, p. 102; *The Hand of Ethelberta*, pp. 1, 2, 121, 183, 211, 224, 424–25.

NOTES TO CHAPTER V

1. *Early Life*, p. 163.

2. T. P. O'Connor, "Thomas Hardy as I Knew Him," *Living Age*, CCCXXXIV (March 1, 1928), 457.

3. Ford Madox Ford, "Thomas Hardy," *American Mercury*, XXXVIII (August, 1936), 440.

4. T. P. O'Connor, quoted by Gertrude Atherton in *Adventures of a Novelist* (New York, 1932), p. 263.

5. Madeleine L. Cazamian, *Le Roman et les idées en Angleterre* ("Publications de la Faculté des Lettres de l'Université de Strasbourg" [Strasbourg, 1923]), p. 252.

6. R. H. Goodale, "Schopenhauer and Pessimism in the Nineteenth Century," *PMLA*, XLVII, 242.

7. Notably J. W. Barlow, *The Ultimatum of Pessimism* (1882); T. B. Kilpatrick, *Pessimism and the Religious Conscience* (1883); J. R. Thomson, *Modern Pessimism* (1885); C. Williams, *Modern Pessimism, Its Cause and Its Cure* (1885). Cf. W. H. Mallock, *Atheism and the Value of Life* (1879); to which there were numerous replies; E. B. Darling, *The Value of This Earthly Life;* Anon., *The Value of Life.* Two articles by L. S. Bevington on "Modern Atheism and Mr. Mallock" appeared in the *Nineteenth Century*, XXXII, 585–603, 999–1020.

8. Amy Levy, "Impotens," *A London Plane Tree and Other Verses* ("Cameo Series" [New York, 1891]), p. 36.

9. Hardy quotes Browning and Tennyson more often than any of those I have mentioned in the text, but there is no question of any influence by either of them.

10. Beginning of love (see especially Esther Beach's remark, "Nater will find her way very rapid when the time's come for't" [*The Trumpet Major* ("Anniversary Edition," Vol. XII [New York, 1920]), p. 118] and the scene following p. 172). Should not care (*ibid.*, pp. 366, 97); such an ending (*ibid.*, pp. 338, 373–74).

11. *A Laodicean*, pp. 41, 109, 366.

12. Be made possible (*ibid.*, p. 192); Charlotte's more common (*ibid.*, pp. 43, 55). An architect and an idealist, Somerset even had almost exactly Hardy's experience with pedobaptism.

13. Marcus Aurelius (*ibid.*, p. 300); ". . . . force of judgment" (*ibid.*, pp. 367–68).

14. Important to man (*Two on a Tower*, p. vii); to atomic dimensions (*ibid.*, p. 247); a nightmare vision (*ibid.*, pp. 68–69); controls their destinies (*ibid.*, pp. 30–34, 147, 312).

15. "Yearning temperament" (*ibid.*, pp. 102, 5–6, 46, 129, 70); her natural/impulses (*ibid.*, pp. 257–58).

16. Hardy tells us (*ibid.*, p. 258); every important sense (*ibid.*, p. 311).

17. Unhappy second venture (*ibid.*, p. 281); basis for hope (*ibid.*, pp. 12, 81, 100).

18. Predestines human activities (*ibid.*, p. 147); for our understanding (*ibid.*, p. 279).

19. "Hand of necessity" (*The Mayor of Casterbridge* ["Harper's Modern Classics" (New York and London, 1922)], p. 295). Elizabeth Jane's fatalism is mentioned on p. 384, Susan Henchard's on p. 17, Whipple's on p. 113. "Sinister intelligence" (*ibid.*, pp. 345, 219, 144); sinister motivation (*ibid.*, p. 144); ". . . . to a minimum" (*ibid.*, p. 369); ". . . . . drama of pain" (*ibid.*, p. 386).

20. And his wife (*ibid.*, p. 3); superficies of things (*ibid.*, p. 305).

21. *Ibid.*, pp. 109–10.

22. *Ibid.*, pp. 132, 184, 308, 13.

23. Hardy approvingly quotes Novalis' dictum that character is fate (*ibid.*, p. 131).

24. "Doing" is past (*ibid.*, p. 369); and tends to (*ibid.*, pp. 135–36).

25. Own worst accuser (*ibid.*, pp. 36, 143–44, 380); ". . . . I can bear" (*ibid.*, p. 361).

26. Art of renunciation (*ibid.*, pp. 200, 205); in positive pain (*ibid.*, p. 385).

27. To a minimum (*ibid.*, p. 369); of her face (*ibid.*, p. 2); edicts of society (*ibid.*, p. 368); her future husband (*ibid.*, pp. 196–203, 301); like "poor Lucetta" (*ibid.*, pp. 319, 322).

28. I do not consider the short stories in my discussion because they do not give any additional insight into Hardy's reading of life.

29. *The Dynasts*, p. 1.

30. ". . . . Eight million eyes" (*Early Life*, p. 179); "the human forms" (*The Dynasts*, p. 118); ". . . . like an automaton" (*Early Life*, p. 184).

31. *Early Life*, p. 191.

32. *Ibid.*, pp. 219–20.

33. *Ibid.*, p. 232.

34. Preface to *Poems of the Past and Present, Collected Poems*, p. 75.

35. *Collected Poems*, p. 171.

36. Preface to *The Dynasts*, p. viii.

37. Of obtaining it (*Early Life*, pp. 192, 213; "Poems of Rural Life in the Dorset Dialect," *New Quarterly Magazine*, II, 472); gradual progress possible (*Early Life*, p. 216); idea of progress (*ibid.*, pp. 225, 189); the rural poor (*ibid.*, pp. 204, 191, 210, 206–7); "The Dorsetshire Laborer," *Life and Art by Thomas Hardy: Essays, Notes, and Letters Collected for the First Time*, ed. Ernest Brennecke, Jr. (New York, 1925), p. 40. See also *ibid.*, pp. 41, 46, 47.

38. It promises incipiently (*Early Life*, pp. 231, 201); ". . . . of the Universal" (*ibid.*, p. 231).

39. References, direct or implied, to natural selection such as we have noted in *The Mayor of Casterbridge* are common: *A Laodicean*, p. 35; "On the Use of Dialect" (1881), *Life and Art*, p. 114; *Two on a Tower*, p. 76; "The Dorsetshire Laborer" (1883), *Life and Art*, p. 29.

40. "The Pedestrian," *Collected Poems*, pp. 472–73.

NOTES TO CHAPTER VI

1. *Early Life*, p. 272.

2. *Early Life and Letters of John Morley*, ed. F. W. Heist (London, 1927), II, 234

3. Brougham Villiers, *The Socialist Movement in England* (London, 1910), p. 119.

4. Although Charles Reade had presented *Drink*, a drama borrowed from *L'Assomoir*, in 1878, the translation of Zola did not seriously begin until about 1883.

5. An article about Ibsen by Edmund Gosse appeared in the *Fortnightly Review* in 1879, and he was prominently mentioned in Gosse's *Studies in the Literature of Northern Europe* (1879) and Archer's *About the Theatre* (London, 1886).

6. Grant Allen, *The Woman Who Did* (Boston, 1895), p. 141.

7. George Gissing, *The Nether World* (New York, 1929), p. 392.

8. *The Woodlanders* ("Anniversary Edition," Vol. VI [New York, 1920]), pp. 55, 92, 85, 286, 8, 139, 21, 59, 19, 95.

9. *Ibid.*, pp. 24, 168, 15, 376, 233, 51, 73, 296, 245.

10. *Ibid.*, pp. 196, 440. See also *Early Life*, p. 289.

11. *The Woodlanders*, p. 443.

12. *Ibid.*, pp. 350, 367, 369.

13. ". . . . by the INEVITABLE" (*Later Years*, p. 14); ". . . . of human institutions" (*ibid.*, p. 44); ". . . . heart of things" ("Candour in English Fiction," *Life and Art*, p. 77).

14. *Later Years*, p. 44.

15. "Sterling character" (*The Woodlanders*, pp. 264, 267, 404); laws of England (*ibid.*, p. vii, where this intention is admitted in the Preface); "defensive alliance" (*ibid.*, p. 244).

16. *Ibid.*, pp. 260, 366, 248, 340, 418, 428, 198. Hardy would have liked to see Grace Melbury more actively protestant and was angry with her because she was "too commonplace and straitlaced" to go off with Giles (Carl J. Weber, *Rebekah Owen and Thomas Hardy* [Waterville, Me., 1939], p. 32).

17. *Tess*, pp. xvi, xiv.

18. *Ibid.*, pp. 186, 259, 327–28, 408, 34, 199.

19. "Sport with Tess" (*ibid.*, p. 508); unreasoning humanity (*Later Years*, p. 4); of her ancestors? (*Tess*, p. 91); " 'Nature's holy plan' " (*ibid.*, p. 24); ". . . . in a Springe" (*ibid.*, pp. 91, 136, 251); ". . . . towards today" (*ibid.*, p. 435); ". . . . under the sky" (*ibid.*, p. 447); never justified (*ibid.*, p. 455). By statements of the author and his characters the questionableness of the "blessing" of birth is enforced (see *ibid.*, pp. 34, 97, 160, 162, 324, 464). One pessimistic statement made in the novel—and quite out of character—by Tess is almost identical with Hardy's declaration that all is worse than vanity (journal entry for 1876, *Early Life*, p. 148; cf. *Tess*, p. 353).

20. *Tess*, pp. 152, 155, 12, 134, 127, 365, 262, 124, 48–49.

21. *Ibid.*, pp. 20, 48, 114.

22. *Ibid.*, pp. 104, 165, 194, 199, 187, 395, 311.

23. *Ibid.*, pp. 83–84.

24. *Ibid.*, p. 505.

25. ". . . . Such an anomaly" (*ibid.*, p. 108); ". . . . innate sensation" (*ibid.*, p. 115); of her "sin" (*ibid.*, pp. 116, 120, 189); at least tolerable (*ibid.*, pp. 355–56).

26. *Ibid.*, pp. 91, 108, 125–26, 338, 260, 312. Sometimes this conventional standard of judgment of Clare's is combined with the cruelty of the social order at large, as in the case of the eviction of Tess's family by people of "scrupulous character" (*ibid.*, p. 450).

27. *Ibid.*, p. 432.

28. *Ibid.*, p. 338. That this is the main purpose of the novel, both the Preface and the subtitle prove. Aside from the important criticism of social convention cited above, Hardy also attacks again the unfairness of class distinctions (pp. 150, 163–64, 212) and launches the most significant attack upon conventional Christianity contained in the novels (hypocritical Christianity is also criticized in "A Tragedy of Two Ambitions" in *Life's Little Ironies* ["Anniversary Edition," Vol. VIII (New York, 1920)]). The reason for this attack, which excepts the sincere Calvinist Clare (*Tess*, pp. 203–15), is that Hardy feels that creeds attempt to check what in human nature wisdom would be content to regulate (*ibid.*, p. 203) and because he feels that a great deal of bigotry is associated with the practice of so-called "Christianity."

29. *Early Life*, p. 215.

30. *Ibid.*, p. 284.

31. ". . . . To do with reason" (*The Well-beloved* ["Anniversary Edition," Vol. XIII [New York, 1920], p. 88); ". . . . next début" (*ibid.*, p. 97).

32. *Ibid.*, p. 59.

33. *Early Life*, p. 232.

34. *Later Years*, p. 59.

35. *Jude*, p. 45.

36. *Ibid.*, p. 407. Expressed by Jude but in agreement with Hardy's view.

37. *Ibid.*, p. 388.

38. *Ibid.*, pp. 40, 41.

39. *Ibid.*, p. 305. An additional reason for Sue's plea is that she is less fully sexed than Jude and feels that marriage would emphasize this possible cause for estrangement. Because of the convention of the time, this difficulty is only implied in the novel (p. 259), but Hardy's own statement of intention makes clear the meaning (*Later Years*, pp. 41–42).

40. *Jude*, pp. 29, 400, 364, 377.

41. *Ibid.*, p. 482.

42. *Later Years*, p. 40.

43. *Jude*, p. 254.

44. *Ibid.*, p. 419.

45. *Ibid.*, p. 478.

46. *Early Life*, p. 272.

47. *Jude*, p. 388.

48. *Ibid.*, p. 62.

49. *Later Years*, pp. 40–41.

50. I do not discuss the short stories in the text, for, like the shorter tales of the last period, they only incidentally illuminate the philosophic thinking of Hardy.

51. *Early Life*, pp. 243, 294–95.

52. *Ibid.*, p. 282; see also p. 289.

53. *Ibid.*, pp. 294, 303.

54. *Ibid.*, p. 232.

55. *Ibid.*, p. 243.

56. At a concert (*ibid.*, p. 263; see also *ibid.*, pp. 242–43, 270–71, 283–84, and "Why I Don't Write Plays," *Life and Art*, pp. 116–17); ". . . . should be made" (*Early Life*, p. 284).

57. *Later Years*, p. 9.

58. *Ibid.*, p. 283; *Collected Poems*, p. 10. See also *Early Life*, pp. 66, 231; *A Pair of Blue Eyes*, pp. 112, 244; *Far from the Madding Crowd*, p. 16; *The Hand of Ethelberta*, p. 355; *The Woodlanders*, pp. 41, 42, 195, 264, 404.

59. *Early Life*, p. 234.

60. *Ibid.*, p. 305; *Later Years*, p. 9.

61. *Early Life*, pp. 233–34, 308, 296–97, 265, 268; *Later Years*, p. 6. In a letter to Mr. Nevinson for August 5, 1909, Hardy says that he has favored woman's suffrage for a "long time" (an unpublished letter in the Maggs Brothers' Collection).

62. "Lines" (1890), *Collected Poems*, p. 71.

63. "Candour in English Fiction," *Life and Art*, pp. 76–77; *Early Life*, p. 251; "The Profitable Reading of Fiction," *Life and Art*, p. 73; *Early Life*, p. 294.

64. *Collected Poems*, p. 480.

65. *Later Years*, pp. 124–25.

66. W. R. Rutland, *Thomas Hardy: A Study of His Writings and Their Background* (Oxford, 1938), p. 93; *Tess*, p. 203.

67. Rutland, *op. cit.*, pp. 100–102.

68. Hardy's first mention of Ibsen is in 1890 (*Early Life*, p. 294). Hardy is familiar with Zola's work by 1891 as can be seen in "The Science of Fiction" (1891), *Life and Art*, p. 86.

69. Archer, *Real Conversations* (London, 1904), pp. 46–47.

NOTES TO CHAPTER VII

1. "Chance and change" (Preface to *Poems of the Past and the Present, Collected Poems*, p. 75); ". . . . place for man" (*Early Life*, p. 234).

2. *Early Life*, p. 294; *Later Years*, p. 165; *Letters on the War* (London: Privately printed, 1915), p. 5.

3. A letter in the private collection of Sir Sydney Cockerell; F. Lefèvre, "An Hour with Thomas Hardy," *Living Age*, CCCXXV (April 11, 1925), 100; *Later Years*, pp. 162, 165.

4. *Later Years*, pp. 124–25, 270; "A Philosophical Fantasy," *Winter Words*, pp. 123–24.

Index

Abercrombie, Lascelles, 206

Accident and coincidence, 65, 71, 94, 98, 99, 102, 104, 106, 107, 108, 110, 113–14, 116, 120–21, 122, 126, 127, 128, 132, 133, 134, 141, 145, 146, 149, 157, 169, 177, 185; *see also* Chance

Aeschylus, 34, 85, 223

Agnosticism, 137, 155, 156, 193, 199, 203

Aids to Faith, 14, 32

Ainsworth, W. H., 4, 10, 24

Allen, Grant, 139, 157, 161, 165, 166

"Amabel," 58, 67–68, 69, 70

Anglican church (1840–60), 13–16; in Dorset, 16–19

Architecture versus literature, 52–55, 80, 82

Arnold, Matthew, 13, 15, 27, 52, 55, 59, 88, 164

Astronomy, 46, 143–44

"At a Bridal," 65, 68

"At Waking," 69, 70

"At the Word 'Farewell,' " 79–80

Aurelius, Marcus, 142, 156, 159; *see also* Renunciation, virtues of

Automatism, 153, 155, 157, 159, 190

Bagehot, Walter, 34, 222–23

Barnes, William, 4, 11, 12

Beach, Joseph Warren, 94

Bentham, Jeremy, 51

Bible, the, 3, 4, 5, 13, 15, 20, 22, 24, 35, 37, 39, 40, 47 n., 186

Brennecke, Ernest, 11

Browning, Robert, 51, 59, 89, 138, 139, 160, 215

Bulwer-Lytton, Edward, 35

Byron, George Gordon, 35, 52

Carlyle, Thomas, 50, 51, 53, 61, 162, 193, 214

Cazamian, Madeleine L., 13, 138

Chambers, Robert, 27, 28

Chance, 63, 64, 65, 66, 67, 68, 69, 70, 71, 73, 77, 95, 99, 104, 108, 111, 112, 116, 120, 121, 124, 126, 127, 128, 131, 132, 133, 141, 144, 145, 149, 152, 154, 157, 169, 170, 177, 179, 185, 190, 192, 197, 198, 202; *see also* Accident and coincidence

"Chapel-Organist, The," 58

Character and fate, 148–49, 150, 157, 175–76, 177–78, 185, 186, 188, 190

Chew, Samuel, 2, 225

Circumstance, 103, 104, 106, 111, 112, 120, 121, 124, 126, 128, 132, 144, 146, 153

Class allegiance, 55, 56, 214

Class consciousness, 73, 105, 116, 117, 131–32, 142, 169, 171, 184, 192

Clifford, William K., 89, 134

Colenso, John William, 32, 46

Coleridge, Samuel T., 50

Collins, Wilkie, 94

Comte, Auguste, 51, 156, 160, 192

"Confession to a Friend in Trouble, A," 25, 66

"Crass casualty," 64, 65, 77, 97, 104, 126

Curse of consciousness, 66, 67, 72, 77, 96, 98, 99, 102, 103, 106, 121–22, 123, 124, 126, 129, 134, 141, 142, 149, 155, 159, 175, 182–83, 184

"Darkling Thrush, The," 208–9

Darwin, Charles, 26, 27, 28–30, 32, 34, 38, 40–44, 45, 47, 48, 49, 64, 65, 68, 70, 71, 88, 89, 92, 97, 104, 109, 126, 127, 132, 138, 139, 148

"Dawn after the Dance, The," 69

Desperate Remedies, 12, 54, 55, 83, 93–98, 101, 102, 112, 129, 130

Determinism, 92, 126–28, 133–35, 146, 147, 151, 152, 153, 154, 155, 156, 157, 158, 166, 167, 168, 173–74, 183, 190, 195, 197, 199, 201, 205

"Dicing Time," 65, 125, 132

Dickens, Charles, 15, 16, 34, 55, 75, 114, 202, 215

Disillusionment: with Christian faith, 33–48, 56, 59, 81, 212; about human relationships, 58–59; about love, 56–58, 69, 70; with own ability, early, 56

"Ditty," 66

"Domicilium," 6, 11, 35

"Doomsters," 61, 63, 72, 104, 127, 132

Dorset County Chronicle, 16, 17, 18, 35

"Dorsetshire Labourer, The," 23 n.

"Dream of the City Shopwoman, The," 66, 67

Dryden, John, 3

Dumas *père*, Alexander, 4, 24

Dynasts, The, 3, 45, 48, 64, 125, 140, 146, 152, 153, 154, 155, 171, 182, 191, 195, 203, 204, 205, 209–12, 214, 215

Early optimism, 22–23, 26, 47

Early religious belief, 3, 12, 19–22, 26, 47, 128, 212

Ecclesiastes, Book of, 24, 35, 87

Eliot, George, 13, 74, 75, 83, 90, 149, 157, 202, 215

Elliot, G. R., 2, 23

Ellis, S. M., 5–6

"Epitaph," 1

Essays and Reviews, 14, 26, 27, 30–33, 34, 35, 38, 39–40, 44, 47, 90

"Evil characters," 97, 98, 167–68, 176, 184, 190

Exideuil, Pierre d', 70, 217

Far from the Madding Crowd, 83, 84, 91, 107–13, 116, 118, 130, 146, 171

Fatalism, 95, 96, 99, 101, 133–34, 156, 157, 166, 173–74, 197, 199, 201

"Fire at Tranter Sweatley's, The," 71

Firor, Ruth M., 12

"For Life I Had Never Cared Greatly," 1

Ford, John, 6

"From Her in the Country," 66

Gaskell, Elizabeth Cleghorn, 75, 98–99

Gibbon, Edmund, 37

Gifford, Emma Lavinia (the first Mrs. Hardy), 78–81, 83–85, 137

Gissing, George, 139, 157, 164–65, 166

"God's Funeral," 20

Godwin, William, 50

Goodale, R. H., 138

Goodwin, C. H., 40

Gosse, Edmund, 139, 161, 164

Grant, James, 4, 24

Hand of Ethelberta, The, 23, 113–18, 119, 123, 124, 130, 131, 132, 134, 142, 171

"Hap," 47, 48, 52, 61, 62, 65, 77, 95, 157

Hardy, Florence Emily (the second Mrs. Hardy), 204

Hardy, Sr., Thomas, 7, 9, 19

Hardy, Sr., Mrs. Thomas, 7, 10, 19

Harper, C. G., 11

Harrison, Frederick, 51

Hartmann, Eduard von, 90, 159, 196–97, 198

"He Never Expected Much," 1

"He Wonders about Himself," 195, 200

Hedgcock, F. H., 2, 86

Hegel, Georg, 192, 193

"Heiress and Architect," 62, 66, 77

"Her Dilemma," 58, 69, 72

"Her Initials," 69

"Her Reproach," 77

Hicks, Granville, 56

Homer, 4, 24, 34, 212

Horace, 4, 35

"How I Built Myself a House," 35

Huxley, Thomas Henry, 28, 29, 30, 33, 43, 45, 49, 59, 83, 87, 89, 138, 139

"I Found Her Out There," 206–7

"I Was the Midmost," 2, 23

Ibsen, Henrik, 164–65, 197

Iconoclastic forces (1870–78), 88–93

Idealistic pantheism, 125, 190–93, 197, 199, 205, 215

Imaginative sympathy, 105, 106, 116, 179–80

Immanent Will, 64, 91, 125, 126, 128, 132, 146, 147, 152, 154, 155, 159, 183–84, 186, 189–91, 195–96, 198, 203, 204, 205, 210, 211; see also "Unconscious Propensity"; "Unfulfilled Intention"

"Impercipient at a Cathedral Service, The," 21

"In Childbed," 22

"In Tenebris," 2, 7, 23, 45

"In Time of 'The Breaking of Nations,' " 209

Indiscretion in the Life of an Heiress, An, 25, 73

James, G. P. R., 4, 24

Jefferies, Richard, 33, 139

Johnson, Samuel, 3, 24

Jowett, Benjamin, 39

Jude the Obscure, 2, 23, 51, 62, 118, 137, 161, 171, 183–89, 200, 202, 210, 214

Kant, Immanuel, 191, 193

Keats, John, 85, 215

Laodicean, A, 23, 25, 141–43, 150

Lefevre, Jacques, 205

Lewes, George Henry, 27

"Lines" (1890), 194

"Long Have I Framed Weak Fantasies of Thee," 216

"Louisa in the Lane," 8

"Love the Monopolist," 25

Lyell, Charles, 30, 33, 46

Macaulay, Thomas Babington, 54

McDowall, Arthur, 1–2

Macmillan, Alexander, 54, 55, 83

"Man He Killed, The," 209

Mann, Thomas, 93, 215

Martineau, James, 27

Marx, Karl, 211

Mayor of Casterbridge, The, 147–52, 154, 157, 166, 168, 171, 177, 190, 198, 202

"Melancholy temperament," 6–9, 52

Meliorism, 72, 73, 74, 75, 76, 77, 92, 111–13, 119, 120, 123, 124, 130–

32, 133–35, 136, 139, 142, 143, 146, 151, 152, 154, 155, 156, 157, 158, 159–60, 169–73, 178–80, 183, 187–90, 193–95, 197, 198–99, 205, 213; *see also* Social criticism

"Memorial Brass, The," 58

"Memory and I," 1, 2, 23

Meredith, George, 49, 54, 55, 86, 94, 114, 138, 165, 203

"Midnight on Beechen, 187–," 8, 82

Mill, John Stuart, 32, 44–45, 51, 53, 61, 88, 91, 132, 164

Milman, Henry Hart, 27, 37

Milton, John, 212

"Minute before Meeting, The," 25

Morley, John, 88, 139, 163

Morris, William, 117, 163, 165, 214

"Mother Mourns, The," 203

Moule, Henry, 19, 46

Moule, Horace Mosley, 5, 35, 36, 37, 38, 46, 48

Natural law, 65, 104, 106, 110, 111, 112, 120, 121, 124, 126, 127, 128, 144, 145, 146, 152, 154, 157, 167, 169, 170, 179, 184, 185, 186, 190, 192, 202

Natural selection, 6, 41–44, 64, 65, 72, 87, 92, 93, 97, 104, 114, 126, 127, 129, 148, 149, 167, 169, 177, 185, 186, 210

Natural versus social law, 151, 170–73, 178–80, 188–90, 194–96

Nature, 63, 64, 65, 66, 67, 68, 70, 77, 87, 93, 97, 104, 105, 113, 120, 125, 126, 128, 130, 131, 134, 148, 151, 170, 175, 176, 177, 178, 179, 182, 183, 190, 194, 212

"Neutral Tones," 57, 69, 77

Newman, John Henry, 14, 16, 17, 33, 35, 48

O'Connor, T. P., 137

Optimism, early nineteenth-century, 49, 50, 51

Origin of Species, 15, 26, 27, 28–30, 32, 34, 35, 38, 40–44, 47, 64, 68–69, 71, 88, 90, 210

Ovid, 4

Oxford movement, the, 14, 16, 17, 22

Pair of Blue Eyes, A, 25, 58, 83, 93, 101–7, 108, 112, 116, 125, 136, 127, 129, 130, 131, 134

"Paradisaic tendency," 23–26, 47, 103

Patmore, Coventry, 83

Pattison, Mark, 39

Peasant "philosophy," 12, 13, 26, 42–43, 64, 95, 96, 98, 101, 108, 173–74

"Pedestrian, The," 158–59

Pessimism (1878–86), 138–39

"Pessimism" (Hardy), 1, 6, 8, 13, 63, 64, 70, 71, 73, 77, 85, 86, 87, 90, 93, 100, 102, 103, 109, 111, 114, 115, 118, 119, 120, 123, 124, 128, 129, 131, 132–34, 137, 139, 157, 158, 159–60, 166, 173, 183, 186, 198–99, 200, 201, 202, 204, 205, 213

"Philosophical Fantasy, A," 205, 206

"Philosophy" (Hardy): 1865–70, 62–77; 1870–78, 125–35; 1878–86, 152–60; 1886–95, 190–99

Plato, 191, 193

"Poor Man and a Lady, A," 70

Poor Man and the Lady, The, 53, 55, 59, 61, 73, 74, 75, 76, 93, 112, 118, 119, 123, 131, 162, 166

"Postponement," 58, 70

Powell, Baden, 40

"Radicalism" (Hardy), 73, 74, 75, 76, 117, 119

Renan, Ernest, 46

Renunciation, virtues of, 124, 142, 143, 150, 151, 154, 156, 159, 169; *see also* Aurelius, Marcus

Replies to "Essays and Reviews," 14, 32

"Retty's Phases," 77

Return of the Native, The, 23, 82, 85, 88, 90, 92, 93, 118–25, 126, 127, 132, 134, 142, 146, 171, 175, 192, 201, 214

Revolution in theology and science (1860–65), 27–33

"Revulsion," 58, 82

Ridder-Barzin, Louise de, 13, 217

Ruskin, John, 35, 116, 162

Rutland, W. R., 12, 45, 47 n., 73, 91, 137, 159, 196

St. Pierre, Bernardin de, 3, 24

"San Sebastian," 58

Saturday Review, the, 28, 29, 30, 31, 32, 35, 38, 46

Schopenhauer, Arthur, 44, 46, 63, 70, 71, 86, 89, 90, 132, 138, 139, 154, 158–59, 192–93, 196, 197

Seclusiveness of Hardy, 56, 86

Sensational devices in novels, 94, 98, 101, 107–8, 141

Sensitiveness of Hardy, 6, 8, 26, 43, 44, 48, 86, 87

Sexual selection, 68, 97–98, 99–100, 102, 103, 104, 106, 108–10, 115, 121–22, 126, 127, 129–30, 133, 134, 140–41, 144–46, 147, 148, 149, 152, 154, 159, 167–68, 169, 176–77, 181–82, 184

Shakespeare, William, 4, 5, 34, 47 n., 54, 152

Shaw, George Bernard, 163, 165, 166, 214

"She," 192

"She to Him," 58, 65–66, 69

Shelley, Percy Bysshe, 23, 24, 35, 47, 75, 182, 214, 215, 223

Sherman, Stuart Pratt, 56

"Sick Battle-God, The," 204

"Singer Asleep, A," 60

Social criticism, 73, 74, 75, 76, 105, 111, 116, 117, 119, 120, 123, 130–32, 134, 142, 146, 151, 152, 156, 158, 169, 173, 178–80, 184, 185, 187–90, 193–95, 197, 198–99; *see also* Meliorism

Social protest (1886–95), 162–66

Sophocles, 34, 125, 198, 223

Spencer, Herbert, 27, 30, 45, 59, 87, 89, 91, 132, 138

Stephen, Leslie, 43, 88, 90, 91–93, 119, 132, 158, 166

Stevenson, Lionel, 223, 224

"Sunday Morning Tragedy, The," 58

Swift, Jonathan, 86

Swinburne, Algernon Charles, 60–62, 75, 76, 89, 139, 214

Temple, Frederick, 39, 50

Tennyson, Alfred, 30, 50, 51, 59, 79, 139, 215

Tess of the D'Urbervilles, 11, 23, 25, 111, 118, 161, 171, 173–80, 196, 197

Thackeray, William Makepeace, 15, 35, 54, 164, 202, 215

Thirlwall, Connop, 27, 50

Thomson, James, 86, 89

"To an Actress," 66–67, 72

"To-Be-Forgotten, The," 203

"To an Impersonator of Rosalind," 72

"To Outer Nature," 2, 7, 22

"To the Unknown God," 155, 207–8, 216

Tolstoy, Leo, 214

Trollope, Anthony, 35, 59, 202, 223

Trumpet Major, The, 137, 140–41

"Two Men, The," 66, 68, 71, 92, 102

Two on a Tower, 46, 143–46, 152, 154, 155, 157, 168, 198

Tyndall, John, 89

"Unborn, The," 5, 22

"Unconscious Propensity," 154, 159, 191, 194–95; *see also* Immanent Will

Under the Greenwood Tree, 3, 11, 18, 25, 83, 98–100, 101, 102, 112

"Unfulfilled Intention," 167, 169, 170, 205; *see also* Immanent Will

Virgil, 3, 4, 34, 54

Walpole, Horace, 54

"Weathers," 206

Webb, Clement, 13

Weber, Carl, 2, 73

Well-beloved, The, 180–83, 191, 193, 202

West, Rebecca, 55

Westminster Review, the, 15, 27, 29, 30, 31

"When I Set Out for Lyonnesse," 80

Whitman, Walt, 54

Wilberforce, Samuel, 14, 16, 29, 31, 32, 33, 35, 45

Williams, Rowland, 39

Wilson, H. B., 40

Woodlanders, The, 23, 166–73, 197, 200

Wordsworth, William, 50, 53, 61, 174

Working-class movement (1865–67), 75–76

Young, G. M., 74

"Young Man's Epigram on Existence, A," 62, 77

"Young Man's Exhortation, A," 62, 71, 77

Zola, Émile, 164–65, 197